THE FETAL TISSUE ISSUE
MEDICAL AND ETHICAL ASPECTS

POPE JOHN CENTER TASK FORCE ON HUMAN FETAL TISSUE TRANSPLANTATION

FETAL TISSUE BANK COMMITTEE

Maria Michejda, M.D. (Chair)
Senior Staff Associate
International Center for Interdisciplinary Studies
of Immunology
Georgetown University School of Medicine
Washington, DC

Joseph A. Bellanti, M.D.
Director
International Center for Interdisciplinary Studies
of Immunology
Georgetown University School of Medicine
Washington, DC

Julianne Byrne, Ph.D.
Project Director
Boyne Research Foundation
Washington, DC

Christopher DeGiorgio, M.D.
Assistant Professor of Neurology
University of Southern California
School of Medicine
Los Angeles, CA

D. Theodore Eastlund, M.D.
Medical Director
American Red Cross Tissue Services
St. Paul, MN

Robert E. Flynn, M.D.
Chairman
Board of Directors
Caritas Christi
Waltham, MA

Thomas Murphy Goodwin, M.D.
University of Southern California
School of Medicine
Department of Obstetrics & Gynecology
Women's Hospital
Los Angeles, CA

William M. Holls, M.D.
Department of Obstretrics and Gynecology
University of Tennessee Hospital
Knoxville, TN

Sister Margaret John Kelly, D.C., Ph.D.
St. John's University
Jamaica, NY

Lawrence Kromer, Ph.D.
Department of Anatomy & Cell Biology
Georgetown University Medical Center
Washington, DC

Kevin Lafferty, Ph.D.
University of Colorado
Barbara David Center for Childhood
Diabetes
Denver, CO

Ann LeBelle, D.M.D.
Committee on Labor and Human Resources
U.S. Senate
Washington, DC

Salvatore Mancuso, M.D.
Department of Gynecology
Universita Cattolica del Sacro Cuore
Agostino Gemelli Hospital
Roma, Italia

Edmund D. Pellegrino, M.D.
John Carroll Professor of Medicine and Medical Ethics
Georgetown University
Washington, DC

Jacek Piatkiewicz, Ph.D., M.D.
Chairman of the Legislative Committee
of the National Medical Council of Poland
Warszawa, Poland

Ronald Riner, M.D.
Vice President for Clinical Services
Daughters of Charity National Health System
St. Louis, MO

Robert Stevenson, M.D.
Director, (Retired) American Tissue Culture Association
Rockville, MD

Sister Mary Jacob Yelcho, C.S.A.
Providence Hospital Foundation
Columbia, SC

ETHICS COMMITTEE

The Reverend Albert S. Moraczewski, O.P., Ph.D. (Chair)
President Emeritus
Pope John Center
Braintree, MA

Hadley Arkes, Ph.D.
Ney Professor of Jurisprudence and American Institutions
Amherst College
Amherst, MA

The Reverend Benedict Ashley, O.P., Ph.D.
Professor of Moral Theology
Aquinas Institute of Theology
St. Louis, MO

James Bopp, Jr., J.D.
Bopp, Coleson & Bostrom
Attorneys at Law
Terre Haute, IN

The Reverend J. Daniel Cassidy, O.P., Ph.D.
Providence College
Providence, RI

Peter J. Cataldo, Ph.D.
Director of Research
Pope John Center
Braintree, MA

The Reverend Ronald Lawler, OFM Cap., Ph.D.
Rector
Holy Apostles Seminary
Cromwell, CT

William E. May, Ph.D.
Michael J. McGivney Professor of Moral Theology
John Paul II Institute for Studies on Marriage & Family
Washington, DC

The Reverend Patrick Norris, O.P., M.A.
Center for Health Care Ethics
St. Louis University, Medical Center
St. Louis, MO

The Reverend Russell E. Smith, S.T.D.
President
Pope John Center
Braintree, MA

THE FETAL TISSUE ISSUE

MEDICAL AND ETHICAL ASPECTS

Edited by
PETER J. CATALDO
ALBERT S. MORACZEWSKI, O.P.

THE POPE JOHN CENTER

NIHIL OBSTAT: Reverend James J. O'Donohoe, J.C.D.

IMPRIMATUR: Bernard Cardinal Law January 25, 1994

The Nihil Obstat and Imprimatur are a declaration that a book or pamphlet is considered to be free from doctrinal or moral error. It is not implied that those who have granted the Nihil Obstat and Imprimatur agree with the contents, opinions or statements expressed.

Library of Congress Cataloging-in-Publication Data

The Fetal tissue issue : medical and ethical aspects / edited by Peter
   J. Cataldo, Albert S. Moraczewski.
      p. 191   cm.
   "Results of the Pope John Center Task Force on Human Fetal
Transplantation."
   Includes bibliographical references and index.
   ISBN 0-935372-37-7
   1. Fetal tissues—Transplantation—Religious aspects—Catholic
Church.   2. Catholic Church—Doctrines.   3. Fetal tissues—
Transplantation—Moral and ethical aspects.   I. Cataldo, Peter J.,
1956–   .   II. Moraczewski, Albert S., 1920–   .   III. Pope John
XXIII Medical-Moral Research and Education Center. -Task Force on
Human Fetal Transplantation.
RD120.9.F47   1994
241'.6425—dc20   94-6927
                                                                         CIP

Contents

Members of the Pope John Center Task Force on Human
Fetal Tissue Transplantation. ii

Preface
        Edmund D. Pellegrino xi

Introduction
        Peter J. Cataldo
        Albert S. Moraczewski, O.P. xv

Chapter 1—Fetal Tissue Transplantation: Miscarriages and
        Tissue Banks
        Maria Michjeda 1

Chapter 2—Fetal Tissue and the Question of Consent
        Hadley Arkes 15

Chapter 3—Is the Biological Subject of Human Rights Present
        from Conception?
        Benedict Ashley, O.P. and
        Albert S. Moraczewski, O.P. 33

Chapter 4—Fetal Tissue Transplantation and Moral Complicity
        with Induced Abortion
        James Bopp, Jr.. 61

Chapter 5—The Principles of Cooperation in Catholic Thought
        Russell E. Smith 81

Chapter 6—The Determination of Fetal Death in Miscarriage: Its Ethical Significance for Fetal Tissue Transplantation
Peter J. Cataldo and T. Murphy Goodwin 93

Chapter 7—The Management of Ectopic Pregnancies: A Moral Analysis
William E. May 121

Chapter 8—Justice and Allocation of Resources: A Look at Fetal Tissue Research and Therapy
Patrick Norris, O.P. .149

Chapter 9—The Good Things Sought in the Fetal Tissue Project: Should Catholic Institutions Cooperate in This Plan?
Ronald Lawler, O.F.M.Cap 169

Afterword
Bernard Cardinal Law 177

Appendix A 181

Appendix B. 183

Appendix C. 185

Index 187

The Catholic moral tradition posits that certain concrete negative norms derived from biblical revelation and natural law are always and unexceptionally to be observed. This is a position sometimes difficult and even painful to uphold when compromise of these norms would benefit many people. As a consequence, many—some Catholics among them—attempt to justify breaches of Divine and natural law for reasons of compassion.

This is preeminently the situation today in the case of the experimental and therapeutic use of tissue obtained from electively aborted fetuses. On this view, it is shameful, cruel, and even immoral to waste fetal tissues that could alleviate, or even cure, a variety of serious and disabling diseases. It is reasoned that since the abortions would have been performed anyway, fetal tissues should be used for a humanitarian purpose. One might even oppose abortion, the argument continues, but at least turn it to some good. This viewpoint is supported by the popular press, the media, and many professional ethicists. Most recently, it received the approbation of the Clinton Administration which has lifted the ban on fetal tissue experimentation. As a result, we seem poised for a further descent into the moral maelstrom which began with *Roe v. Wade.* That descent is the consequence of the secular, relativist, and utilitarian cast of modern morality which is inimical to any conception of an objective moral order. The dangers of this kind of moral reasoning have clearly been set forth by John Paul II in his recent encyclical *Veritatis splendor.*

Against the secular view, the Catholic tradition holds to an order of morality that is theologically and philosophically grounded in certain principles derivable from Divine and natural law. On this view, however good the putative consequences of fetal transplantation may be, those consequences cannot justify even remote cooperation with the intrinsically evil act of elective abortion. There is nothing wrong *per se* in the use of fetal tissues, but they must be procured by means which do not involve the direct killing of the fetus.

The essays in this volume provide a fulsome exposition of the way this position flows from the principles of the Catholic moral tradition. Catholics, and others for whom elective abortion is more than a matter of private choice, will find here a coherent, well-reasoned account upon which to ground a response to the complex moral questions raised by the potential for both good and harm inherent in fetal tissue transplantation.

These essays begin where substantive discourse in biomedical ethics must begin, i.e., with a review of the biological and technical facts. Maria Michejda's opening article reviews the many potential uses for tissue from the fetal brain, bone marrow, pancreas, or thymus. She shows the advantages and disadvantages of tissues from both elective abortions and miscarriages. She makes a good case for the establishment of collection networks and tissue banks for miscarriages (spontaneous abortions). These present a morally viable alternative which, to date, has been inadequately examined because aborted tissue is easily available. Furthermore, many in the field do not acknowledge the profound moral issues at stake—or simply ignore them.

The most profound, crucial, and divisive of these issues is the moral status of the fetus. Ashley and Moraczewski carefully review the most recent biological knowledge about embryogenesis. They conclude that individuation occurs biologically when fertilization is complete. On these grounds, they assert that ". . any individuated organism which is genetically of the species *homo sapiens* is a person." They show, too, that the biological data are compatible with traditional philosophical conceptions of substance and unity as well as the theological conception of soul and God's creation of that soul. From all these perspectives, the human zygote and embryo are deserving of preservation, nurturing, and protection from harm. Experimentation on the embryo for any purpose except possible therapeutic benefit to that embryo is accordingly unacceptable. Setting fourteen days, or any other dividing line between licit and illicit experimentation is biologically, philosophically, and theologically indefensible.

The other papers in this volume deal with ethical issues that, in one way or another, flow from this fundamental concept of the inviolability of the embryo and fetus. For example, a woman who consents to elective abortion has agreed to an act of violence against the fetus. This act disqualifies her as a surrogate who can give valid permission for the use of that fetal tissue (Hadley Arkes).[1] Another example is offered by James

---

[1] Names of authors of the pertinent essays in this volume are in parentheses.

Bopp: any cooperation with, or encouragement of, the act of elective abortion such as is requisite in the way tissues are procured, is morally illicit. Indeed, on the principles of cooperation promulgated in the Catholic tradition, the use of electively aborted fetuses is shown to be morally indefensible (Russell Smith). Moreover, even if fetuses from miscarriages are used, it must be certain that they are dead before tissues can be removed (Peter Cataldo and Thomas Goodwin). It is also morally wrong to use tissues removed by salpingostomy or following the use of methotrexate since both procedures involve direct killing of the embryo (William E. May).

Christian charity should impel Catholic institutions to establish tissue banks for miscarriages (Ronald Lawler). Catholic principles of charity and justice must be given consideration in the allocation of tissues for transplantation if tissue banks are set up to collect tissues from miscarriages. Those principles include the principles of distributive justice and the preferential option for the poor as promulgated in Scripture, recent Papal encyclicals, and the teachings of the National Conference of Catholic Bishops (Patrick Norris).

Taken together, these essays constitute a compendium of some of the most crucial principles in Catholic moral teaching as they have been developed, deepened, and expanded in recent years. They make clear how fundamentally different that tradition is from the secular, utilitarian, and libertarian bias of so much of contemporary biomedical ethics. The Catholic tradition and its consistent advocacy for the protection of human life in all its stages must be authentically represented in the debate about the moral uses of all biological knowledge. It is the most potent deterrent to further depreciation and dehumanization of human life, in general, and of the vulnerable human *in utero*, in particular.

Unfortunately, many Catholics today are unfamiliar with the principles that undergird the Church's position on human life issues. Catholic universities no longer systematically teach those principles. Misplaced compassion, unreasoning humanitarianism, and uncritical confusion of liberty with license may lead uninformed Catholics to pro-choice positions or the conclusion that since an electively aborted fetus is already dead, its tissues may be used with moral impunity.

Educated Catholics cannot be indifferent to the way the unprecedented capabilities of modern human biology are used. They are compelled in charity and justice and by the obligation of evangelization to take part in public policy debates about human life issues, from abortion and the use of aborted fetal tissue to euthanasia or assisted suicide and the permutations and combinations of surrogate parenting. Educated Catholics have a moral obligation to present the Catholic perspective cogently and authoritatively.

The unprecedented powers conferred on humanity by advances in biology are expanding daily. Their potential for moral good and harm are so enormous that they must be contained within ethical boundaries. In defining those boundaries, the Catholic moral tradition must play a central role—particularly in our morally diverse, and increasingly secular, times. It is a role important not just for Catholics, but for the good of the whole human community—especially its most vulnerable members.

Edmund D. Pellegrino

This volume is in large measure an analysis of the convergence of the two universal moral obligations regarding human life upon the medical issue of human fetal tissue transplantation. These obligations are the duty to conserve human life and the duty not directly to kill innocent human life. Specifically, the work attempts to answer the ethical question whether both obligations toward human life can be fulfilled in the procurement and transplantation of human fetal tissue obtained from miscarriages.

In general, the utility of human fetal tissue for transplantation is dependent in part on its immunological acceptability and the retention of its functioning capacity. If, therefore, no conflict is to occur between the obligations to conserve human life and the inviolability of human life, and if the most viable fetal tissue must be obtained for successful transplantation, determining the moment of death for the fetus is pivotal to the reconciliation of medical and ethical concerns. As we will argue, it is gravely immoral directly to take the life of the fetus (even during its last moments of life) in order to have useful tissue that is viable for conserving the life of another. However, one may remove tissue from a dead fetus in order to conserve the life of an individual who may benefit from such a transplantation. John Paul II summarized well the general moral dilemma which is faced by the issue of human fetal tissue transplantation in an address to a conference of the Pontifical Academy of Sciences:

> This is the very problem you are considering. How does one reconcile respect for life—which forbids any action likely to cause or hasten death—with the potential good that results for humanity if the organs of a dead person are removed for transplanting to a sick person who needs them, keeping in mind that the success of such an intervention depends on the speed with

which the organs are removed from the donor after his or her death? At what moment does that which we call death take place? That is the crux of the matter. In essence, exactly what is death? (John Paul II, 1990: 524)

Catholic Church teaching has continually upheld the obligations not to kill innocent human life directly and to conserve human life. These obligations are evident from God's revelation of the sacredness of human life and also from the Natural Law. These moral obligations apply to all human life at each and every stage of development, including the stage of life at which fetal tissue is used for transplantation. These obligations are also absolute, that is, without exception: the inviolability of innocent human life is binding on all free moral agents in all circumstances, and the duty to conserve life is always binding but with a fulfillment proportionate to the circumstances. These obligations apply both to those responsible for the lives of the human fetus and the lives of those who might be helped by fetal tissue transplantation. Vatican II reaffirmed our obligations both to new and mature innocent human life, declaring in *Gaudium et spes* that,

> God, the Lord of life, has entrusted to men the noble mission of safeguarding life, and men must carry it out in a manner worthy of themselves. Life must be protected with the utmost care from the moment of conception: abortion and infanticide are abominable crimes (Vatican II, 1965).

The key concepts in this teaching are: a) that life is a gift from God the Creator; b) that safeguarding the gift is inherent to its entrustment from God; and c) that the particular developmental stage of life is, as such, irrelevant to the duty to conserve life. The teaching of *Gaudium et spes* was reiterated in the *Declaration on Procured Abortion,* particularly with respect to the fact that our moral obligations toward life are not differentiated according to developmental stages:

> The right to life is no less to be respected in the small infant just born than in the mature person. In reality, respect for human life is called for from the time that the process of generation begins. From the time that the ovum is fertilized, a life is begun which is neither that of the father nor of the mother; it is rather the life of a new human being with his own growth. It would never be made human if it were not human already (CDF, 1974: 13).

It is equally important to note that the *Declaration* construes the inviolability of human life as something which is owed to the preborn human being as a person. The teaching on the inviolability of innocent human life is not based simply on the fact of human generation but on the basis that certain protections are due to the individual as a person. The *Declaration* teaches that the right to life and personhood are mutually inclusive. Where there is human life, according to the *Declaration,* there is an individual who must be respected as a person **and** whose life must be safeguarded: "The first right of the human person is his life . . . It does not belong to society, nor does it belong to public authority in any form to recognize this right for some and not for others. . . ." (CDF, 1974: 11). "It is at all times the task of the State," the *Declaration* teaches later, "to preserve each person's rights and to protect the weakest" (CDF, 1974: 19). In 1987 *Donum vitae* reflected and expanded this same teaching: "The gift of life which God the Creator and Father has entrusted to man calls him to appreciate the inestimable value of what he has been given and to take responsibility for it. . . ." (CDF, 1987: 5). *Donum vitae* states that the Magisterium has not adopted a philosophical argument for the beginning of a personal presence, but like the *Declaration,* it does teach that human life from the moment of fertilization must be respected and treated as a person with all the rights of a person, including the right to life:

> Thus the fruit of human generation, from the first moment of its existence, that is to say from the moment the zygote has formed, demands the unconditional respect that is morally due to the human being in his bodily and spiritual totality. The human being is to be respected and treated as a person from the moment of conception; and therefore from that same moment his rights as a person must be recognized, among which in the first place is the inviolable right of every innocent human being to life (CDF, 1987: 14).

The duty to conserve the life of the unborn child is also derived from the same respect for him or her as a person: "Since the embryo must be treated as a person, it must also be defended in its integrity, tended and cared for, to the extent possible, in the same way as any other human being as far as medical assistance is concerned" (CDF, 1987: 14).

These two duties we have toward the human fetus, the duty not to kill directly and the duty to conserve life, are the same duties we have toward the recipients of human fetal tissue, such as Parkinson's, Alzheimer's, or diabetic patients or those with certain blood disorders. The debilitating physical or psycho-social conditions of the Parkinson's and Alzheimer's patient do not take precedence over the sacredness of their lives as being created in the image of God; nor can these conditions snuff out the primordial inclination to conserve life, and, therefore, the corresponding natural law obligation we have on their behalf.

As noted above, this volume is concerned with the resolution to the apparent conflict between two moral obligations: the duty to conserve life and the duty not directly to kill innocent human life. It has been shown that the transplantation of certain fetal tissues has the potential of saving the lives of many persons afflicted with a variety of disorders. However, up to the present time these fetal tissues are being largely obtained from fetuses who have been electively aborted. The essays in this volume seek to show that 1) it is immoral to use for transplantation purposes tissues obtained from induced abortions; 2) tissues obtained from miscarriages (spontaneous abortions) can be a suitable source for transplantations and would be ethically acceptable; and 3) in order to acquire a sufficient amount of high quality tissues from miscarriages networks of cooperating hospitals would be required.

Several chapters are devoted to establishing the first point: it is immoral to use tissues from induced abortions. **Ashley and Moraczewski** provide the solid foundation for the argument by carefully considering the question: "Is the biological subject of human rights present from conception?" Phrasing the question in that manner avoids an unnecessary digression into the nature of personhood and permits the ready use of biological data and criteria to establish the presence of an organism. Thus the evidence firmly supports the existence of an individuated human organism which is genetically a member of *Homo sapiens* from the time that the process of fertilization is completed just prior to the first cleavage of the zygote. Certain philosophical and scientific terms are correlated by the authors so that philosophical and theological principles can be applied to the biological data. The spiritual soul, both as the principle of human biological life and as the principle of intellectual cognition and free will, has to be directly created by God—it cannot as such evolve from, or be reduced to, matter. The soul is the reason that the human organism can be, and indeed is, the proper subject of moral rights and responsibilities.

Arkes argues that in the case of induced abortions, the subject who is making the donation of his or her tissues is not in a position to give appropriate consent. Nor can the mother of the child who has freely elected to abort her child; she does not have the required status to give such a consent.

Furthermore, as **Bopp** clearly demonstrates, transplantation therapy using tissues from elective abortions is unavoidably tainted by the immorality of such abortions. The requirement for fresh, high quality tissues necessarily leads to some level of cooperation between the abortionist and the fetal tissue researcher. There is complicity with both past and future induced abortions. Other factors such as the financial gain involved in the process tends to further dehumanize our culture.

Clearly, then, there is a need to explore alternative sources of fetal tissue, sources that would not carry the taint of abortion with it. One of these sources that have been suggested is tissue from ectopic pregnancies. **May** examines the condition of ectopic pregnancy and the various methods which have been proposed for its treatment. He judges that the use of salpingostomy is not an ethically acceptable way of treating ectopic pregnancies and should not be used for transplantation purposes.

Since the obtaining of fetal tissue is the usually the work of several persons, the issue of cooperation emerges. **Smith** looks closely at the traditional principle of cooperation and at its distinctions, formal and material, proximate (immediate) and mediate, contingent and necessary. Applying the principle and its distinctions, he concludes that the use of tissue from induced abortions could be material but that it would be proximate, contingent and mediate; it would not be justifiable ethically because the value of fetal tissue research would be outweighed by the value of the innocent life which had been deliberately destroyed.

Having established that tissue from electively aborted fetuses is not ethically acceptable, another source for medical and ethical consideration would be fetuses which have been spontaneously aborted, that is, miscarriages. The remaining chapters examine this source in light of the second and third factors given above; namely, that tissues obtained from miscarriages can be a suitable source for transplantations and would be ethically acceptable, and that in order to acquire a sufficient amount of high quality tissues from miscarriages, networks of cooperating hospitals would be required. The first question which arises here is whether such tissues would be useful for transplantation purposes. Up to this time the assertion had been made in both public and medial literature that tissues from miscarriages generally would not be suitable, and if a few specimens were, there would not be a sufficient and steady supply of such tissues. This is a requisite to carry on any kind of systematic program in fetal tissue transplantation. **Michejda** reviews the literature as well as her own contribution to the subject of fetal tissue transplantation. She observes that to this date there has not been a serious and adequate review of alternative and ethically more acceptable sources of fetal tissue for transplantation purposes. Current trends indicate that fetal tissue is being increasingly used in the treatment of a variety of disorders.

Contrary to popular views, tissues from electively aborted fetuses are often not as good as that obtainable from miscarriages. Dr. Michejda cites evidence that about 7% of miscarriage tissues would be suitable for transplantation purposes. However, to acquire an adequate amount of such tissues from the 850,000 miscarriages which occur annually in hospitals in this country, networks of tissue banks and hospitals need to be created. Such networks would be responsible not only for the collection of tissues from satellite hospitals but also for their processing, certification, storage and distribution.

A major requirement for the use of fetal tissues is that the fetus is dead before any tissue is removed. This concern is examined by **Cataldo and Goodwin.** Obviously, the usual medical criteria for the determination of death generally are not applicable in the case of very young fetuses. Consequently other criteria need to be developed for fetuses at various stages of development. A balance has to be struck between the protection of innocent life and the needs of others for the conservation of life. Death may not be declared prematurely nor may such a declaration be unjustifiably delayed with the resulting deterioration of the tissue and the consequent loss of its utility for transplantation. In light of this double requirement criteria are proposed for the determination of fetal death, and recent efforts to redefine life and death with respect to the unborn are examined.

Even if it is granted that tissues obtained from miscarriages would be both medically and ethically acceptable, there remains a further question. **Norris** considers the matter from the point of view of social justice. Would tissues from such networks—say, sponsored by Catholic hospitals—be made available to the poor? Or would this be another example of discrimination? Applying the requirements for social justice, Norris concludes that it could be possible to set up such a network for the collection and distribution of fetal tissues for transplantation purposes in such a manner that the needs of all requiring such treatment could be met, even though it must be admitted that the current health care delivery system in the United States does not meet the criteria for social justice. For the purpose of making a final evaluation of the proposed network, **Lawler** completes the volume by taking a broad view of the various goods that may be achieved through fetal tissue transplantation and those goods which may be threatened by this work.

The chapters of this book take the reader through a maze of scientific, medical, and ethical concerns associated with the use of fetal tissues for transplantation in the management of a number of disorders which to date have not been treated satisfactorily. It is hoped that what is presented here will truly benefit those in need of such treatment as well as provide an ethical guide for those who have to make the critical decisions in this particular arena of medical research and practice.

This volume is the result of work of The Pope John Center Task Force on Human Fetal Tissue Transplantation which held meetings and conducted research from June 1992 to January 1994. We conclude by expressing our gratitude to all those members of the Task Force (listed on pages ii-v) whose expertise, dedication, and collaboration enabled its goals to be realized. While each member has made a valuable contribution, each and every view expressed in this book does not necessarily represent the views of each member of the Task Force.

A particular word of thanks goes to those at the Pope John Center: to Father Russell Smith, S.T.D., President, for his guidance and leadership of the project; to Father David Beauregard, O.M.V., Ph.D., Director of Publications, for his valuable editorial advise and work with the manuscript of this volume; to Sister Margaret Mary Turner, R.S.M., M.S.A., Director of Development, for her indispensable work of organizing the logistics of the Task Force meetings and for securing a grant in support of the Task Force; to Mrs. Doris Amirault, Secretary, for her diligent efforts in assisting with the typescript of the book; to Mrs. Jeanne Burke, Assistant to the President, Mr. Donald Powers, Business Manger, and Miss Barbara Sullivan, Secretary, for their generous assistance with the work of the Task Force. We are also very grateful for the helpful comments made by Julianne Byrne, Ph.D. A special note of gratitude also goes to an anonymous benefactor of the Task Force and to the Our Sunday Visitor Institute for the award of a generous grant towards the work of the Task Force.

Peter J. Cataldo
Albert S. Moraczewski, O.P.
Editors

References

Congregation for the Doctrine of the Faith. (1974). *Declaration on Procured Abortion.* Boston: Daughters of St. Paul.

Congregation for the Doctrine of the Faith. (1987). *Donum vitae.* Boston: St. Paul Editions.

John Paul II. (1990, 11 January). Address to the Pontifical Academy of Sciences, December 14, 1989. *Origins*, pp. 523–525.

Vatican II. (1988). Gaudium et spes n. 51. In A. Flannery, O.P. (Ed.), *Vatican Council II: The Conciliar and Post Conciliar Documents.* Boston: St. Paul Editions.

Chapter 1

FETAL TISSUE TRANSPLANTATION: MISCARRIAGES AND TISSUE BANKS[1]

Maria Michejda

Editors' Summary: To date there has not been an adequately serious and systematic review of alternative and ethically more acceptable sources of fetal tissue for transplantation. This situation may be due to the premature and inadequately substantiated judgment that tissues from spontaneously aborted fetuses (miscarriages) would not be suitable, either qualitatively or quantitatively. This chapter brings together the medical and scientific evidence which shows the increasing importance of fetal tissue and cells in the treatment of a wide variety of

---

[1]The Introduction to this chapter was drafted by Albert S. Moraczewski, O.P.

disorders not only of the born human person but also for the management of several disorders in the fetus. It also presents evidence which argues that high quality fetal tissues in sufficient quantities (for research) could be obtained from miscarriages by means of a suitable network set up for this purpose. It is estimated that about 90% of the 1.6 million induced abortions performed annually in the United States occur in the first trimester. In contrast, out of a total of some 840,700 miscarriages annually (in the late 1980s) about 30% of these are caused by uterine anomalies and occurred in the second trimester. In principle, miscarriages can take place at any time during pregnancy while induced abortions usually take place during the first trimester. For many transplantation purposes fetal tissue from the second trimester is required. It is unlikely that electively aborted fetuses could supply the needed amount. The use of tissues from induced abortions is also limited by the fact that tissues from elective abortions is often contaminated (75%). The use of oxytocin and prostaglandins may induce free radical damage to the tissue resulting in ischemic changes in the tissue which would impair significantly the process of engraftment. Although the viability of miscarriage tissues may be only about 7–10%, they may well be of superior quality because they are rarely damaged. In order to obtain an adequate supply of useful fetal tissue from miscarriages networks of tissue banks need to be established. These would require suitable protocols and trained personnel for the retrieval, collection, processing, storage, and distribution in order to ensure adequate amounts of high quality tissue suitable for transplantation.

INTRODUCTION

Recent advances in transplantation research involving human fetal tissues such as neural and lymphoid tissues, bone marrow, liver, pancreas and thymus (Michejda, 1992), have led to major ethical and legal controversies. Consequently, federal funding for fetal transplantation research, particularly that involving neural tissue was banned by the Reagan Administration in 1988, and the ban was sustained by the Bush Administration. As a consequence, fetal tissue transplantation became a social and political issue, linked to the ethical and legal problems of abortion. The issue of fetal tissue transplantation polarized society, and resulted in major efforts by some politicians to lift the ban[2], or others to modify it by appropriate amendments[3]. In the meantime, transplantation research utilizing human fetal tissue from elective abortions was carried out and funded by non-federal, private sources.

---

[2]Congressional Record-March 31, 1992. 4460–4488
[3]Sen. Hatch's Amendment No. 1749.

2

In 1990, the Office of Technology Assessment (OTA) of the U.S. Congress released a report on the potential use of human fetal tissue for the treatment of certain neurological disorders (U.S. Congress, Office of Technology Assessment, 1990). This report pointed out that at the date of writing only Parkinson's disease had reached the stage of clinical human research while for the other neurological disorders such as Alzheimer's disease, stroke, and spinal cord injury, research was still at the level of basic science and animal experimentation. One of the recent studies carried out by a group of investigators at Yale university on the use of fetal tissue transplants in the management of patients with Parkinson's disease showed diminished symptoms of parkinsonism during 18 months of evaluation (Spencer, Robbins, Naftolin et al., 1992). These effects were observed after unilateral intracaudate grafting of fetal neural tissue containing dopamine neurons. Similar improvements in patients with severe parkinsonism were reported by a group from the University of Colorado (Freed, Breeze, Rosenberg, et al., 1992). However, the best results were achieved by a team from Lund University in Sweden on patients with severe parkinsonism induced by the drug MPTP (1-methyl-4-phenyl-1,2,3,6-tetrahydropyridine). The bilateral fetal mesencephalic grafting in two patients (43 yr ♂, 30 yr ♀) resulted in significant long term improvement of motor function (Widner, Tetrud, Rehncrona, et al., 1992). However, the Swedish investigators, who in fact had initiated fetal tissue transplantations nearly 15 years ago and probably have the highest level of experience in this area, have recently emphasized that the complete cure for parkinsonism is not available at present. Only certain improvements of motor function can be achieved (Lindvall, 1991). These investigators believe that in order to obtain "cures" of parkinsonism, considerably more research needs to be carried out. The transplantation procedures need to be optimized, especially with respect to an increase of brain bilateral sites in which neural grafts are inserted, the location of these grafts and the volume of the engrafted neural tissue. Also, the optimal gestational age of the engrafted tissue is an important consideration (Lindvall, 1991; Sawle, Bloomfield, Bjorklund, et al, 1992).

Many studies have been carried out in experimental animal models during the last fifteen years which contributed to a better understanding of fetal neural tissue characteristics and provided basis for clinical trials of fetal neural tissue transplantation (Freed, De Medinocelli, and Wyatt, 1985; Bjorklund, Olson, Seiger, and Lindvall, 1988; Hitchcock, Kenney, Clough, Huges, Henderson, and Detta, 1990; Stromberg, Bygdeman, Goldstein, Seiger, and Olson, 1986; Wictorin, Clarke, Bolam, Brundin, and Gustavili, 1990; Brundin, Barbin, Strecker, and Isacson, 1988; Carvey, Ptak, Lo, Linn, Buhrfiend, Goetz, and Klawans, 1991). Recently some studies have suggested the use of viral vectors or encapsulated oncogenic viruses, which release neuronal growth factors and cause multiplication of neurons and enhancement of neuronal growth (Bredesen, Manaster, Rayner, et al. 1991). These studies while very interesting are still very much in the experimental stage. On the other hand, xenotransplantation, where the donor is of different species from the recipient, may be useful particularly when there is a shortage of human donors. In fact, xenotransplantation has been successful in transplantation of bone marrow (Michejda, Peters, and Bellanti, 1992). There were some attempts to use neural tissue xenographs in animal models (Cadet, Kujirai, Berger, et al., 1991). However, in case of neural tissue it may be more difficult to achieve beneficial results because of significant evolutionary differences between animal and human central nervous systems.

Fetal tissue transplantation offers many exciting, therapeutic prospects. However, the ethical problem inherent in the use of fetal tissue from elective abortions, coupled with the impending scarcity of healthy tissues caused by early induced abortions, (discussed later in this chapter), lead to the inevitable conclusion that the only acceptable and available source of these tissues in the future will be from miscarriages.

On the basis of the experimental animal data and clinical trials it is now clear that utilization of fetal tissue in various therapeutic modalities can be very effective (The AMA Council on Scientific Affairs and the Council on Ethical and Judicial Affairs, 1990; Touraine, Raudrant, Royo, et al., 1991; Michejda, 1988; Gale, 1987; Kuhn, Wachs, and Ruckert, 1990). However, more consideration and study of the whole question of fetal tissue procurement needs to be undertaken. It will be especially important to examine the alternatives to tissues from elective abortions. Tissue procurement from miscarriages is such an alternative, which has the virtue of being immediately ethically acceptable and, in the long run, more medically viable.

CURRENT RESEARCH EFFORTS

The long and emotional debate over the utilization of human fetal tissue in transplantation entered a new phase during the first fortnight of the Clinton administration with the lifting of the ban on the use of human fetal tissue in research. During this long debate, as mentioned above, fetal tissue procurement was linked closely with the controversial issue of abortion. Moreover, the fetal tissue banks for tissue from miscarriages established by the Presidential Executive Order in May, 1992

4

were closed in 1993 by the NIH Revitalization Law[4]. The 1992 Presidential Executive Order resulted from the public reaction against elective abortion as a source of tissue, and was supported by newly obtained data on the volume and characteristics of fetal tissue from miscarriages (Michejda, 1988; Byrne, et al.; 1985: Byrne, 1992; MacKenzie, et al, 1988; Thorne and Michejda, 1989)[5]. The major objective of the five banks which were established by NIH, was to carry out feasibility studies to evaluate the existing volume of viable tissue from miscarriages and ectopic pregnancies. Clearly, useful tissue had to be free of any contamination and infection, and to be cytogenetically normal. Unfortunately, the planned two-phase project for these banks was never completed. Results from only the first six months of existence of the tissue banks are currently being evaluated at NIH[6]. However, some preliminary data were discussed at the meeting of the American Association of Tissue Banks in Boston (Aug. 22–25, 1993). The initial results presented by two groups were inconsistent. One study indicated that 40–46% of miscarriages may provide tissue suitable for transplantation research[7], but the other study indicated that no viable tissue was found from 65 referrals[8]. These differences, however, may be attributed to different methods of tissue collection, availability of resources as well as methods of storage of aborted tissues.

Currently, our group at Georgetown University is in the process of collecting and testing the viability and function of fetal bone marrow harvested from miscarried fetuses during the second trimester of pregnancy[9]. Our preliminary studies have shown good viability of healthy stem cells from bone marrow extracted from prematurely delivered non-surviving fetuses from various stages of gestation. These data indicate that some marrow and other tissues from various miscarriages can be a resource for transplantation tissue. However, collection and evaluation of the tissue in the tissue banks as well as the short term

---

[4]Public Law 103-43, the National Institute of Health. Revitalization Act of 1993, 103P.L.43; 1993 S.l; 107 Stat 122(103rd Congress, first session).
[5]See also footnote 3 above and Goodwin, T.M. and Kovacs B., unpublished data.
[6]Dayton, D. NIH report on fetal tissue banks, unpublished data.
[7]Low, W.C., Eastlund, T. Vishing, B.A. et al.: "Assessment of Human Fetal Tissue from Spontaneous Abortions for Potential Cell Transplantation Therapies." Abstract, Amer. Assoc. Tissue Banks Meeting, Boston, 1993.
[8]Gage, H., Mueller, B., Krohn, M. et al.: "Evaluation of Fetal Tissues from Spontaneous Abortions and Ectopic Pregnancies for Banking and Transplantation". Abstract, Amer. Assoc. Tissue Banks meeting, Boston, 1993.
[9]Michejda, M., Goodwin, T. M., and Verma, U. : Bone Marrow Harvested from Miscarriages: Stem Cells Viability and Function. (In preparation for publication).

and long term preservation should be optimized. These problems are being studied in several other laboratories as well.

Very disturbing in the early debate on alternative sources of fetal tissue (which was always more political than scientific), were the emotions and lack of objectivity, as well as lack of true scientific inquiry which frequently jeopardized scientific integrity. Many members of the scientific community promoted exclusively the use of tissue harvested from elective abortions as the only optimal source of donor tissue. Unfortunately, there has been almost a complete lack of information about any alternative source of fetal tissue, such as those derived from miscarriages. The only retrospective study on the assessment of the incidence of miscarriages as a possible alternative to be explored for fetal tissue comes from the Georgetown University laboratory (Thorne, et al., 1989). On the other hand, much of the information of the characteristics of electively aborted tissue were based on *in vitro* studies and on very limited experience *in vivo*. This is particularly true for neural tissue of different gestational ages, and less for the hematopoietic stem cells. There was no interest in tissue from miscarriages, which was always labeled as "fetal waste," and which until recently was totally disregarded as a potential source of suitable donor tissue.

In view of the increasing demand for fetal tissue for potentially life saving transplantations it is necessary to review the current knowledge on fetal tissue characteristics in general and in particular its quality when harvested from elective abortions and from miscarriages.

TISSUES FROM ELECTIVE ABORTIONS AND MISCARRIAGES COMPARED

It has been recognized that fetal tissues have distinctive biological and therapeutic properties. These biological properties include: 1) an extensive capacity to produce trophic substances and growth factors which promote cell growth, survival and regeneration of the damaged tissue and/or cell; and 2) an ability for rapid cellular growth, proliferation, differentiation revascularization and reinnervation (Lund, 1976; Michejda, 1988; Stromberg, Bygdeman, Goldstein, Seiger, and Olson, 1986).

Immature fetal tissue also has special immunologic characteristics. These properties of fetal tissue make the fetus the ideal transplant donor *and* the ideal transplant recipient (Michejda, 1990; Flake, Harrison, Adzick, and Zanjani, 1986; Michejda, Peters, and Bellanti, 1991). In fact, fetus to fetus transplantation does not require immunosuppressive therapy to prevent transplant rejection.

6

Fetal tissue research has led to the development of many exciting advances in transplantation immunology, which, in turn, have led to the development of new therapeutic modalities (Barrett and McCarthy, 1990). For many years embryonic tissue has been the source of cells which could be cultured. These cell lines were very important for the study of cell-cell interaction and gene expression in developmental biology. The early polio vaccine was derived from human fetal kidney cells, and even now human fetal cells are frequently used to study the mechanisms of viral infections, including AIDS. For over ten years, transplantations of human stem cells obtained from fetal liver, thymus, pancreas, lymphoid tissue, brain and bone marrow, have been utilized in the experimental treatment of numerous genetic diseases and inborn errors (Meng, Fei, Gu, et al., 1985; Krivit and Paul, 1986). These have included various hemoglobinopathies, immunodeficiencies, metabolic or lysosomal storage diseases and neurologic degenerative diseases (see Table 1). Thus, transplantation of fetal tissue, involving therapeutic stem cell reconstitution, is the forerunner to the genetically engineered cell therapy (Touraine, J. L., Roncarolo, Royo, and Touraine, F., 1987).

Since the mid 1970's there has been strong evidence that experimental treatment with fetal pancreatic cells (islets of Langerhans) in diabetic patients may, under special conditions, restore pancreatic function and secretion of insulin (Hullet, Falany, Love, et al., 1987). Important advances in neurobiology, which have occurred in the last 20 years, and which have been spurred in large part by transplantation of neural tissue, have led to dramatic advances in the understanding of fetal neural tissue characteristics, particularly its great capacity for plasticity, regeneration and self-repair (Lund, 1976; Michejda, 1988; Michejda, 1984). Recent reports of the transplantation of brain cells in Parkinson's disease and an attempt to restore the secretion of the neurotransmitter dopamine in the affected area of the brain are very promising (Lindvall, et al., 1992). It is conceivable that in the near future fetal tissue transplantation may be a treatment of choice for Parkinson's, Huntington's and Alzheimer's diseases, epilepsy, spinal cord injury and other inborn or acquired neurological diseases (Harris, Cotman, 1984; Fishman, 1986). The scope of fetal tissue transplantation is expanding rapidly, and now includes antenatal treatment of the fetus.

Advances in diagnostic techniques, such as ultrasound imaging and the development of various biologic markers, have provided a new basis for antenatal diagnosis and treatment. In this approach, the fetus is recognized as the patient and since fetal treatment seeks to prevent anomalies before they become irreversible, could be considered to be a new aspect of preventive medicine (Michejda and Pringle, 1987; Harrison,

7

1990). Detection of specific disorders by molecular genetic methods have made *in utero* fetal stem cell transplantation an increasingly important treatment method for the future.

There are many significant advantages of intrauterine stem cell transplantation as a method of treatment of a sick fetus. These include: fetal immunoincompetence, which obviates the need for immunosuppression, no graft-versus-host disease, sterile environment for the transplant, as well as the presence of the previously mentioned high levels of trophic and growth factors (Michejda, 1990).

One of the earliest successful attempts of *in utero* transplantation of fetal tissue was carried out in rhesus monkeys in 1981, later in baboons (Michejda, et al., 1992; Michejda, et al., 1981), and more recently in sheep and monkeys (Slotnick, Crobleholme, Anderson, et al., 1988). In 1991 three successful intrauterine stem cell transplants in human fetuses with severe immunodeficiency diseases and one case with Hunter's disease diagnosed *in utero* (mid-gestation) were reported (Touraine, Raudrant, Royo, et al., 1991)[10]. It is clear now that human fetal hematopoietic stem cell engraftment to the defective fetus at a specific time of gestation of the donor and recipient may result in rapid stem cell reconstitution.

The future of novel life saving therapies involving fetal tissue transplantation depend on the availability of healthy fetal tissue harvested at a specific gestational age of the donor. Thus, it is crucial to review briefly the current status of fetal tissue volume and availability, its gestational age characteristics, epidemiology and prognostication of its availability in the future.

It is estimated that there are 1.6 mil. abortions performed annually in USA (Hernshaw, 1990). Most of them take place during the first trimester (up to 90%), and about 10% in the second trimester (Milunski, 1986). However, those late abortions are usually performed for maternal and/or for fetal health reasons. On the other hand, it is estimated that one in seven recognized pregnancies (approx. 15%) terminates in miscarriage. A strong trend for increasing incidence for miscarriages has been reported more recently by the National Center for Health Statistics. In terms of raw numbers the National Survey of Family Growth in 1982 estimated 750,000 per year (Thorne, et al., 1989). In the late 1980's these figures increased to 840,700 per year (Kuhn, et al., 1990). The etiology of miscarriages is multifactorial. However, it is generally be-

---

[10]Krivit, Zanjani: "In utero transplantation of hemopoietic stem cells in humans" in *New Therapies for Lysosomal Storage Diseases*, 1991 (in preparation), personal communication.

lieved that genetic abnormalities in fetuses or structural abnormalities of the uterus, which interfere with the normal developmental process, contribute to most miscarriages. Moreover, it is now widely accepted that about 50% of all aborted fetuses are chromosomally abnormal (Milunski, 1986).

On the other hand uterine anomalies are the most important single group of maternal abnormalities known to cause miscarriage during second trimester. While no precise data on incidence exist, uterine anomalies are thought to cause as many as 30% of miscarriages, and consist of congenital abnormalities, intrauterine adhesions, and cervical incompetence. Additional causes of abortion are endocrine problems, immunological incompatibility, psychogenic abortion, and trauma. Also environmental factors such as radiation and other toxins or teratogens can contribute to miscarriage (Huisjes, 1984).

The viability of tissue from miscarriages is as low as 7–10% (Byrne, et al., 1985; Byrne, 1992; MacKenzie, 1988)[11]. In principle, miscarriages can occur any time during pregnancy. Thus, they can provide tissue of various gestational ages while elective abortions are more restricted to first trimester (Milunski, 1986). First trimester abortions are a generally unsuitable source of hematopoietic stem cells and of islets of Langerhans because their ontogenic development requires tissue which is derived from fetuses of 20 wks (and over) gestation (Metcalf and Moore, 1971; Michejda, Peters, de Vleeschouwer, and Bellanti, 1990). Thus, fetal bone marrow, as well as islets and major fetal organs, require second trimester donors. It is unlikely that tissue from second trimester elective abortions will provide sufficient amounts of healthy tissue. Additionally, recent reports indicate that tissue harvested from electively aborted fetuses are highly contaminated (75%) due to the methods of abortive intervention and the rapid expulsion of the fetus with the resulting rupture of the fetal abdominal wall and other surface areas (Gottesdiener, 1989). Vital fetuses from miscarriages and tissues collected shortly after death may in fact have superior qualities because they are rarely damaged (Huisjes, 1984; Gottesdiener, 1989). Utilization of oxytocin and prostaglandins may also induce free radical damage of the tissue resulting in hypoxia and ischemic changes in the tissue which could impair the process of engraftment significantly. Thus, there are many problems associated with abortive techniques and with the quality of the harvested tissues. These problems traditionally were grossly overlooked and must be addressed in the future.

---

[11]See also Goodwin and Kovacs in footnote 5 above.

9

TISSUE COLLECTION NETWORK

In view of the various limitations of both elective abortions and miscarriages as sources of fetal tissue for transplantation (Hammerslough, 1992), the establishment of tissue collection network and banks for short term tissue storage and extensive evaluation seems to be inevitable. This concept was initially proposed and discussed at the Eleventh Bishops' Workshop in Dallas (Michejda, 1992).

Establishment of fetal tissue banks is not a new concept. The first such bank was established at the Royal Marsden Hospital in London in order to collect "dead fetuses" for transplantation to patients with leukaemia (Michejda, 1992). In the USA there are a number of small tissue banks which collect various cadaveric tissues to serve the needs of the individual surgeons who established them. The largest "free-standing" tissue bank in the USA is located in Virginia Beach, VA (Virginia Tissue Bank). It has its own air transportation and "crew" for recovery of various tissues, particularly fresh cadaveric bone tissue. Currently, there are no well established fetal tissue banks in this country which are solely devoted to collection of various fetal tissues from miscarriages.

There is another compelling argument for the exploration of miscarriages as a source of transplantable tissue. The advent of early abortifacient drugs suggests that electively aborted tissue may become scarce. Furthermore, it is likely that when the use of those types of drugs becomes widespread only embryonic tissue (if any) will be available, which is for most cases unsuitable for transplantation.

Careful tissue screening and uniform high quality control is critical to the progress of broad therapeutic applications. The process of cytogenetic screening of chromosomal abnormalities now can be accelerated by utilization of fluorescence in situ hybridization (FISH). However, viral screening may require up to 3 weeks, while HIV screening requires over 4 weeks. The need for high quality control cannot be compromised by therapeutic bone marrow urgency. Thus, the establishment of tissue banks is necessary for safe and effective utilization of fetal tissue in the future. Failure to do that may lead to loss of high quality control which will result in loss of confidence in the utilization of fetal tissue in novel therapeutic modalities.

The need for fetal tissue banks is well recognized by the research community involved in transplantation research. Most recently there are strong suggestions by some to continue to support the five fetal tissue banks established by NIH, or from others to develop a comparable method of banking and processing of fetal tissue harvested predominantly from elective abortions (Cohen and Jonsen, 1993).

Table 1. Utilization of Fetal Tissue Transplants for Treatment of Various Diseases

Transplantation of Neural Tissue	Transplantation of Pancreas	Transplantation of Liver alone or with Thymus	Transplantation of Bone Marrow
Parkinson's disease	Diabetes type I	Immunodeficiencies	Erythrocyte disorder
Alzheimer's disease		Mucopolysaccharidoses	Lymphocyte disorder
Huntington's disease		Mucolipidoses	Granulocyte disorder
Epilepsy			Lysosome storage disorder
Spinal cord injury			Malignancies
Schizophrenia			AIDS

The problem of sources of fetal tissue for therapeutic transplantation will remain controversial. In the future, it will be particularly difficult for those patients for whom fetal tissue transplantation could provide a life saving treatment and who for moral reasons are against utilizing fetal tissue from elective abortions. The recent rapid progress in biological sciences, and in the new therapies, which emerged from them, has moved ahead of the currently accepted ethical guidelines. Thus, there is an urgent need to establish sound bioethical grounds which may in the future provide an ethical framework for the legal guidelines needed to regulate these new therapies.

References

AMA Council on Scientific Affairs and the Council on Ethical and Judicial Affairs. (1990). Medical Application of Fetal Tissue Transplantation. *JAMA*, *263*(4), 565–70. Barrett, J., & McCarthy, D. (1990). Bone Marrow Transplantation for Genetic Disorders. *Bone Marrow Transplantation*, *3*, 116–131.

Bjorklund, A., Olson, L., Seiger, A., & Lindvall, O. (1988). Toward a Transplantation Therapy in Parkinson's Disease. *Ann NY Acad Sci*, *495*, 658–661.

Bredesen, D., Manaster, J., & Rayner, S. e. a. (1991). Functional Improvement in Parkinsonism Following Transplantation of Temperature-Sensitive Immortalized Neural Cells. *Nerurology*, *41(Supl l)*, 325.

Brundin, P., Barbin, G., Strecker, R., Isacson, O., Pronchiantz, A., & Bjorklund. (1988). Survival and Function of Dissociated Rat Dopamine Neurones Grafted at Different Developmental Stages or After Being Cultured In Vitro. *Dev. Brain Res.*, *39*, 233–243.

Byrne, J. e. a. (1985). Morphology of Early Fetal Deaths and Their Chromosomal Characteristics. *Teratology*, *32*, 297–315.

Byrne, J. (1992, 17 July). Miscarriage Study (letter). *Science*, p. 310.

Cadet, J., Kujirai, K., & Berger, K. e. a. (1991). Differential Effects of Three Clones of the Human Neuroblastoma, SKN-SH, After Transplantation in the Rat Model of Semiparkinsonism. *Neurology*, *41 (Supl. 1)*, 326.

Carvey, P., Ptak, L., Lo, E., Lin, D., Buhrfiend, C., Goetz, C., & Klawans, H. (1991). Levodopa Reduces the Growth Promoting Effects of Striatal Extacts on Rostral Mesencephalic Tegmentum Cultures. *Exp. Neurol.*, *114*, 28–34.

Cohen, C., & Jonsen, A. (1993). The Future of the Fetal Tissue Bank. *Science*, *262*, 1663–1665.

Fishman, P. (1986). Neural Transplantation: Scientific Gains and Clinical Perspectives. *Neurology*, *36*, 389–393.

Flake, A., Harrison, M., Adzick, N., & Zanjani, E. (1986). Transplantation of Fetal Hematopoietic Stem Cells in Utero: The Creation of Hematopoietic Chimeras. *Science*, *233*, 776–78.

Freed, W., De Medinocelli, L., & Wyatt, R. (1985). Promoting Functional Plasticity in the Damaged Nervous System. *Science*, *227*, 1544–1548.

Freed, C., Breeze, R., & Rosenberg, N., et al. (1992). Survival of Implanted Fetal Dopamine Cells and Neurologic Improvement 12 to 46 Months After Transplantation for Parkinson's Disease. *N. Engl. J. Med.*, *327*, 1549–1555.

Gale, R. (1987). Fetal Liver Transplantation in Aplastic Anemia and Leukemia. *Thymus*, *10*, 89–94.

Gottesdiener, K. (1989). Tranplanted Infections: Donor-To-Host Transmission with the Allograft. *Ann Intern Med, 110,* 1001–1006. Hammerslough, C. (1992). Estimating the Probability of Spontaneous Abortion in the Presence of Induced Abortion and Vice Versa. *Public Health Reports 1992, 107,* 269–277.

Harris, E., & Cotman, C. (1984). Brain Tissue Transplantation Research. *Appl Neurophysiol, 47,* 9–11.

Hernshaw, S. (1990). Induced Abortion: A World Review. *Family Planning Perspectives, 22*(2) *1990.*

Hitchcock, E., Kenney, B., Clough, C., & Hughes, R. (1990). Stereotactic Implantation of Foetal Mesencephalon (STIM): The UK Experience. *Prog. Brain Res., 82,* 723–728.

Huisjes, H. (1984). *Spontaneous Abortion.* Edinburgh: Churchill Livingstone.

Hullet, D., Falany, J., & Love, R. e. a. (1987). Human Fetal Pancreas-A Potential Source for Transplantation. *Transplantation, 43,* 18–22.

Krivit, W., & Paul, N. (1986). Bone Marrow Transplantation for Treatment of Lysosomal Storage Diseases. *Birth Defects, 22,* 1–189.

Kuhn, F., Wachs, J., & Ruckert, J. e. a. (1990). Tissue Bank of Human Fetal Pancreas. *Transplan Proc, 22,* 683–684.

Landsdorp P.M., Dragowska W., & Mayani H. (1993). Ontogeny-Related Changes in Proliferative Potential of Human Hematopoietic Cells. *J Exp Med, 178,* 787–779.

Lindvall, O. (1991). Transplants in Parkinson's Disease. *Eur Neurol, 31 (suppl 1),* 17–27.

Lindvall, O., Widner, H., & Rehncrone, S., et al. (1992). Transplantation of Fetal Dopamine Neurons in Parkinson's Disease: One-Year Clinical and Neurophysiological Observations in Two Patients with Putaminal Implants. *Ann Neurol, 31,* 155–165.

Lindvall, O., Widner, H., & Rehncrona S., e. a. (1992). Transplantation of Fetal Dopamine Neurons in Parkinson's Disease: One-Year Clinical and Neurophysiological Observations in Two Patients with Putaminal Implants. *Ann Neurol, 31,* 155–165.

Lund, R. (1976). *Development and Plasticity of the Brain.* New York: Oxford University Press.

MacKenzie, W. e. a. (1988). Spontaneous Abortion Rate in Ultrasonographically Viable Pregnancies. *Obstet Gynecol, 71,* 81–83.

Meng, P., Fei, R., & Gu, D., et al. (1985). Allogeneic Fetal Liver Transplant in Acute Leukemia. In R. Gale, J. Touraine & G. Lucarelli (Eds.), *Fetal Liver Transplantation* (pp. 281–285). Pesaro.

Metcalf, D., & Moore, M. (1971). Embryonic Aspects of Hematopoiesis. In A. Neuberger & E. Tatum (Eds.), *Frontiers of Biology-Haematopoietic Cells* (pp. 172–271). Amsterdam: North Holland Publishing Co.

Michejda, M., Bacher, J., Kuwabara, T., & Hodgen, G. (1981). In Utero Allogeneic Bone Transplantation in Primates: Roentgenographic and Histologic Observation. *Transplantation, 32,* 96–100.

Michejda, M. (1984). Intrauterine Treatment of Spina Bifida: Primate Model. *Z Kinderchir, 39,* 259–61.

Michejda, M., & Pringle, K. (1987). New Advances in Fetal Therapy. *Fet Ther., 1,* 165–67.

Michejda, M. (1988). Utilization of Fetal Tissue in Transplantation. *Fetal Therapy, 21*(3), 129–134.

Michejda, M. (1988). CNS Repair. In M. Harrison, M. Golbus & R. Filly (Eds.), *Unborn Patient* (pp. 565–580). San Francisco, New York: Grune and Stratton, Inc.

Michejda, M. (1990). Primate Models for the Study of Prenatal Diagnosis and Treatment of CNS Defects. In C. Romanini, E. Symonds, H. Wallenburg & H. Prechtl (Eds.), *Experimental Models in Perinatal Research* (pp. 1–18). Cardiff: Parthenon Publishing.

Michejda, M., Peters, S., de Vleeschouwer MHM, & Bellanti, J. (1990). New Approaches in Bone Marrow Transplantation. *Fet Diag Therap., 5*(1), 40–56.

Michejda, M. (1992). Transplant Issues. In R. E. Smith (Ed.), *The Interaction of Catholic Bioethics and Secular Society* (pp. 115–130). Braintree: The Pope John Center.

13

Michejda, M., Peters, S., & Bellanti, J. (1992). Xenotransplantation, Bone Marrow Transplantation and Stem Cell Reconstitution. *Transplantation, 54*, 759–762.

Milunski, A. (1986). *Genetic Disorders and the Fetus. Diagnosis Prevention and Treatment.* New York: Plenum.

National Center for Health Statistics: Vital Statistics Series (6, Vol. 41). (1992).

Rice, H., Hedrick, M., & Flake, A. e. a. (1993). Bacterial and Fungal Contamination of Human Fetal Liver Collected Transvaginny for Hematopoietic Stem Cell Transplantation. *Fet. Diag. Ther., 8*(1), 42–47.

Sawle, G., Bloomfield, P., & Bjorklund A., e. a. (1992). Transplantation of Fetal Dopamine Neurons in Parkinson's Disease: PET (18F)6-L-Fluorodopa Studies in Two Patients with Putaminal Implants. *Ann Neurol, 31*, 166–173.

Slotnick, R., Crobleholme, T., & Anderson, J. e. a. (1988). Stable Hematopoietic Chimerism Following In Utero Stem Cell Transplantation. *Am J Human Genetics, 43*(1–3), A133.

Spencer, D., Robbins J., & Naftolin et al. (1992). Unilateral Transplantation of Human Fetal Mesencephalic Tissue into the Caudate Nucleus of Patients with Parkinson's Disease. *N. Eng. J. Med., 327*, 1541–1543.

Stromberg, I., Bygdeman, M., Goldstein, M., Seiger, A., & Olson, L. (1986). Human Fetal Substantia Nigra Grafted to the Dopamine-Denervated Striatum of Immunosuppressed Rats: Evidence for Functional Reinnervation. *Neurosci Lett., 71*, 271–276.

Stromberg, I., Bygdeman, M., Goldstein, M., Seiger, A., & Olson, L. (1986). Human Fetal Substantia Nigra Grafted to The Dopaminedenervated Striatum of Immunosuppressed Rate: Evidence for Functional Reinnervation. *Neurosci Lett., 71*, 271–276.

Thorne, E., & Michejda, M. (1989). Fetal Tissue from Spontaneous Abortions: A New Alternative for Transplantation Research. *Fetal Diagnosis and Therapy, 4*, 37–42.

Touraine, J., Ronsarolo, M., Royo, C., & Touraine, F. (1987). Fetal Tissue Transplantation, Bone Marrow Transplantation and Prospective Gene Therapy in Severe Immunodeficiencies and Enzyme Deficiencies. *Thymus, 10*, 75–81.

Touraine, J., Raudrant, D., & Royo, C. e. a. (1991). In Utero Transplantation of Hemopoietic Stem Cells in Humans. *Transplant Proc, 23*, 1706–1708.

Touraine, J., Raudrant, D., & Royo, C., et al. (1991). In Utero Transplantation of Hemopoietic Stem Cells in Humans. *Transplant Proc, 23*, 1706–1708.

U.S. Congress, Office of Technology Assessment. (1990). *Neural Grafting: Repairing the Brain and Spinal Cord.* Washington, D.C.: U.S. Government Printing Office.

Unborn Patient. (1990). Philadelphia: W.B. Saunders.

Wictorin, K., Clarke, D., Bolam, J., Brundin, P., Gustavii, B., Lindvall, O., & Bjorklund, A. (1990). Extensive Efferent Projections of a Species-Specific Neurofilament Market and Anterograde Axonal Tracing. *Prog Brain Res., 82*, 391–399.

Widner, H., Tetrud J., & Rehncrona, S., et al. (1992). Bilateral Fetal Mesencephalic Grafting in Two Patients with Parkinsonism Induced by 1-Methyl-1,2,3,6-Tetrahydropyridine (MPTP). *N. Engl. J. Med., 327*, 1556–1563.

14

FETAL TISSUE AND THE QUESTION OF CONSENT

Hadley Arkes

Editors' Summary: Arkes recalls for us that in the mind of Lincoln, Hamilton, and Madison the "right of human beings to be governed by their own consent is the 'father of all principles'." Contained therein is the right to be informed about, and freely to consent to, medical treatment.

Unlike the situation for our Founding Fathers, these claims today are not based on human nature but on an ungrounded premise of autonomy which has been fashioned to be the groundwork for the "new rights of privacy" from which could be drawn the "right" to abortion and the "right" to die. Beings, i.e., human beings, who can give and understand reasons about matters of right and wrong deserve to be treated differently from those beings such as animals who cannot. But autonomy and consent have moral limits which determine what we can do to others and what we can allow to be done to ourselves. Although, as Locke noted, we may be in a state of natural liberty, it is not a state of license—one does not have the right to destroy himself or another.

With regard to fetal tissue, we are dealing with "donors" who do not have the competence to donate. But is this arrangement for the good of the fetus or for others? The drive to collect fetal tissue has been powered and justified by the prospect of a palpable good—the treatment of Altzeimer's disease, Parkinson's, and the like. But a woman may have no moral right to consent to the destruction of her child for the purpose of providing fetal tissues for another person. If she has decided to have an abortion, it is a decision not to be a mother, and hence she has no moral basis for giving consent to what happens to the child.

The movement for a Uniform Anatomical Gift Act was propelled by an interest in overcoming the barriers of the common law and the natural reluctance on the part of people to donate the parts of their own bodies. However, the very principle of the obligation to rescue, used to justify procurement of tissue from an unconsenting fetus, really argues for the rescue and protection of the unborn child. Furthermore, even if the child is "going to die anyway" through abortion, there is no moral justification to become accomplices to the abortion by making use of this tissue. Only in the case of a miscarriage or the death of a child who was delivered prematurely in an effort to save that child could a parent or guardian become morally responsible for donating the child's tissues.

Abraham Lincoln made the point with sobriety, with no touch of hyperbole, that the proposition "all men are created equal" was the "father of all principles" among us. That proposition was the central proposition of the Declaration of Independence, and it was put forth in that document, not as an expression of "opinion," but as a self-evident truth. By a self-evident truth, the Founders meant a truth that was *per se nota;* as Alexander Hamilton explained, it was a proposition containing "an internal evidence which, antecedent to all reflection and combination, commands the assent of the mind." This truth of the Declaration provided the ground for that universal right, proclaimed in the Declaration, of human beings to be governed only with their own consent. James Madison would later refer to that central truth of the Declaration as an "absolute" truth.[1] And with the same understanding, Lincoln would remark that "the doctrine of self-government is right—absolutely and eternally right."[2]

This right of human beings to be governed by their own consent would seem to be the "father of all principles" of consent, including that claim more familiar in our own day, the claim of a patient to consent to the medical treatment that is administered to him. That claim of a right

---

[1]See the annals of Congress, June 8, 1789, or the passage reprinted in Schwartz (1971: 1029).

[2]Speech in Peoria on the Kansas-Nebraska Act (September 1854) in Basler (1953: 265).

to consent entails the further claim of the right to be "informed" about the nature of the treatment. As Aristotle observed, an act taken in ignorance may not exactly be a "voluntary" act (Aristotle: 1110b18–1111al and ff.). It is not that the act is "involuntary"—that it is caused by forces utterly beyond the control of the actor. But rather, an "action" involves intention, choice, reflection. If a patient does not understand the real purpose or end of a medical procedure, it is hard to say that he "intends" the end that is implied in that procedure. If he is not alert to its hazards, he does not reckon knowingly the prospect of this procedure to attain a "good" for him, or to preserve his own well-being. To consent, then, out of ignorance, is not to consent at all.

These claims have become familiar in our own day, and yet they have been removed from the moral framework that supplied, for the American Founders, their meaning and coherence. For the American Founders, these claims sprung from "truths," and those truths were grounded in human nature, or in the "laws of reason." But in our own day, the doctrine of informed consent has been drawn from a premise of "autonomy," detached from any claims about human nature, or even from any claim to its own truth.[3]

That claim of autonomy has been fashioned to provide the groundwork for new rights of privacy, which could entail in turn a right to abortion, and a "right to die." These claims have been fashioned for the sake of resisting the intrusions of the law, for governments were more willing to intervene in these domains when they were swollen with the conviction that they were vindicating moral truths, grounded in nature. For the writers in our new jurisprudence, "nature" is mainly an invention; what we take to be "nature" is really "socially constituted" from place to place according to the conventions that are dominant in any country. And in their estimate, the law that began with "nature" had the political function of preserving a patriarchal order, marked by the subordination of women. A law that would install, for women, a right to abortion, would sweep away all legal restrictions based on "nature" or on claims to moral truth. In its place would be put new rights of "autonomy," inhering in "persons." Those rights would entail the right to elect—or reject—any medical procedures, as a reflection of the right of any person to be the sovereign judge of the reasons that are finally good enough to justify the performance of surgery on her body.

But where was this right to "autonomy" anchored? And what made it "right"? In the new jurisprudence, that claim to autonomy was simply

---

[3]I have set forth this argument more fully in some of my own pieces; the reader may see Arkes (1987: 421–422); and Arkes (1990: 599–615).

stipulated, without offering a proof, or drawing lines of reason from deeper principles. As the saying went, there were no "foundations" for moral judgments, and therefore, no foundations for these new "rights" in the law. We were asked simply to posit, or stipulate, as a premise, the notion that human beings claimed a certain respect, as persons, to be treated as ends in themselves, and that they deserved as much freedom as practicable to pursue their own ends. But for anyone who was reluctant to accept these stipulations, there were no truths that could command his assent and establish these rights as truly "rightful."

The new jurisprudence, anchored in "autonomy," claimed some connection to Immanuel Kant, for Kant did seek to find a ground of moral judgment that would not depend merely on generalizations about human nature, drawn from records of experience. But for Kant, claims of right and autonomy were contained in a distinctly moral framework, governed by the laws of reason. And even though Kant sought to move beyond narrowly empirical accounts of human nature, the moral laws were to be drawn, as he said, from the very idea of "a rational creature as such."

After all, even in the world of the new jurisprudence, not all beings could claim rights of "autonomy" and informed consent. Even the professors of this new law will not sign labor contracts with dogs and horses. That is to say, we will not seek the "consent" of these creatures before we rule them, or before we authorize surgery upon them. Eventually, we back into an ancient understanding: that beings who can give and understand reasons deserved to be ruled in a manner notably different from beings who cannot understand reasons over matters of right and wrong. Beings who can understand reasons deserve to be ruled only through the rendering of reasons or justifications. They have a right, in other words, to hear the reasons, and to consent to the terms on which they are governed. We do not make this provision for dogs, horses, and other animals, and for the same reason, we do not enter the charade of seeking their consent to surgery. For they are patently unable to deliberate about the ends of the surgery, and to weigh their own interests.

The right of autonomy, the right to be governed only with one's own consent, was a right that arose only for "a rational creature as such." But then the paradox: It was in the very nature of these beings that they had access to an understanding of right and wrong, and if they understood the things that were "wrong," they understood the things they were not free to choose even in the name of their own autonomy. As Aquinas and Lincoln taught, we cannot coherently claim a "right to do a wrong." If it is wrong in principle to make slaves of other human beings, then it is wrong to make a slave of oneself, and nothing in one's own "consent" could efface the wrongness of the arrangement. As the saying used to go, this was one of those rights that we were incompetent to waive or to "alienate" even for ourselves.

This logic of "unalienable" rights marked the moral limits to the claims of autonomy and consent, and therefore it marked the limits to the kinds of things we were free to order up for others as well. We could show here, for example, if we had the space, that we could not rightfully order the death of any person on account of his deafness. We could show that "deafness" was an affliction utterly wanting in moral significance: From a person's deafness we could not draw any inferences about his goodness or badness, and for that reason, we could not draw any judgment on whether that person *deserved* to live or die. But if deafness could not supply a ground of justification for taking the life of any other person, it could not supply a justification for the taking of our own life. And if we would not be justified in ending our own lives on account of our deafness, it would have to follow that we could not transfer to any of our relatives a license of "substituted judgment" to end our lives on account of our deafness. On the basis of our own "autonomy" we could not transfer to others a power of "consent" to end our lives for reasons we could not rightly invoke ourselves, even in the name of our own autonomy.

This recognition may be breaking through again of late, but it is worth reminding ourselves that it is rooted in understandings that run back to the Founders, and to the ancients, to the first books of moral philosophy. Even Locke, who thought that our rights of consent began with our ownership of ourselves—even Locke understood that suicide, or self-killing, would be as wrongful as the unjustified killing of any other person. That is, our supposed ownership of ourselves did not provide a "right to do a wrong" even to ourselves. Man might be in a state of natural liberty, "yet it is not a state of license: though man in that state have an uncontrollable liberty to destroy himself" (Locke, 1690: Sec.5). And since he has no right to destroy himself wrongly, he may not alienate or transfer such a right to anyone else:

> Nobody can give more power than he has himself, and he that cannot take away his own life cannot give another power over it . . . [N]o man can by agreement pass over to another that which he hath not in himself a power over his own life (Locke, 1690: Secs. 23, 24).[4]

---

[4]In an earlier, unpublished manuscript on "The Law of Nature," Locke had been willing to fill out a rather different notion of the "ownership" of ourselves, and he made it even clearer that nothing in the control of ourselves diminished in any way our responsibility to a moral law outside ourselves:

The same premises that established, then, our right to be governed by our own consent established that we had no right to consent to things that were wrongful. These understandings were comprehensible to us in the past, and as I say, they are breaking through again today, for they mark the only moral framework in which the issues of "consent" in medicine can attain their coherence. And when this framework of understanding is set in place once again, it must make the most profound difference for the question of consent and fetal tissue.

With the donation of fetal tissue, we are dealing with "donors" who do not have the competence to "donate," and they are not accorded the moral standing of donors. In that respect alone, there is nothing novel here. The law often encounters beings who do not have the competence or maturity to tender their own consent. They may include infants, animals, and persons who are retarded, infirm, or critically wanting in the competence to manage their own affairs. In those instances, someone else may be recognized as a guardian or superintendent, to make decisions on behalf of a being in need of care. But that guardianship is recognized as a moral office: The authority is not assigned to the guardian to dispose of the body and assets of the ward to further the profit of the guardian. The guardianship is a trust, which is justified by a need to make decisions directed to the preservation and the well-being of the ward. Parents are invested with the authority to decide on the surgeries performed on their minor children, but that authority may be overridden if parents seek to withhold blood transfusions or other treatments that may be necessary to preserve the lives of their children. Even the owners of dogs may be restrained from torturing their own animals, and it goes without saying that they do not have the authority to order, from a veterinarian, the kind of surgery that would simply inflict a gratuitous suffering.

When the extraction of fetal tissue is approached with these understandings, the first question of course is whether the procedure is designed to serve the good of the fetus, or the child. In the case of a child who has died, or who is about to die, through a miscarriage, there is no

---

Since god is superior to all things, [and] he holds as much right and authority over us as we cannot hold over ourselves, since we owe to him and to him alone our body, soul, life, whatever we are, whatever we possess, and also whatever we can be it is right that we live [obedient] to the prescription of his will.

See Locke, *Questions Concerning the Law of Nature*, in Horwitz, Strauss Clay, and Clay (1990: 211, 213).

prospect of attaining a good for the child, and so the problem must shift to the question of whether the tissue of the child is being extracted for the purpose of advancing a legitimate end. It is not idle to point out that we would never countenance the eating of this flesh, or the use of this tissue in making lamp shades or soap. For we have had vivid reminders, in the reach of our own experience, that members of our species have not been above these "uses" of tissue, drawn from beings they recognized quite readily as human. In several states, there are statutes that bar the commercial sale of fetuses, as a species of traffic in the flesh of humans, or as a commerce that reduces the "parts" of human beings to commodities. Those statutes make sense only if we are alert to the fact that it is human tissue that is bought and sold. That point is covered over in the description of the sources as "fetuses," as indeed that term is used to cover over the nature of the lives that are taken in abortions. But these small recognitions, breaking through the fictions of the law, remind us that there may still be restrictions on the uses of tissue drawn from children in the womb. The persistence of these provisions in the law seem to mark the fact that there will be necessary, lingering concerns about the treatment of this tissue, regardless of how the subjects may be described.

In the recent controversy, the drive to collect fetal tissue has been powered and justified by the prospect of a palpable good: the treatment of Alzheimer's disease, Parkinson's, diabetes, and certain spinal cord injuries.[5] And indeed, the prospects here seem so rich in possibilities that they would justify the efforts to make use of this tissue, if it can be decently or justly collected. In the case of miscarriages and the deaths that result from ectopic pregnancies, that medical use could provide an ample justification. But the question of consent and justification must be gravely altered with the case of elective abortions. If the abortion is ordered solely for the sake of extracting the tissue, then the life of a child is being sacrificed for the sake of serving the interests of another. The usual notions of self-defense are out of place here, for the child poses no distinct threat to the lives of the people who might benefit from its tissue. The child bears no *mens rea*, no guilty mind, no intention of harming the people who might make use of its tissue. She could be said to "threaten" the life of another only by withholding the tissue that may be of use to another. But in that respect, the child holds back nothing that would not be available in any other child with useable tissue. And in

---

[5]See, for example, the account offered by Senator Orrin Hatch in Hatch (1992: S4467–68). See also chapter one of this volume.

that respect, too, the child would pose no "threat" to the user that the user is not posing, in turn, to the child, by seeking her death as an attendant consequence of seeking her tissue.

But in point of principle, it is not as all clear as to why the life of the child is not worth preserving, quite as much as the life of that adult who would seek the use of her tissues. She has done, after all, no wrong, which could warrant the destruction of her life; and there is no ground of principle on which to say that she has a life any less worth living than the life of anyone else. In that event, it would not matter in the least that a pregnant woman has "consented" to the extraction of tissue from her child. If there is no ground that justifies the destruction of the child in these circumstances, the pregnant woman would have no right to consent to this procedure and order the destruction of the child.

Of course, we are addressing this question at a time when people have been given a license by the Supreme Court to order an abortion at any stage of the pregnancy, for virtually any reason or interest that moves the pregnant woman. Let us suppose then that the woman had ordered up an abortion anyway, perhaps because this was an inconvenient pregnancy, or because, for one reason or another, the child was not "wanted." In that event, the pregnant woman would have reckoned her interests, weighed them on a scale with the interests of the child, and come to the judgment that the child had no interest she felt bound to respect. Or to put it more precisely, let us say that she came to the judgment that her own interests or needs, even the interests of her own convenience, overrode any claim on the part of the child to have its life preserved. Under those conditions, it would seem to be clear beyond shading that the woman has made a decision not to be a "mother" in any sense that defines the office and the relation: She will not bring the child through to birth; she will not sustain the child after birth; she will not take on the functions of nurturance and protection that we associate with parents. Beyond that, she will not even take the minimal responsibility of placing of the child in the hands of people who are willing to offer that care and nurturance.

It is hard to imagine, in sum, a situation in which a woman would sever more decisively her connections to the child and the claim to stand, in the life of that child, in the position of a "mother" or even a guardian. In that event, it is not only an extravagant presumption, but a logical inversion, for this woman to claim the office now of a mother, or parent, in "consenting" to the use of tissue drawn from the child, or collecting a royalty for its use. For she would have overthrown the premises that stand behind the usual claim on behalf of parents, namely, that her decisions are governed by an overriding concern for the health and well-being of the child.[6] It is worth pointing out that this conclusion could stand, regardless of whether we accepted the current laws on abortion: For it should be clear that the woman who has ordered up the abortion has given a powerful, unequivocal sign that her decisions on the child are not animated by an interest in preserving the life and health of the child. If that meaning is not clear in abortion, nothing is clear. But in that case, it should be quite as clear that she could not meet the minimal moral conditions that would be necessary to the authority of a "parent" in consenting to surgeries, or disposing in any way of the body of the child.

That conclusion might seem a bit jarringly out of line with the currents of our time, but we need to remind ourselves here that there has been something novel, and a touch bizarre, in the currents of our time. As recently as thirty years ago, there was no settled assumption in the law about the "right" of anyone to "consent" or "donate" the parts of his own body, let alone the parts of any other person. We have moved rapidly into the age of *Roe v. Wade*, euthanasia, and procedures even more refined in the transplantation of bodily organs. The ready acceptance of these new surgeries has produced, in turn, a discourse similarly unburdened with any sense of the novel or the problematic. People may speak readily about the donation of organs, and women describing themselves as "mothers" may claim a right to dispose of tissues drawn from the fetuses they would discard, as though nothing remarkable were taking place. But this strainless improvising has been attended by remarkably little in the way of explicit reasonings, on the same plane of seriousness, to settle the rights and wrongs of the matter.

Against the recent trends in surgery and law, it is rather curious to consider that there was almost no sense, in the common law, of any right of property over a dead body and its parts. For that reason, there was no clear sense that anyone had a right to make a "donation." And so Blackstone could remark that there were grounds for prosecuting the thieves who steal a shroud from a grave, for the shroud "is the property of those, whoever they were, that buried the deceased: but stealing the corpse itself, which has no owner (though a matter of great indecency) is no felony, unless some of the gravecloths be stolen with it" (Blackstone, ed. 1979: 216).[7] With the same understanding, Blackstone observed in

---

[6]For an extended statement of his position, one could hardly do better than the statement offered by James Bopp and Fr. James Burtchaell in their dissent on the *Report of the Human Fetal Tissue Transplantation Research Panel*, NIH (Bopp and Burtchaell, 1988: 45–70; especially 47–50).

[7]Originally published in 1769.

another place that "the heir has a property in the monuments and escutcheons of his ancestors, yet he has none in their bodies or ashes; nor can he bring any civil action against such as indecently at least, if not impiously, violate and disturb their remains, when dead and buried" (Blackstone, ed. 1979: 429).

Certain "rights" have been ceded as a kind of annex to the duties of those people who finally bear the responsibility for arranging the burial or disposal of the body. In that respect, as one commentator wrote, the American courts have been willing to designate a corpse "as property under certain circumstances and in [a] very limited sense."[8] But obviously, the law has been ready to honor the wishes, expressed by the decedent before his death, on the arrangements for his own burial and the disposal of his body. That we honor the stipulations made, on these matters, in a will, would seem to mark our respect for that elementary right of property that a person may claim in himself—indeed, in that right which Locke regarded as the foundation of all other claims of property. That we honor the claim even on the part of a person no longer alive would seem to indicate, quite powerfully, that his rights over his body do not vanish with his own bodily death. One team of legal commentators ran perhaps more deeply than they knew when they observed that "the roots of the unique position of the dead body in a world of 'property' must lie in something extrinsic to the dead body itself."[9]

The source of rights, once again, must lie in principles that are not material in nature. Those rights do not vanish upon death because the principles themselves do not decompose. But of course the principles that establish the rightful uses of the body may also establish the wrongful uses, and so they may place limits on the kinds of things that a person is free to will, even in the name of his property in his own body. In this vein, the Attorney General of California pronounced the judgment, in 1980, that a person would not have a constitutional right to place his body into cryogenic suspension with the hope of being thawed out, and animated again, at a more promising moment.[10] But the judgment, in this instance, seems to be drawn from the ancient notion of an "unalienable" right: We are enjoined not to take our lives on untethered speculations, for the same reason that we are enjoined not to destroy our lives knowingly in an act of suicide.

---

[8]Cited in Steven M. Cooper, "Consent and Organ Donation," 11 *Rutgers Computer & Technology Law Journal* 559, at 578 (1985).

[9]Sideman and Rosenfeld, "Legal Aspects of Tissue Donation from Cadavers," 21 *Syracuse Law Review* 825, at 826 (1970), cited in *ibid.*, at 577 n. 103.

[10]See 63 *Opinions of the Attorney General* (California) 879 (1980).

When our techniques of surgery suddenly ran, then, beyond the state of our law; when the possibilities emerged for transplanting eyes and kidneys; the common law cast up all kinds of barriers of hesitation. Hence, the move in the late 1960's to overcome the reservations of the common law with a new, "uniform law on anatomical gifts." The reservations and silences of the common law were discouraging the gift of organs, and those inhibitions were amplified by the variations cast up in the laws as the transactions moved beyond the bounds of the separate States. There was a need, at the very least, to insure that a donation, made according to the laws in one State, would be honored in another. The solution seemed to lie in a Uniform Anatomical Gift Act, which was approved by the National Conference of Commissioners on Uniform State Laws, and the American Bar Association, in August, 1968.[11] Within two years, that model statute had been enacted, with only minor revisions, in 47 States. By 1973, all of the States and the District of Columbia had placed this statute on their books.

And yet, in spite of this orchestrated effort on the part of the legal profession to remove the subtle barriers and encourage these novelties in medicine, the members of the public held to their venerable inhibitions. In the face of this encouragement, elaborately choreographed, they persisted in their reluctance to tender their consent. It was not that they were held back by any dim prejudices clinging from the past. The American Council on Transplantation commissioned a survey by the Gallop organization in 1985, and the survey revealed that 93 per cent of the Americans in the sample knew about the transplantation of organs. Of those Americans, amply tutored, 75 per cent approved of the concept of donating organs. And yet, only 27 per cent indicated that they were likely to donate their own organs, and only 17 per cent had actually bothered to fill out "donor cards" or prepare the legal documents. Of the people who were likely to donate organs, only half had mentioned their intentions to members of their families—even though the permission of the family would usually be sought before organs were removed.[12] In the abstract, these Americans would not detach themselves from the liberal sentiments of the age. But when it came to their own cases, these Americans, much given to high sentiments, still evidently had trouble in conceiving the project in terms that would not entail a certain dismemberment. And that prospect still had a tendency to de-

---

[11]8A *Uniform Laws Annotated* 16, and for the provisions of the statute, see 30ff. (1983).
[12]See the Report of the Task Force on Organ Transplantation (April 1986) cited in 8A *Uniform Laws Annotated;* 1992 Supplementary Pamphlet, 4.

flect people to less mordant thoughts, and more cheerful schemes, for pursuing the public good.

But while the public remained stodgy, there had been a dramatic enhancement in the techniques for performing transplants. There were powerful, new immunosuppressive drugs, such as Cyclosporine, and there were notable improvements in the techniques for transplanting organs and tissues. The ironic result was a widening of the gap between the demand and supply.

With more people able to use the organs and tissues, and with the continued aversion of the public, there were about 8,000 to 10,000 people now waiting for transplants.[13] These new, obdurate facts seemed to exert further pressure for a Reform of the Reform: There would now be a 1987 version of the Uniform Anatomical Gift Act, to overcome the points of hesitation, and make it far easier to gather the consent of persons to the donation of their organs. It would not be necessary any longer to have the addition of witnesses, or the consent of the next of kin, if a donor had made out a proper document to authorize the removal of organs. There would be a further aid to the identification of donors through the duty to search for the documents of a gift. Hospitals would also take it as a new part of their routine to raise with their patients the question of donating organs.[14]

Still, these subtle encouragements would not alter the fundamental structure of "consent," and for some critics, the supply of organs did not promise to improve dramatically until there was a more critical shift in the presumptions that governed these transactions. For in the presence of silence or doubt, it was not to be presumed that consent had been tendered. The act of consent had to be explicit, and solemnly offered. If the donor could not sign a letter of consent, the letter could be signed by another person, but in the presence of two witnesses, "at the direction and in the presence of the donor and of each other."[15] But for the sake of encouraging donations, or relieving the anxieties that surrounded these gifts, it was thought important to make it easy for the donor to change his mind, to revoke his gift. He could sign a new statement; he could make an oral statement in the presence of two witnesses; he could simply convey his wishes, in any form, to a physician or surgeon in the course of a terminal illness; or he could send a signed statement to the donee, withdrawing the gift. Again, the burden of explicitness attached

---

[13]See *ibid.*, 4–5.
[14]*Ibid.*, at 5.
[15]*Ibid.*, Section 2, at 12.

to the giving of consent, and the paths were to be cleared for the withdrawal of consent.

However, there was, in the Anatomical Gift Act, an extended list of the persons who could be authorized to donate organs and tissue when the intentions of the decedent were unknown. The law established, in fact, a hierarchy of people who could exercise this new franchise to allocate this new property: First came the spouse, followed by the adult sons or daughters, and then by either parent of the one who had died. If there were no living parents, the authority would shift to an adult brother or sister, then to a grandparent, and finally to a guardian. No person lower in the hierarchy could make the donation if the authorities could find a person higher in the list of precedence. But what is more important, any authorization made by a person lower in the list would be superseded if any person higher in the list objected to the donation of the organs. And no one, anywhere on the list, was to authorize a gift if he knew that the decedent had indicated wishes to the contrary.[16]

Behind this hierarchy of titles lay an unstated assumption: namely, that the people bearing these relations to the decedent were more likely to be attached to his interests. That assumption, of course, was notably less than an apodictic truth. There are people, after all, who have not inspired affection or loyalty, even among their closest relatives. Even when the proxies are animated by a devotion to their relative and a zeal for the public good, the deeper question has yet to be answered: How do these relatives claim a right to authorize the dismembering of his body, in a project he never sanctioned, and dispose of the body in this way as a part simply of their responsibility to arrange for its decorous burial?

But even if we put that vexing matter aside, we ought to notice that the structure of consent remains largely the same. If people still remain reluctant to dwell, with a morbid precision, in planning for their own dismemberment, even the changes in the law do not promise a wave of new donations. One commentator has been moved then, as I suggested, to urge a decisive switch in presumptions: In the presence of silence or the absence of opposition, it might be presumed now that the decedent had consented to the donation of his organs.[17] The writer would bring forth, as the compelling ground for this shift, a substantial public interest in the salvaging of tissues and organs. The new calculus of utility would have, in its scale, the large numbers of people (say, 8,000 to 10,000) whose lives could be saved, or ameliorated, by these acts of retrieval. We would have, on the one side, an immense good to be done,

---

[16]See *ibid.*, at 17 (Section 3).
[17]See Steven Cooper, *supra*, note 18, at 571, and generally, 569–88.

and many lives to be saved. On the other side, we would have persons who had registered no explicit objections if their organs would be used to save the lives of others.

And with the prospect of saving the lives of particular persons, the courts have acted, in some signal cases, to impose surgeries even on patients who had emphatically refused their consent. Two of the more celebrated cases involved Jehovah's Witnesses, who had refused on religious grounds to have blood transfusions: In *Raleigh Fitkin-Paul Memorial Hospital v. Anderson* (1964),[18] a court ordered the blood transfusion for a woman in the thirty-second week of pregnancy, for the sake of saving her unborn child. The court did not claim the authority to intervene for the sake of saving the woman's own life. In this case, the interests of the mother and the child were so connected that the court could not act for the child without affecting the mother. But in a related case the same year, at Georgetown Hospital in Washington, Judge Skelley Wright was willing to order a blood transfusion solely for the interest in saving the life of the patient.[19]

Still, in these cases, the calculus was tilted decisively: There was a life to be saved with timely action, where the needs of the patient were precisely known. And the subject who was compelled to undergo surgery was not forced to risk her own life as she was recruited for the rescue. Indeed, in these cases, the unwilling subject had her own life saved through the surgery. These kinds of cases usually come to us in a broader framework, under the "obligation to rescue," and they may lend themselves to this reckoning of interests: We may compel people at times to go to the rescue, or lend their aid in a rescue, when they are not compelled to risk an injury comparable to the injury we are seeking to avert. An unsteady swimmer could not be obliged to plunge to the rescue of a man drowning, for he could not be obliged to risk his own, innocent life in the effort to save another.[20] And so, when the donors of organs have been faced with danger, or the serious impairment of their own condition, the courts have leaned decisively in the other direction. In *McFall v. Shimp,* in 1978, a court in Pennsylvania refused to order a man to donate some of his bone marrow to his cousin. In this case, there was reason to believe that the donor was uniquely situated to save the life of his relative, and indeed the plaintiff died soon after the suit had

---

[18]42 N.J. 421, 201 A. 2d 537.

[19]See Application of President and Directors of Georgetown College, 331 F. 2d 1000 (D.C. Cir.).

[20]For the discussion of these cases, and the principles that govern them, see Arkes (1986: 292–99).

failed.[21] The court marked its aversion to the defendant, but it saw no practicable way of overriding the primary right of the defendant to offer, or withhold, this consent to the surgery on himself.

What might we establish, then, if we sought to collect the strands from this record and bring them to bear on the problem of fetal tissue? For one thing, we would begin with the most pronounced aversion to any arrangement for extracting tissue from subjects who are not in a position to render their own consent. That aversion would be deepened in cases in which the subject is not treated through the surgery, but deliberately killed as an inescapable part of the procedure for removing the tissue. And yet, the circumstances of the case could mesh with the current provisions of the Anatomical Gift Act if the child died in a miscarriage, without any design to bring about its death. For then, when the removal of the tissue will cause no further injury, any number of people may be authorized, under the law, to make a donation of that tissue, that it may yet yield a practicable good.

The most radical proposal, to switch the presumptions that govern consent, would be unavailing on this matter. In fact, it would argue even more powerfully in another direction: When we set in place the facts and principles that enjoin the obligation to rescue; when we weigh the interest in saving life, against the injury that is threatened to the "rescuer"; we could hardly arrive at the conclusion that a child in the womb should have its life sacrificed in order to relieve the condition of another person, whose life it does not threaten, and whose condition it does not strain. The same principles would argue even more compellingly on the other side: that there is an obligation to rescue *the child* from the elective abortion. On the one hand, the child is faced with certain death, and on the other, the woman ordering the abortion may be threatened with injuries that are dramatically less than fatal. She may be faced with embarrassment or the derangement of her plans, or she may be faced with the inconvenience of several months in carrying a child to term. Some of these discomforts may be felt acutely, but none of them stands on the same plane as the injury that is threatened for the child. And if the conclusion flows from the comparison of these interests, the conclusion would seem plain: The woman would be obliged to bear these costs and rescue the life that she is uniquely in a position to save.[22]

When it comes, then, to the matter of fetal tissue, we find that the most audacious argument finally turns against itself: The most radical case for extracting tissue from donors without their consent would de-

---

[21]See 10 Pa. D. & C. 3d 90 (Eq. Ct. C.P. Allegheny Co.).
[22]For an argument in this vein, see Arkes (1986: 397-403).

pend on the principles that enjoin the obligation to rescue, and those principles would not sweep away the inhibitions on using the tissues drawn from unborn children. They would enjoin us, rather, to turn away even more firmly from elective abortions and the destruction of the child.

If a family treats a child as a commodity to be discarded, then it should go without saying that the transaction may come under the kinds of rules that govern the discarding of other materials. For one thing, the child may not be discarded in ways that create nuisances for the community. Of course, the family may dispose of certain goods by selling them. But we retain at least enough of a sensibility on this matter to put restraints on the selling of human fetuses and their parts. If a serious program of research takes hold with the use of fetal parts, there will no doubt be exchanges for these scarce parts, and we should not be surprised if some bids are attended by offers of cash or other payments. It may be impossible to suppress these transactions, but the law may at least withhold its endorsement. It may refuse to recognize the legitimacy of this commerce, and simply in holding back, in refusing to enforce these "contracts," the law may render these arrangements more hazardous and discouraging.

If fetuses are to be discarded and not sold, then the woman who chooses an abortion should make it clear, in the formalities of abortion, that she has indeed discarded the child and its tissue. In that event, the tissue will come into the possession of a clinic or surgical facility, where the abortion is performed. If there is an active commerce in this tissue, then there will no doubt be exchanges for cash, which will affect the profitability of the enterprise. Even when the laws of a State forbid the "sale" of this tissue, it will still be necessary to pay for the procedures and administration, and the transactions may be described, as they are in Minnesota, as "renditions of service." If there is money to be made in this business, some clinics will be offering abortions at lower prices for the sake of luring in the material they can sell, in turn, later. In this manner, the donors may be compensated, in the form of lower prices, on other services. Still, the community may prefer that the transactions take this indirect character, rather than encouraging people to sell their own fetuses and making them suggestible to the notion of redeeming their offspring for cash.

As much as practicable, the decision on abortion should be detached from any incentive to make the tissue available for research. That concern was taken quite seriously by the panel on Human Fetal Tissue Transplantation, of the National Institutes of Health, in 1988, and it has even carried over to the drafters of the new legislation on the use of fetal tissue: In both cases, there was an effort to establish a procedural

30

barrier between the decision on abortion and the retrieval of the tissue. The concern here was that the prospect of rendering a "public service" could finally tilt the judgment of a woman who was poised, indecisive, on the threshold of an abortion. The prospect of "aiding research" could be used as a casual device for sweeping away those moral reservations that may still offer a wholesome inhibition on the choice of an abortion. And so, under the current proposals, the decision on abortion is to be insulated from any judgment about the use of fetal tissue, and from any decision to donate the tissue to a beneficiary known to the pregnant woman.

It was made clear by the dissenting members of the panel of the NIH that these were, at best, the procedures that would come into play where the laws still protected, at every point, the right to order an abortion at any stage of the pregnancy, and for any reason. But these are not the procedures that should be in force in any Catholic hospital, or in any institution that would regard abortion as morally portentous. We are persuaded that abortion involves, in almost all cases, the unjustified taking of a human life, and in that event, we would be governed by that ancient maxim of the law, that it is never permissible to profit from wrongdoing. Even if many of these children are "going to die anyway" in abortions, that wrong would not permit us to become accomplices in their death by making use of this tissue, which could be gathered only through the commission of a grave wrong. And again, no "consent" tendered by a pregnant woman, could efface the nature of this wrong, and render this use of the tissue, in our eyes, as morally tenable.

We are left then, necessarily, with the path of pursuing this research through means that are morally defensible. And that means that we are confined, in the first place, to the tissue drawn from miscarriages, or from children who were extracted from the womb earlier in an effort to save their lives. Under those conditions, there would be no evident strain in considering just who would have the authority to consent to the extraction and use of the tissue. The parents or guardians who intended the birth and nurturing of the child, the guardians who were governed up to the last moment by the dominant interest in preserving the life of the child, would have a clear moral standing to tender a consent, in place of the child, and make a gift of this tissue.

References
Aristotle, A. *Nicomachean Ethics.* Book III.
Arkes, H. (1986). *First Things.* Princeton: Princeton University Press.
Arkes, H. (1987, May). "Autonomy" and the "Quality of Life": The Dismantling of Moral Terms. *Issues in Law & Medicine.*

Arkes, H. (1990, September). When Bungling Practice Is Joined to Absurd Theory: Doctors, Philosophers, and the Right to Die. *The World & I.*

Blackstone, W. (1979). *Commentaries on the Laws of England* (Vol. 4). Chicago: University of Chicago.

Bopp, J., & Burtchaell, J. (1988). *Report of the Human Fetal Tissue Transplantation Research Panel* (Vol. 1). Washington, D.C.: National Institutes of Health.

Hatch, O. (1992, 31 March). *Congressional Record.*

Locke, J. (1690). *Second Treatise on Civil Government.*

Locke, J. (1990). *Questions Concerning the Law of Nature* (R. Horwitz, J. Strauss Clay, & D. Clay, Eds.). Ithaca, N.Y.: Cornell University Press.

Schwartz, B. (1971). *The Bill of Rights: A Documentary History* (Vol. 2). New York: Chelsea House and McGraw Hill.

The Annals of Congress. (1789, 8 June).

The Collected Works of Abraham Lincoln (R. P. Basler, Ed.) (Vol. 2). (1953). New Brunswick, N.J.: Rutgers University Press.

Chapter 3

IS THE BIOLOGICAL SUBJECT OF HUMAN RIGHTS PRESENT FROM CONCEPTION?

The Reverend Benedict Ashley, O.P.
The Reverend Albert S. Moraczewski, O.P.

Editors' Summary: This essay seeks to provide an answer to the question posed by the title. Beginning with a summary of the current controversy, the authors review the best biological data currently available. To this material they apply philosophical and theological principles and arrive at an affirmative response to the question.

The current controversy swirls around the issue of abortion. The Catholic Church, along with other churches, strongly opposes abortion because it sees abortion as a usurpation of the absolute dominion God has over the universe and all its parts. As moral agents, human beings share as a gift the task of bringing new human beings into the world. But such activity is limited by moral laws discoverable by careful investigation of reality and by a humble listening to God's word.

*While the Church has not defined the precise time of hominization, evidence argues that it occurs at the completion of fertilization. Cognizant of the problems associated with attempts to define "personhood" in an objective manner, the essay focuses on establishing biological criteria so that any individuated organism which is genetically of the species, **Homo sapiens sapiens** is a person. Although objections have been raised to the notion of hominization at fertilization, these can readily be answered in light of available data.*

The relevant data includes details about the formation of the zygote, the timing and sequence of cleavages, the multiplication, differentiation and compaction of blastomeres within the zona pellucida, and implantation. All these data argue for the existence of a human organism from the completion of fertilization. The phenomena of twinning and fusion are reviewed and seen as exceptions to normal occurrence of a single conceptus.

To apply philosophical and theological principles to the biological data it is necessary to correlate certain philosophical and scientific terms, such as substance, unity, and organism. Soul as a theological concept is recognized as being both a spiritual principle and the substantial form of the material body. By no means are these incompatible concepts or entities. But as a spiritual being the soul cannot arise from matter. Hence it is necessary that God create each soul when the material substrate is suitable to be informed by a spiritual principle. At this point there is present a biological subject, i.e., the human organism, capable of sustaining human rights.

Introduction

The issue as to when an individual human person comes into existence is a critical one. Upon the timing of this event depends the response one gives to the question as to when a human being becomes the subject of rights—both natural and civil. If an individual human being is not, and does not become, a subject of the natural rights accruing to a human person until some stage *after* conception, then during that interval of time it is not really secure from unjust attacks on its life or integrity. Furthermore, one is then left with the task of determining by some generally acceptable criteria the precise point when personhood arises or is conferred by societal agreement.

This chapter proposes to explore this issue and to arrive at a response based on the best biological evidence currently available. It will begin with Part I, a discussion of the current controversy. A presentation of the data will constitute Part II, while Part III will provide a philosophical and theological interpretation. Part IV will include a summary and conclusion.

PART I: THE CURRENT CONTROVERSY

OPPOSITION TO ABORTION

Christian churches, notably the Catholic Church, oppose abortion because it is a usurpation of the absolute dominion the Creator possesses over all of creation including human persons (CDF, 1974). The Creator has given to humans the mission of cooperating with Him in the completion and governance of the universe, but no authority to go beyond the limits set by His plans and purposes. The nature of these limits must be carefully explored by ethics. Man and woman cooperate with God in the creation of human persons, but their rightful role is to engage in normal sexual intercourse (or mutually agree to abstain from it) within marriage. They have no right to use their ova or sperm to produce children except through this conjugal act (CDF, 1987), nor to interfere with the normal reproductive process once begun (Paul VI, 1968). Hence abortion which deliberately terminates the reproductive process already begun is a very serious sin, even if that process has not yet produced a human being. It is all the more serious if it has produced a human being whose life is then terminated. Therefore, although the Church's opposition does not stand or fall with the determination of exactly when a human person, a subject of human rights, comes into existence, it is nonetheless a question of very great importance.

TIME OF HOMINIZATION

The document of the Congregation for the Doctrine of the Faith, *Declaration on Procured Abortion* (1974) in a footnote (#19) left open the question of the time of "animation" or "hominization" of the fetus. But its later *Instruction on Respect for Human Life in its Origin and on the Dignity of Procreation* (1987, I,1) stated that the view which holds that hominization takes place at conception (i.e. completion of fertilization of the zygote) is highly probable according to present biological knowledge.

Today, however, the pressures for *in vitro* fertilization as a remedy for sterility, and for embryo experimentation, as well as continued insistence on abortion as a back up for post-rape treatment, etc., have led many to identify "conception" with implantation, to introduce the term "pre-embryo," and to argue for "delayed hominization." This motivation is suspect, and tends to color the interpretation of the biological data. Consequently, it is important to approach this problem as objectively and scientifically as possible.

35

DEFINITION OF PERSON

Because the term "person" is understood in different ways in modern philosophy, it is not easy to formulate a clear statement of the problem under debate. Since Descartes, for many philosophers "person" means "a self-conscious subject" (see Derr, 1990; Ashley, 1990). Hence, some argue that while the pregnant woman clearly is a "person" since she is self-conscious and capable of free decisions, her still unconscious fetus is not yet a "person." Consequently, the mother has all the fundamental human rights but the child does not. Others argue that "personhood" is essentially a "social construct," so that a "person" is determined at a particular time and place by public opinion or the courts, provided that the criteria used are not purely arbitrary. Thus, the Supreme Court in *Roe vs. Wade* (1973) spoke of the fetus as "potential human life."

Such arguments are too subjective and inconsistent to be altogether satisfactory. Today few would deny that women and blacks and Jews are persons with all the basic human rights, although in the past in certain regions one or other of these groups of human beings were denied personhood. What is accepted today as true and right is not merely a matter of social construction, but rests on the objective fact of membership in the same human species. Moreover, most people today vigorously defend the human rights of the severely disabled and of children because they are members of our species. Nor do we assert that we lose our human rights when we are asleep or comatose. Consequently, it seems more reasonable first to determine whether it is valid to define a "human person" by biological criteria, so that any living individuated organism which is genetically of the human species is a "person" "endowed with inalienable rights," no matter of what age or condition. This leaves us then with the question of looking at the biological data, interpreting them in biological terms, and subsequently analyzing the scientific evidence in philosophical and theological terms.

OBJECTIONS TO HOMINIZATION FROM CONCEPTION

The first phase of the hominization controversy took the form of an attempt to revive the premodern embryology of Aristotle and St. Thomas Aquinas with its concept of "delayed hominization" (Donceel, 1970; Pastrano, 1977). According to this ancient theory, the embryo passes through stages of vegetative and animal ensoulment before arriving at the human stage when the body is sufficiently developed for the "infusion of the spiritual soul" by the immediate action of the Creator. Proponents of this theory generally locate hominization as late as the formation of the human brain, or even concurrent with the activity of the cerebral cortex. The popularity of this theory of delayed hominization has also been supported by Karl Rahner who thought that the fact that 50% of embryos [Wilcox, (1989) reduces the number to 31%] miscarry could not be reconciled with Christian views on God's providence over the human person if these embryos are human persons. (Rahner was apparently also unaware that about 50% of these miscarriages probably had such severe chromosomal defects that they need not be considered human beings because the matter would not be a suitable substrate for receiving or sustaining a human soul.)

Unfortunately this theory (of delayed hominization), as usually presented is thoroughly inaccurate not only as to the modern biological data, but even as to the reasoning of Aristotle and Aquinas. Their theory was based on two "factual" biological assumptions which we now know to be wrong: (a) that the material cause of the embryo was menstrual blood which was homogeneous and without any structure of its own, and hence required to be formed in a series of progressive steps by some external agent; (b) that this formative agent was the semen which remained in the womb, separate from the menstrual blood, forming it first as a vegetative entity, and then as a animal entity, and finally as a proximately human body (see Ashley, 1976).

Criticism of this out-dated and far-fetched "delayed hominization theory" led to a second phase of the controversy, based on the notion of a distinction between "genetic" and "developmental" individuation. Among its proponents have been the theologian, Richard McCormick, S.J. (1990), and the physicians Drs. Grobstein (1988) and Cefalo (see Bedate, 1989). It has been even more elaborately developed by Fr. Norman Ford, in his *When Did I Begin?* (1988), and by Thomas Shannon and Fr. Alan Wolter, O.F.M. (1990).

These views admit that the zygote is genetically individuated. Grobstein (1988), however, argues that personal individuation is a gradual process that is completed only at maturity. Ford (1988) is more philosophically sophisticated, but is impressed by the fact that twinning can occur after conception but before implantation. Consequently he puts forward the theory that although the zygote is individuated it divides into a number of distinct individuals only loosely aggregated within the *zona pellucida*. It is only when these loosely aggregated *blastomeres* compact that they form the human individual who retains identity till adulthood. He also points to the possibility of "chimaera" and concludes that the totipotentiality of preimplantation cells to form new individuals precludes hominization before the implantation period.

Bedate and Cefalo (1989) argue from existence of hydatidiform moles and teratomas that genetic individuation is not sufficient since these entities arise from zygotes. This argument, however, seems definitively refuted since it is now known that the so-called "zygote" in question is radically defective from the outset (Szulman, 1978, 1987; Moraczewski, 1990). However, these authors (i.e., Bedate and Cefalo) have another argument of a very different type. They point out that since the embryo cannot develop without receiving additional information from the mother after implantation (no convincing data is cited in support), it is wrong, they assert, to say that the genetic endowment of the zygote determines the destiny of the embryo.

Since the biological difficulties raised against hominization taking place at conception seem to lie primarily in the so-called "pre-embryo" phase (i.e., prior to implantation), it is to this topic we will primarily address ourselves. (It should be noted that some consider that conception is initiated with implantation because, they say, the woman is "pregnant" only when the embryo has implanted in her.) We will first list the relevant data, and then turn to a philosophical and theological discussion of these data.

PART II: THE DATA

The following are the relevant data currently available with regard to the different phases of embryogenesis (Moore, 1988; Gilbert, 1991; Larsen, 1993):

FORMATION OF THE ZYGOTE

1) While both oocyte (ovum) and spermatozoon (sperm) each contribute half of the nuclear genetic material of the future zygote, the ovum alone contributes additional genetic factors found in its cytoplasm (i.e., mitochondrial genes), while the spermatozoon contributes almost no cytoplasm to the zygote.

2) From what is known of infrahuman reproduction it is probable that the human ovum already has a certain polarity (which may be conditioned also by the entry point of the spermatozoon) that persists in the zygote, so that the zygote before cleavage is already polarized.

3) When a human spermatozoon penetrates the ovum, the ovum normally within a few seconds becomes impervious to other spermatozoa. The penetrating spermatozoon initiates a new level of metabolic activity in the ovum without which it will not develop into a viable organism.

4) The zygote is constituted and begins to function as a distinct organism only when the membranes of the paternal and maternal pro-nuclei have broken down and their respective chromsomes have intermingled. If this chromosomal intermingling is not effected, development will soon come to an end.

CLEAVAGE

1) The zygote begins its first cleavage about 24 hours or sooner after the entry of the spermatozoon. The orientation and timing of the cleavages of the embryo are species specific and therefore genetically determined. Before the nuclear genes of the zygote become fully activated, maternal cytoplasmic genetic factors seem to control the orientation and timing of the first few cleavages of the zygote. Nevertheless, cleavage would not take place normally if the zygotic nucleus were not already present, so the nuclear genes must also play some role in initiating and controlling these cleavages.

2) After the first cell cleavage subsequent early cleavages of the human embryo (and of mammalian embryos in general) do not take place simultaneously (Gilbert, 1991:90), so that the sequence is not 2, then 4 . . . blastomeres (cells formed by the cleavages), but 2, 3, 4 . . . blastomeres, which suggests that even at the 2-cell stage there is something of the polarity clearly observed in infrahuman species in which after the first division one blastomere is clearly differentiated from the other. Note also that since the blastomeres receive different portions of the cytoplasm of the zygote, and this cytoplasm was by no means uniform (it was already markedly differentiated in the ovum), they are not truly identical. Although the blastomeres are not differentiated as regards the nuclear genome, they are by no means undifferentiated as regards their cytoplasm.

THE BLASTOMERES

1) In the early stages of embryonic development, all cells remain "totipotent" in the sense that if some cells are lost they can be replaced by the remaining cells by a process called regulation. As development continues, however, they become more and more differentiated so that they lose the capacity to produce any but cells of their own type. This differentiation is probably produced by processes that progressively "turn off" certain of the genes which remain in all (or almost all) somatic cells but in an inactivated state.

2) As already stated, up to the 8-or 16-cell stage cleavage seems to be under direct control of maternal cytoplasm factors (yet, e.g., in mouse and goat, the switch from maternal to zygotic control occurs at the 2-cell stage [Gilbert, 1991: 91]), and the blastomeres seem totipotent and undifferentiated. But these cleavages do not enlarge the embryo, but simply subdivide the original cytoplasm derived from the ovum. Hence, different blastomeres receive different portions of the maternal cytoplasm and are thus somewhat differentiated.

3) Although the blastomeres first seem simply to be held together by the jelly-like *zona pellucida* which surrounds them as a kind of soft shell but fall apart if it is removed, they remain in direct contact with each other as a *morula* of cells having *microvilli*. Very soon the blastomeres compact tightly together *to form an outer layer of cells*, the trophoblastic cells and an inner mass of cells, the embryoblast. The latter is then protected from outside forces by the outer layer. The zygote began dividing on the first day. By the third day the solid *morula* of some 16 blastomeres has formed, then it takes in fluid, and a fluid-filled cavity begins to form. By the fourth day it has become a blastocyst, differentiation of trophoblast and inner cell mass already having taken place; on the fifth day the *blastocyst* enzymatically lyses a hole in the zona pellucida and appears to squeeze through or "hatch" (Larsen, 1993; Gilbert, 1991: 96). Thus the blastocyst is *active*, not passive, in the process and on the sixth day it implants in the uterine wall.

4) Even in the very brief period before compaction into the blastocyst takes place, the blastomeres do not exist in isolation, but are somehow in communication with each other and with the morula as a whole. Otherwise the cleavages would not take place in a regularly timed sequence, nor would the gene products necessary for compaction and other changes be prepared in proper sequence. If there were not this inter-communication among the blastomeres, either cleavage would halt or *by reason of their totipotentiality each would develop into a distinct organism*. That they do not do so but instead continue development as a single organism implies that the genetic program includes instructions which normally prevent separate development. Apparently more than one embryo develops only when such controls fail (twinning). Thus "totipotentiality" is not absolute, but conditioned by the relation of a given blastomere to the other blastomeres within the zona. Even if it is true (which is not certain) that in the early cleavages *no* differentiation has taken place by the deactivation of genes, there is at least differentiation in the *positional differences* of the blastomeres (and perhaps by the different portions of the maternal cytoplasm which they received, as already noted). Thus the totipotentiality of the blastomeres means only that their genes remain capable of full activation and hence of causing reg-

ulation, but not that they are totally identical in all respects. Also, if a nondisjunction of two members of a chromosome pair occurs during early cleavage, an embryo with two or more cell lines with different chromosome numbers is produced (*mosaicism*).

5) The positional differentiation of the blastomeres becomes obvious when some of the blastomeres become enclosed in the interior of the morula by others on its exterior. The interior cells then become the *inner cell mass* and the exterior cells the *trophoblast* which becomes eventually the embryonic membranes and placenta. These exterior cells (the trophoblast) protect the embryo formed out of the inner cell mass and enable it to implant in the lining of the maternal uterus. The trophoblast, however, is not an organism other than the embryo, but a differentiated part or organ of the embryo; it is a part of its body, although a temporary and eventually disposable one at birth. It is genetically identical with the embryo, and unable to develop unless the embryo remains present within it.

6) The inner cell mass which develops into the permanent body of the embryo at first consists of a few cells only (and some of them later become incorporated in the trophoblast), compared with the many cells which go to form the trophoblast. The trophoblast must develop first because until it does the organism cannot implant, and until it implants it cannot obtain the nutrition necessary for it to attain the cellular volume necessary if it is to become highly differentiated and organized. Since these cells of the inner cell mass are still relatively undifferentiated, they remain for a time totipotent.

IMPLANTATION

1) After gastrulation the three cell-layers, from which all the adult organs of the organism will develop, are differentiated, and its structural axis from head to tail is clearly established by the appearance of the primitive streak which will become the central nervous system. Thus by the time implantation is established the plan of the human body, programmed from conception, is manifest.

2) It is species specific to the human species for the mother to bear only one offspring at a time. The incidence of twinning in the United States is about 1.2% (Sadler, 1985: 103). This is an evolutionary adaptation to the fact that the extremely complex body of the human child requires a long period of gestation and greatly stresses the mother. More than one child is difficult to carry, to deliver, and to nurse. Moreover, the crowding in the womb of more than one fetus is disadvantageous. It is probable, therefore, that human genes include a factor which not only

prevents multiple conceptions (as for fraternal twins) but also prevents identical twinning. Twinning, therefore must be the result of a genetic defect or of some developmental accident. There is evidence (Philippe, 1985) that at least in many cases twinning is caused by the interaction of a genetic disposition and an environmental factor. Thus the biological interpretation of this phenomenon must begin with the fact that the human conceptus normally develops without twinning:

a) Twinning which can take place even after the ninth day when implantation has already occurred (Gilbert,1991: 58) cannot occur after the embryo has become so differentiated that its cells have lost their totipotentiality or power of extensive regulation, i.e., adaptation of existing cells to new functions so as to replace missing parts. It has been shown that in some invertebrates this power of regulation is lost very early, because the parts of the organism are already so differentiated that their whole embryological destiny is already determined. If such a part is isolated it will simply develop into an isolated organ. But in higher animals the power of regulation is retained longer. This is in line with the fact that such organisms are more structurally and functionally *unified* so that the cells are in closer communication with each other and information of the loss of one cell can be communicated to the whole organism and to its constituent cells which can then be adapted to take its place.

b) Twinning cannot occur after gastrulation has begun because by that time the basic structure of the body is laid down, confirmed by the appearance of the primitive streak. Some sets of identical twins are surrounded by a single set of membranes (the chorion and the amnion). This indicates that in their case twinning took place by a division of the inner cell mass after the chorion and amnion had been formed. Other sets of identical twins share only a common chorion but each have their own amnion, which means that the split took place between day five and day nine. Others have separate sets of both membranes which indicates twinning before the trophoblast had differentiated, so that each twin separately produced its own set of membranes.

c) A related phenomenon, certainly observed in subhuman organisms, and perhaps in the human species, is the formation of a "chimera" by fusion of two embryos at an early stage, so that they become a single organism, with a mosaic of cells of different genetic composition. Biologically this is no more puzzling than the surgical transplantation of organs, except that it takes place at a very early stage when the power of regulation is still greater than in the adult.

d) The biological explanation of twinning (which has still not been thoroughly researched) is that it is due either to (1) an *internal* cause, namely, a genetic defect in the normal mechanism that prevents separation of (a) the blastomeres or (b) the cells of the inner cell mass; or (2) due to interference by some *external* cause with the normal development of the blastocyst. Some still totipotent cell or cells of an embryo X become separated from X, and by means of their power of regulation restore the equivalent of the cells remaining in X by further cleavage and adaptation, and thus become a new, complete organism X'. Concurrently, X (the initial organism) by the same power of regulation restores the cells which it has lost to X'. Thus result two genetically *almost* identical individuals, X and X' of which X is a few hours or days older than X'. We say "almost identical" because X and X' may differ in the genetic factors contained in the material cytoplasm of which they have received different portions. This twinning process can be considered a regression to the asexual reproduction found in plants and some lower animals, resulting from a defect in the normal mode.

PART III: PHILOSOPHICAL AND THEOLOGICAL INTERPRETATION

DEFINITIONS

What is meant by a "philosophical interpretation" of scientific facts? Scientific descriptions are generally obtained by *artificial observation*, i.e., by special techniques involving instruments such as microscopes, thermometers, etc., isolation of the object observed from its natural environment, alteration of the object by dissection, dying, etc., and controlled experimentation. Because such procedures change the natural object in the very process of examination, they presuppose *natural observation* made by the human senses. Therefore, since the results of natural observation are presupposed by the interpretation of artificial data, they require careful analysis if the interpretation of artificial data is to be free of prejudice and distortion.

A "theological interpretation" usually presupposes such a philosophical analysis of scientific data, but adds considerations derived from "revelation" contained in the Bible and Christian Tradition.

CORRELATIONS

In order to pass from the analysis of the data of natural observation to that of artificial observation and vice versa, it is necessary to *correlate* philosophical and scientific terms. There are various sets of philosophical terms, depending on the philosophical tradition to which one is committed. We will make use of terms of an Aristotelian or scholastic type, because (a) these are the common heritage of Western philosophy; (b) for historical reasons they are easiest to correlate with theological terms. The correlations will be approximate, yet useful for the problem in hand.

The philosophical term "living substance" correlates with the biological term "organism." A "substance" is something which is unified in itself (i.e., not a mere collection or mixture of other substances) and is capable of relatively independent existence (i.e., not a part of another substance). A "material" substance is a "body" spatially extended (having "parts which have only boundaries in common") and subject to being changed by forces exerted on it by agents external to itself. (We say "relatively independent" because all things in the universe are connected and related, and no living substance can continue to exist except in an appropriate environment). Yet it is obvious that a dog is not part of the atmosphere it breathes, the earth it runs on, or the food it eats although dependent on them to survive.

"Living" substances are distinct from non-living substances in many ways, but notably in their capacity to assimilate nourishment from the environment and incorporate it into their cells and tissues by metabolic activity, to develop themselves from rudimentary to adult structures, to maintain homeostasis, and to reproduce themselves. Admittedly there are border-line cases (e.g., viruses—or at least some of them such as the bacteriophage T4 in which it is not easy to distinguish the living from the non-living), but this does not invalidate these distinctions.

LIFE STRUCTURES AND FUNCTIONS

The life "functions" are not possible without differentiated "structures" of the substantial material body. Thus at a given point of time a

44

living substance is both a relatively static system of parts and a dynamic system of functions performed by these parts. By its function of self-development it gradually elaborates and coordinates its structure so that its functions become more effective and precise with time until full maturity is reached and subsequently decline and death set in.

By reason of the evolutionary development of living substances some species exhibit much more elaborate life-systems than others. The more elaborate they become the more necessary and feasible becomes the *unification* of each system. Thus in higher organisms a long developmental process is necessary as it progresses from a very simple and relatively disunified structure to a highly complex and tightly unified structure.

In every unified material system such as a mature complex organism, e.g., a paramecium, oak tree, or cat, the functioning of the different parts or "organs" of the system must be under some type of "central control" or the coordinated and harmonious function of the parts would fail. Since every function requires some organic structure, this means that in living things there is always an "organ of central control" (henceforth OCC), although it is to be expected that this OCC itself also undergoes gradual differentiation and unification in proportion to, and synchronous with, the organism as a whole before maturity is reached.

CONSTITUTIVE ASPECTS OF ORGANISMS

Among living things "animals" are distinguished from "plants" in a number of ways, but especially by their capacity to take in information from the environment ("sensation") and respond to it by adaptive movements, e.g., to seek food, to avoid enemies, to find mates, etc. (Again there are borderline cases such as the tropisms of some plants and the relative immobility of some animals such as sponges). The ability of sensation, of course, requires differentiated sense organs corresponding to various kinds of stimuli, mechanical, chemical, and electromagnetic. All animals have at least the sense of touch, but most animals have several senses. The correlation of these senses requires some central organ where information is stored, processed, integrated, and accessed (a central nervous system, or more precisely a brain in the developed human).

From the foregoing it follows that an organism comes into existence at a critical point in time when the matter of which it is composed becomes sufficiently organized so that it forms a functioning unity which is relatively independent of every other substance and begins to carry on at least some of the functions characteristic of living substances. Of these, the most fundamental is *the capacity to maintain homeostasis while at the same time (provided it is not yet already mature) developing itself toward maturity.* Hence it is confusing and wrong to say that the processes leading up to this critical point, i.e., the formation of a new organism, are part of the life process of that organism (e.g., to say that the lives and reproductive activities of the parent organism are the same as the life of their offspring). It is also confusing and wrong to say (as did *Roe v. Wade),* that an human embryonic organism in the process of developing itself to maturity is only "potential life." It is in fact an *actually* living organism, although only *potentially* a mature organism; it is an actual human life with a potential.

How is it possible to determine when a given body is alive and when it is dead? Obviously from the preceding, the empirical proof that an organism exists (i.e., is alive) is evidence that it is carrying on life functions, at least the function of homeostasis and (if immature) self-development. The former dependence on heart-death and the present general acceptance of brain-death as another proof of the death of the human organism, illustrates this point very well. Brain-death is the most accurate criteria—when properly understood and competently applied—because in the mature human organism, it is clear that the brain is the OCC. It is perfectly logical, therefore, to conclude that *the clearest proof of the existence of the human organism at the beginning of life is the existence of an OCC which at least at the earliest stage of life manifests itself by the maintenance of homeostasis and continued development.* (This explains the ancient theory of Aristotle and Aquinas of "delayed hominization." Since they believed that the heart, not the brain, was the central organ of sensation and therefore the OCC, they held that the human organism comes into existence only with the appearance of a primordial heart in the embryo.)

Today there is no doubt that in the mature human organism it is the brain, and not the heart, which is the OCC (a fact made clear even to natural observation by the sight of persons living with artificial hearts). But since an organism is self-developing, and the lowest level of function of the OCC is not sensation but the maintenance of homeostasis and self-development, it is necessary to push this argument backwards to the question as to whether the brain had a precursor, i.e., when an OCC first appeared in the matter out of which the organism is constituted.

At this point we have to enter into the interpretation of the now available embryological data already listed. Up until the point at which the pro-nuclei of the ovum and spermatozoon have fused to form the zygote, there is no evidence that would suggest the existence of a OCC for the material (namely, the ovum and spermatozoon) supplied by the parents. The sperm and ovum have existed as quite distinct entities, but not as "living substances" in the sense defined (a complete organism),

46

but rather as separable parts of the two parental organisms. The existence of the spermatozoon outside the body of the male parent, and of the ovum as a separated body in the oviduct of the female parent after ovulation, is very brief, and neither have the capacity to develop into a mature fertile organism. They had best be considered as "separated instruments" of the parent organisms which are "alive" only with a kind of residual life, like the temporary life of some cells and tissues in a corpse after death, although ovum and spermatozoon in their instrumental capacity transmit life at a high rather than a minimal level.

The fact that fertilization is a complicated process that requires some time does not negate the fact that only at the critical point of completion can we say that a new organism has been "conceived." The existence of a distinct organism is an all-or-none, not a gradual event. It is evident from the data, however, that sometimes this process never reaches completion and a consequent miscarriage occurs. [According to Sadler (1990: 33) it is estimated that "as many as 50% of all pregnancies end in spontaneous abortion and that half of these losses are due to chromosomal abnormalities." Wilcox (1988: 189) reduces the number of miscarriages to 31%.] Thus the defective entity which results from a failure of the fertilization process is not an organism in the sense defined, since it has *no* capacity to develop to maturity, but has only a residual life which makes possible some cell proliferation and even some differentiation as in teratomas and hydatidiform moles (see Moraczewski, 1990: 94).

In the constituted zygote what is the OCC that enables the organism to maintain itself and develop toward maturity? The data seem to make it obvious that the OCC is the *nucleus* of the zygote which contains the principle genetic program which controls the *total* development of the organism and which ultimately controls the development of the brain which then takes over as the OCC. Moreover, the nucleus is not merely the "program" or "blue-print" for control, as is sometimes said, but is also the effective *agent* of control which produces the structures of the organism in conformity with this program.

OBJECTIONS TO THE ABOVE INTERPRETATION

There are, however, certain difficulties against the foregoing interpretation of the data. The first is that although the nucleus contains the vast majority of the genetic factors, it does not contain them all, since the maternal cytoplasm also makes a unique contribution. Furthermore, there is evidence (Gilbert, 1991: 500) that it is these maternal factors which control the first few cell cleavages, and not the nucleic genes. This difficulty can be answered, however, by pointing out that this phenomenon is intelligible in light of what is going on at this very early phase of development. The primary activity at this time is not the growth of the organism in volume, nor differentiation of its parts, but the subdivision of the cytoplasm into increasing the number of daughter cells derived from the mother so that there can be a sufficient number of distinct parts (cells) for differentiation to begin. Moreover, the maternal cytoplasmic genes do not operate except in the milieu of the total organism and in the presence of the nucleic genes. Consequently, it must be presumed that these genes are exerting *some* controlling influence on the operation of the cytoplasmic genes, although our present knowledge has not defined exactly what this influence is. If this were not the case, the *continuity* of development from completion of fertilization to the time when control by the nuclear genes becomes quite obvious could not be explained. Thus the most probable interpretation is that the work of the cytoplasmic genes is subordinate to that of the nuclear genes, but is more obviously manifest at this early stage of development.

A further difficulty is the objection made by Ford (1988) that the blastomeres are totipotent and, when separated, are capable of developing into complete organisms as occurs in the phenomenon of monozygotic twinning before the formation of the trophoblast or afterwards by the division of the inner cell mass. Ford claims also that in the blastocyst stage the cells are only juxtaposed to each other within the zona pellucida without any significant intercommunication that would indicate they are parts of one organism, rather than several organisms each in its own right. The data, however, do not support this interpretation:

a) The cleavages merely subdivide the cytoplasm; the blastomeres they produce generally do not develop into new adult organisms.

b) Nor is the totipotentiality and power of regulation of the individual cells surprising, since this is characteristic of the earliest stages of organic development, when a proliferation of cells is required before they can become differentiated into different types of tissues and organs.

c) Moreover, they are only *relatively* totipotent, since they develop into distinct organisms only when they have been abnormally separated from the parent organism, in which case their power of regulation accounts for the development of a twin by asexual reproduction (i.e., from the separated cells) and the restoration of the lost part (cells) of the original twin.

48

d) As long as the blastomeres remain within the original organism they are differentiated at least *positionally*. This suggests that from the first they are in some kind of communication with each other since they very soon compact and form the blastocyst according to a definite sequence of events determined by the nuclear and cytoplasmic genes. The sequence of mammalian cleavages argues for the same point (see Gilbert, 1991: 90–1).

e) The most telling argument of all against Ford is that if his hypothesis were correct, then since the blastomeres are totipotent and (according to that hypothesis) not in communication with each other within the zona pellucida, they should each develop into a mature organism. But in fact they do so only if they are *separated* from the others. This shows that at least some interaction is taking place between them within the zona pellucida which restrains them from individually developing as *whole* organisms and normally directs them collectively to remain *parts* of a single organism continuous with the zygote.

But how is it possible to say that after the first cleavage there is an OCC when not only the cytoplasm is subdivided, but also there is a mitotic division of the nucleus of the zygote into two or more nuclei? Does not then the nucleus (the original OCC) divide into several OCC's? (This is Norman Ford's hypothesis.) Two better hypotheses are available: The more probable is that at the first cleavage, one of the blastomeres (namely the one which is first to divide at the second cleavage) is established as *dominant* and from its divisions arise the inner cell mass (see Gilbert, 1991: 94 note). An alternative hypothesis is that it is not the nucleus of the zygote but the entire *genome* which it contains that is the primordial OCC of the organism and which provides the effective agency and the information for the construction of the brain which then becomes the OCC of the mature organism. Originally this genome is contained in the single nucleus of the zygote which is thus the OCC of the primal organism. When the zygote begins to cleave into a number of cells, the genome is replicated in the nuclei of each of these cells. Consequently the OCC becomes the whole collection of these nuclei acting *conjointly—because of the common genome*—until this group of cells becomes sufficiently differentiated so that some of them can be selected to constitute the OCC and others the remainder of the organism. Our present data does not seem to enable us to determine exactly when this takes place, although it is clear that the cells which differentiate into the trophoblast are *not* part of the OCC, but that it is either the inner cell mass or some part of that mass which is the OCC. Certainly when the primitive or neural streak forms it is clear that we have the primordial central nervous system differentiating to become the OCC of the total organism. Thus such evidence as we have gives us an outline scenario of the gradual differentiation of the OCC at the organic or multicellular (as distinguished from the organellic or intra-cellular) level of differentiation.

Does the fact that twinning can take place after the formation of the trophoblast by division of the inner cell mass, or the fact that this mass consists of so few cells compared to the trophoblast, raise further difficulties? It is not strange that in mammals the developing organism produces a temporary organ system of the chorionic and amniotic membranes and placenta in order to obtain nourishment from the mother, at a very early stage of its development. Since it begins as a one-celled organism, the body of the fetus cannot be maintained alive for long or its organs differentiated without ample nourishment from the mother, and this supply must be available very early. Hence the first life task of the organism is to construct the trophoblast; other differentiation can wait. Consequently only a few cells need to be present as the primordium of the embryo proper. Since at this stage somatic differentiation has just begun and the cells are few, twinning remains possible just as it was before the differentiation of the trophoblast.

THEOLOGICAL CONSIDERATIONS

We have now arrived at the point of concern for a theological interpretation, although our reasoning remains philosophical: "What of the 'infusion' of the human soul?" The term "infusion" is unfortunate since it smacks of a Platonic dualism in which the soul *preexists* the body and then is inserted into it. The Catholic Church has defined (DS, nos. 902, 3002) that the human being has only one soul which is the "substantial form" of the body, it is co-created with the body, and that it is "spiritual," not material in nature. It is also the ordinary teaching of the Church (Pius XII, 1950) that because it is spiritual the human soul is created *immediately* by God, while the body is created by the mediation of the parents and perhaps by evolutionary forces. It seems, however, that the creation of the human person by God should not be considered two acts, one mediate and the other immediate, but a *single act* in part mediated and in part not mediated. Thus, the conception of a child is a human act of cooperation with God, in which God uses the parents as instruments who are principal causes of the body, but only indirectly and dispositively the causes of the soul, since they furnish the occasion for

50

the creation of the soul and thus of the human person, but do not themselves produce the human person as such which results from the union of the two principles.

The term "soul" in traditional philosophy was not confined to spiritual and immortal souls, but to the principle of life in living organisms, whether it be non-spiritual as in subhuman animals, or spiritual as in the human person. It can be correlated, therefore, with the scientific term "organization" of the material of the body, but with the distinction that this organization is not that of a mechanical juxtaposition of parts having independent existence as in a machine, but the organization of a "substance" which is capable of relatively independent existence and exhibits internal differentiation of parts and functions. Thus we speak of an "organic unity" to indicate the total interdependence of the parts of the structural and functional systems which we call an organism. In lower organisms, as we have said, and in early stages of the development of higher organisms, the differentiation and unification of parts although real is relatively weak (hence the phenomena of asexual reproduction and twinning); in higher organisms at maturity this unification is intense. Thus in the mature human organism while the genome remains present in almost every cell of the body (some cells such as mature red blood cells lack nuclei), the OCC has developed into the brain which is in communication with all parts of the body through the nervous system, receiving information from them and sending out controlling messages to them. The circulatory system and the hormones it circulates also have a controlling function but under the control of the brain. Thus the "soul," or unity and organization of the body, is manifest in all its parts, but its integrative function is effected primarily through the brain, so that if the brain dies the body ceases to be ensouled.

To speak of the human soul as "spiritual" and at the same time as the "substantial form" of the body means that as "spiritual," or non-material, it is not spatially extended nor subject to change by material agents. Therefore, it has no spatial parts or organs, although it can have many "powers" or "faculties." As the substantial form of the body it is its unifying organization already described, and its diverse "powers" are simply the unifying structure and function of diverse bodily organs, e.g., the soul's power of sight is simply the living structure of the eye. As it is spiritual, on the other hand, the purely spiritual functions of the soul, namely, the powers of abstract intelligence and of free will, since they transcend material processes (abstract thought cannot be reduced to material images, and free will cannot be determined by physical laws), intellect and will, as such, do not have a physical organ, and thus are not, as so many today suppose, functions of the brain, although there is a relationship. As long as the human soul informs the body, it cannot operate in its natural manner without the instrument of the brain which supplies it with the raw data for intellection and therefore for free willing. Hence we must conclude that God immediately creates the human soul—and the Church so teaches (Pius XII, 1950)—at that moment when a body suitable for organization by the soul as its substantial form is proximately prepared as far as purely biological forces can effect this preparation. By the creation of the human soul God completes the act of organizing the matter of the body and produces a unique human being who is at once bodily and spiritual.

When, then, is the human body proximately prepared for final organization, vivification, and hominization by the unique soul created by God for *this* particular body? In short, "when did I begin?" as a unique person? Only then can we ask whether this human being is the subject of those human rights which belong to human persons. If we seek an objective biological criterion to settle this question of the origin of the human person, we need to ask simply when does an organism which is a member of the human species begin to be. That question will be answered by asking when is the OCC (the genome or whatever the OCC structure may be) which controls the life and development of this unique human being, first constituted? The response: at conception, defined as the completion of fertilization of the ovum by the sperm, and the formation of a unified nucleus of the zygote as its OCC. All that happens afterwards is simply the effective self-construction of the living human person already in existence, unified and organized by the human spiritual soul. Twinning is a developmental accident by which a second (or more) person(s) of identical nuclear genetic (but not cytoplasmic genetic) heritage is produced by a separation of some relatively totipotent cells and the regulation of both individuals to full normality.

In twinning, whence then comes the soul of X′ if the original twin is X? Not by division of the soul of X, since an immaterial principle cannot be divided. The soul of X′ is created by God exactly as is the soul of X, namely, when there exists a body proximately prepared for it. The body of X was prepared by its parents sexually through the instrumentality of their ovum and sperm. The body of X′ was prepared by the same parents acting in the same way, but (because of a genetic defect or developmental accident) with the additional instrumental mediation of the embryo of X acting asexually. Thus X and X′ are equally the offspring of the same parents, but X more directly than X′. That this is not a far-fetched explanation is evident from *in vitro* fertilization, where the child is the child of the parents who produce the ovum and spermatozoon, but only through the mediation of the physician. In the former case, however, the mediation is natural (in the broad sense that includes defective natural processes) and in the second artificial, and ethically not justifiable.

PART IV: CONCLUSION

The issue, which is really at the focal point of numerous and vigorous if not acrimonious debates, is whether the human embryo from its inception is properly the subject of moral rights. In this chapter we have attempted to bring together the biological evidence and philosophical reasoning to determine whether the human embryo even at its initial stages can be, and indeed is, the subject of moral rights recognized in the born human person.

The biological data were used to determine when one can say with security that there is present a human organism which is in clear continuity with the born child and mature adult. Because most of the objections to such a presence *ab initio* involve the first fourteen days of life after fertilization, the chapter devoted its attention to that period of time in the development of the human individual. It was seen that indeed at the time of the completion of fertilization—when the membranes of the parental pronuclei have "disolved" and the new diploid set of chromosomes have been constituted and just prior to the first cleavage—the single-celled zygote is formed and the new organism begins to exist as a distinct individual. As the organism goes through a series of cleavages prior to implantation, which results in an increase in the number of cells (blastomeres), the total volume remains the same because they are encased in an envelope, the *zona pellucida*, which keeps them together and insures that they remain in functional contact with each other.

Initially, the individual blastomeres remain relatively totipotential, that is, each if separated is able to form a new individual capable of developing into an adult individual given the appropriate environment. Parenthetically, it should be noted here that such a separation was accomplished when blastomeres from seventeen human embryos were separated to form 48 distinct, living human embryos which were allowed to continue cleaving until the process was prematurely terminated by their death within six days (Diggins, 1993). Apparently there has been no intention to implant any of these human embryos fashioned by human art. While such "cloning" of human beings may be technically possible, it is morally reprehensible.

Before implantation, the individual blastomeres begin to differentiate. One expression of this is that some cells on the exterior begin to form the trophoblast which eventually will form the chorionic and amniotic membranes as well as participate with the maternal cells to form the placenta. The blastomeres in the interior, fewer in number initially, form the inner cell mass which is the embryo proper and which will develop gradually to be the fetus, the born child and finally the adult individual.

The formation of these various tissues and organs is a smooth process in which there is no true discontinuity although there are identifiable stages such as the shedding of the *zona pellucida,* implantation, formation of the primitive streak, organogenesis, and birth. It is one and the same individual formed from the chromosomes of the two pronuclei which begins as the zygote and continues to grow and differentiate by means of a self-directed and extremely complex process leading finally to the adult person.

No one seriously contests that the adult person has the full range of basic moral rights and does so by virtue of being a member of the human species. Neither is it questioned that the adolescent, the prepuberty youngster, the infant, and the new born child each also has these same basic rights, especially the right to life, for the same reason. Since the development of the individual is a smooth biological process, without radical discontinuity and clear continuity of identity, there is no persuasive biological reason which would deny the possession of these basic rights to the developing individual at *any* stage of the process.

Hence, in light of the preceding discussion the answer to the question posed in the title of this chapter must be in the affirmative: there is present an appropriate subject of moral rights from conception onwards.

References and Selected Bibliography

Alberts, B., Bray, D., Lewis, J., Ralf, M., & Roberts, K. W., James D. (1983). *Molecular Biology of the Cell.* New York: Garland.

Anderson, E., Hoppe, P., Whitten, W., & Lee, G. (1975). In Vitro Fertilization and Early Embryogenesis: A Cytological Analysis. *Journal of Ultrastructure Research, 50.*

Anderson, J. W. (1985). *Three Abortion Theorists: A Critical Appraisal.* Georgetown University.

Ashley, B. M. (1976). A Critique of the Theory of Delayed Hominization. In D. G. McCarthy & A. S. Moraczewski (Eds.), *An Ethical Evaluation of Fetal Experimentation: An Interdisciplinary Study.* St. Louis: Pope John XXXIII Center.

Atkinson, G. M. (1977). Persons in the Whole Sense. *American Journal of Jurisprudence, 22,* 86–117.

Austin, C., & Short, R. (1982). *Reproduction in Mammals, 2nd ed.* Cambridge: Cambridge University Press.

Austin, C. (1989). *Human Embryos: The Debate on Assisted Reproduction.* Oxford: Oxford University Press.

Balinsky, B., & Fabian, B. (1981). *An Introduction to Embryology.* Philadelphia: Saunders College Publishing.

Bedate, C., & Cefalo, R. (1989). The Zygote: To Be or Not To Be a Person. *Journal of Medicine and Philosophy, 14,* 641–645.

Beier, H. M., & Lindner, H. R. (1983). *Fertilization of the Human Egg in Vitro.* Berlin: Springer-Verlag.

Beirnaert, L. (1970). L'Avortement: Est-il un Infanticide?. *Etudes, 333,* 520–523.

Billings, J. J. (1989). *Nota Critica:* 'When Did I Begin?' Anthropotes, *1,* 119–127.

Bole, T. (1989). Metaphysical Accounts of the Zygote as a Person. *Journal of Medicine and Philosophy, 4,* 647–653.

Braude, P., Bolton, V., & Moore, S. (1988, 31 March). Human Gene Expression First Occurs Between the Four and Eight-Cell Stages of Preimplantation Development. *Nature,* pp. 459–461.

Brown, D. (1970). *Bury My Heart at Wounded Knee.* New York: Holt, Rinehart and Winston.

Buckle, S., & Dawson, K. (1988). Individuals and Syngamy. *Bioethics News,* 7(3), 15–30.

Callahan, D. (1970). *Abortion, Law, Choice and Morality.* New York: Macmillan.

Cameron, N. M. D. S. (1990, 3 March). Is the Embryo One of Us?. *The Tablet,* pp. 269–272.

Carlson, B. M. (1988). *Patten's Foundations of Embryology.* New York: McGraw-Hill.

Charter of the Rights of the Family. (1983). Vatican City: Vatican Polyglot Press.

Congregation for the Doctrine of the Faith. (1987). *Instruction on Respect for Human Life in its Origin and on the Dignity of Procreation (Donum Vitae).* Vatican City: Vatican Polyglot Press.

Congregation for the Doctrine of the Faith. (1974). *Declaration on Procured Abortion.* Vatican City: Vatican Polyglot Press.

Conti, B. M. (1985, January). Letters: Ethics, Science, and Embryos: Weighing the Evidence. *The Tablet,* p. 12.

Daly, Thomas V. (1985). The Status of Embryonic Human Life: A Crucial Issue in Genetic Counseling. In N. Tonti-Filippini (Ed.), *Health Care Priorities in Australia,* (pp. 45–57). Melbourne: St. Vincent's Bioethics Centre.

Daly, Thomas V. (1987, March). Identifying the Origin of Human Life: The Search for a Marker Event for the Origin of Human Life. *St. Vincent's Bioethics Centre Newsletter,* 5(1), 4–6.

Daly, Thomas V. (1988, December). Individuals, Syngamy and the Origin of Human Life. *St. Vincent's Bioethics Centre Newsletter,* 6(4), 1–7.

Davidson, E. (1976). *Gene Activity in Early Development.* New York Academic Press.

Defining Human Life: Medical, Legal and Ethical Implications (M. W. Shaw, M.D. & A. E. Doudera, J.D., Eds.). (1983). Ann Arbor, MI: AUPHA Press and American Society of Law and Medicine.

DeMarco, D. (1991, January). Zygotes, Persons, and Genetics. *Ethics & Medics,* 16(1), 3–4.

Denzinger, H. & Schönmetzer, A. (Eds.). (1976). *Enchiridion Symbolorum* (36th ed.). Barcelona: Herder. (DS)

Department of Health and Social Security, G. B. (1984). Report of The Committee of Inquiry into Human Fertilization and Embryology M. Warnock (Ed.). London: Her Majesty's Stationary Office.

Deuchar, E. M. (1975). *Cellular Interactions in Animal Development.* London: Chapman and Hall.

Diamond, E. F. (1991, November). Games People Play with Abortion Data. *Linacre Quarterly,* 58(4), 35–38.

Donceel, S., Joseph F. (1970). Immediate Animation and Delayed Hominization. *Theological Studies, 31*(1), 76–105.

Dunstan, G., & Sellar, M. J. (1988). *The Status of the Human Embryo Perspectives from Moral Tradition.* London: King Edward's Hospital Fund for London.

55

Edwards, R. G. (1980). *Conception in the Human Female.* New York: Academic Press.

Ethics Committee of the American Fertility Society. (1986). *Ethical Considerations of the New Reproductive Technologies, Fertility and Sterility.*

Fisher, R. A. e. a., (1989). Frequency of Heterozygous Complete Hydatidiform Moles, Estimated by Locus-Specific Minisatellite and Y Chromosome-Specific Probes. *Human Genetics, 82,* 259–63.

Fisher, O., Anthony. (1991). 'When Did I Begin' Revisted. *Linacre Quarterly, 58*(3), 59–68.

Flaman. (1991, November). When Did I Begin? Another Critical Response to Norman Ford. *Linacre Quarterly, 58*(4), 39–55.

Fletcher, J. *Morals and Medicine.* Boston: Beacon Press.

Ford, N. (1954). *When Did I Begin?: Conception of the Human Individual in History, Philosophy and Science.* Cambridge: Cambridge University Press.

Ford, N. (1990, 3 February). Letters: Ethics, Science, and Embryos. *The Tablet,* pp. 141–142.

Ford, N. (1990, 13 January). Letters: Ethics, Science and Embryos: Weighing the Evidence. *The Tablet,* p. 46.

Gallagher, C., John. (1985). *Is the Human Embryo a Person: A Philosophical Investigation.* Toronto: Human Life Research Institute.

Gesell, A. (1971). *The Embryology of Human Behavior.* Westport: Greenwood Press.

Gilbert, S. F. (1991). *Developmental Biology.* Sunderland: Sinauer Associates.

Goldenring, J. M. (1985). Denial of Antipregnancy Prophylaxis in Rape Victims. *The New England Journal of Medicine, 3,* 1637.

Goldenring, J. M. (1985). The Brain-Life Theory: Towards a Consistent Biological Definition of Humanness. *Journal of Medical Ethics, 11,* 198–204.

Grisez, G. (1970). *Abortion: The Myths, the Realities, and the Arguments.* New York: Corpus.

Grisez, G., & Boyle, Joseph M. (1979). *Life and Death with Liberty and Justice.* Notre Dame University Press.

Grisez, G. (1990). When Do People Begin? *The Ethics of Having Children: Proceedings of the American Catholic Philosophical Association, 63,* 27–47.

Grobstein, C. (1983). A Biological Perspective on the Origin of Human Life and Personhood. In M. Shaw, Margery W. & J. Doudera, A. Edward (Eds.), *Defining Human Life: Medical, Legal and Ethical Implications* (pp. 1–11). Ann Arbor: American Society of Law and Medicine.

Grobstein, C. (1988). *Science and the Unborn.* New York: Basis Books.

Gurdon, G. (1992, 24 January). The Generation of Diversity and Pattern in Animal Development. *The Cell,* pp. 185–199.

Hannink, J. G. (1975). *Persons, Rights, and the Problem of Abortion.* Michigan State University.

Haring, B. (1976). New Dimensions of Responsible Parenthood. *Theological Studies, 37*(120).

Heaney, S. J. (1992). Aquinas and the Presence of the Human Rational Soul in the Early Embryo. *Thomist, 56,* 19–48.

Hellegers, A. (1973). The Beginnings of Personhood: Medical Considerations. *Perkins Journal, 3,* 11–15.

Hill, D., Strain, A., & Milner, R. (1987). Growth Factors in Embryogenesis. In J. Clarke (Ed.), *Oxford Review of Reproductive Biology.* Oxford: Clarendon Press.

Horvitz, H., & Herskowitz, I. (1992, 24 January). Mechanisms of Asymmetric Cell Division: Two Be or Not Two Be, That Is the Question. *The Cell,* pp. 237–246.

Huarte, J. (1987). *L'Embryon: Un Homme: Actes du Congres de Lausanne* 1986. Lausanne: Centre du documentation civique.

Hume, C. B. (1990, 10 February). The Protection of Life. *The Tablet,* p. 158.

Hursthouse, R. (1988). *Beginning Lives.* Oxford: Basil Blackwell/Open University.

56

Iglesias, T. (1984). In Vitro Fertilization: The Major Issue. *Journal of Medical Ethics, 10*, 32–37.

Ingham, P., & Arias, A. M. (1992, 24 January). Boundaries and Fields in Early Embryos. *The Cell*, pp. 221–2236.

Irving, D. N. (1991). *Philosophical and Scientific Analysis of the Nature of the Human Embryo.* Unpublished Doctoral Dissertation, Georgetown University, Washington, D.C.

Jarmulowicz, M. (1990, 10 February). Letters: Ethics, Science and Embryos. *The Tablet*, pp. 181.

Jessell, T., & Melton, D. (1992, 24 January). Diffusible Factors in Vertebrate Embryonic Induction. *The Cell*, pp. 257–270.

Jessiman, I. (1985). St. Thomas Aquinas and Procreation. *Catholic Medical Quarterly, 36*, 40.

Johnson, K. E. (1989). *Human Developmental Anatomy.* New York: John Wiley and Sons, and Harwal Publishing Co.

Jones, H. W. (1989). And Just What is an Embryo?. *Fertility and Sterility, 52*, 189–91.

Kushner, T. (1984). Having a Life Versus Being Alive. *Journal of Medical Ethics, 10*, 5–8.

Lawler, S., & Risher, R. (1987). Genetic Studies in Hydatidiform Mole with Clinical Correlations. *Placenta, 8*, 77–88.

Locht, P. (Ed.) (1968). *L'Avortement: Actes du Xeme Colloque International de Sexologie.* Louvain: Centre International.

Lockwood, M. (1988). Hare on Potentiality: A Rejoinder. *Bioethics, 2*, 343–352.

Lockwood, M. (1988). Warnock versus Powell (and Harradine): When Does Potentiality Count?. *Bioethics, 2*, 187–213.

Lopata, A., Kohlman, D., & Kellow, G. (1982). The Fine Structure of Human Blastocysts Developed in Culture. In M. Burger & R. Weber (Eds.), *Embryonic Development* (pp. 69–85). New York: Alan R. Liss.

Mahoney, S., John. (1984). *Bioethics and Belief.* London: Sheed and Ward.

Martin, G. (1980). Teratocarcinomas and Mammalian Embryogenesis. *Science, 209*, 768–776.

Marx, J. (1988). A Parent's Sex May Affect Gene Expression. *Science, 239*, 352–53.

May, W. E. (1991, October). Zygotes, Embryos, and Persons Part I. *Ethics & Medics, 16*(10), 2–4.

May, W. E. (1992, January). Zygotes, Embryos, and Persons Part II. *Ethics & Medics, 17*(1), 1–3.

McCormick, R. A. (1981). *How Brave a New World?* Washington, D.C.: Georgetown University Press.

McCormick, R. A. (1987). Notes on Moral Theology: 1986: Dissent in Moral Theology and its Implications. *Theological Studies, 48*, 87–105.

McCormick, R. (1990, 10 March). The Embryo Debate 3: The First 14 Days. *The Tablet*, pp. 301–304.

McCormick, R. A. (1991). Who or What is the Preembryo?. *Kennedy Institute of Ethics Journal, 1*(4), 1–15.

McCormick, R. A. (1991). The Preembryo as Potential: A Reply to John A. Robertson. *Kennedy Institute of Ethics Journal, 1*(4), 303–305.

McGrath, J., & Solter, D. (1984). Completion of Mouse Embryogenesis Requires Both the Maternal and Paternal Genomes. *Cell*, 179–183.

McLaren, A. (1982). *Embryonic and Fetal Development, Reproduction in Mammals.* Cambridge University Press.

Moore, K. L. *Essentials of Human Embryology.* Philadelphia: Decker.

Moore, K. L. (1988). *The Developing Human: Clinically Oriented Embryology.* Philadelphia: Saunders.

Moore, K. L. (1989). *Before We Are Born: Basic Embryology and Birth Defects* . Philadelphia: W.B. Saunders.

Moraczewski, O.P., Albert. (1990). Personhood: Entry and Exit. In R. E. Smith (Ed.), *The Twenty-Fifth Anniversary of Vatican II: A Look and a Look Ahead* . Braintree: The Pope John Center.

Panigel, M., Kraemer, D., Kalter, S., Smith, G., & Heberling, R. (1975). Ultrastructure of Cleavage Staves and Preimplantation Embryos of the Baboon. *Anatomical Embryology, 147*, 45.

Pastrana, O., Gabriel. (1977). Personhood and the Beginning of Human Life. *The Thomist, 41*, 247–294.

Pereda, J., & Croxato, H. (1978). Ultrastructure of a Seven-Cell Human Embryo. *Biology of Reproduction, 18*, 481.

Plachot, M. e. a. (1989). Cytogenetic Analysis and Developmental Capacity of Normal and Abnormal Embryos after IVF. *Human Reproduction, 4*, 99–103.

Robertson, J. A. (1991). What We May Do With Preembryos: A Response to Richard A. McCormick. *Kennedy Institute of Ethics Journal, 1*(4), 293–305.

Sadler, T. (1990). *Langman's Medical Embryology.* Baltimore: Williams and Wilkins.

Sanders, E. J. (1989). *The Cell Surface in Embryogenesis and Carcinogenesis.* Caldwell: The Telford Press.

Shannon, T., & Cahill, L. S. (1988). *Religion and Artificial Reproduction.* New York: Crossroad.

Shannon, T., & Wolter, O., Alan. (1990). Reflections on the Moral Status of the Pre-Embryo. *Theological Studies, 51*, 603–626.

Shea, M. (1980). The Phenomenon of the Human Soul. *The Teilhard Review, 15*(1), 7–11.

Shea, M. (1985). Embryonic Life and Human Life. *Journal of Medical Ethics, 11*, 205–209.

Shea, M. (1987). Ensoulment and IVF Embryos. *Journal of Medical Ethics, 11*, 95–97.

Short, R. (1990, 3 February). Letters: Ethics, Science and Embryos. *The Tablet*, p. 141.

Siebenthal, J. D. (1987). L'Embryon: Une Home: Actes du Congres de Lausanne 1986. *Lausanne: Centre du Documentation Civique*, 91–97.

Singer, P., & Wells, D. (1983). In Vitro Fertilization: The Major Issues. *Journal of Medical Ethics, 9*, 192–195.

Suarez, A. (1989). Der Menschliche Embryo, Eine Person. Ein Beweis. In *Der Status des Embryos*, (pp. 55–80).

Suarez, A. (1989). Ist der Mensch Eine Person in Jedem Zeitpunkt Seines Lebens?. *Schweizerische Arztezeitung, 49*, 2084–2087.

Suarez, A. (1990). Hydatidiform Moles and Teratomas Confirm the Human Identity of the Preimplantation Embryo. *The Journal of Medicine and Philosophy, 15*, 627–635.

Suarni, M., Barton, S., & Norris, M. (1986). Nuclear Transplantation in the Mouse: Heritable Differences Between Parental Genomes After Activation of the Embryonic Genome. *Cell, 45*, 127–136.

Surani, M., Barton, S., & Norris, M. (1984). Development of Reconstituted Mouse Eggs Suggest Imprinting of the Genome During Gametogenesis. *Nature, 308*, 548–49.

Szulmann, A., & Surti, U. (1978). The Syndromes of Hydatidiform Mole. I. Cytogenetic and Morphologic Correlations. *American Journal of Obstetrics and Gynecology, 131*, 665–671.

Tauer, C. (1984). The Tradition of Probabilism and the Moral Status of the Early Embryo. *Theological Studies, 45*, 3–33.

Taylor, M. A. (1982). *Human Generation in the Thought of Thomas Aquinas: A Case Study of the Role of Biological Fact in Theological Science.* S.T.D. Dissertation, Catholic University of America. Ann Arbor: University Microfilm International.

Tonti-Filippini, N. (1989, August). A Critical Note. *Linacre Quarterly, 56*(3), 36–50.

Tooley, M. (1983). *Abortion and Infanticide.* Oxford: Clarendon Press.

Trosko, J. E. (1991). 'Jump Junction' (Gap Junctions): New Answers, New Questions. In W. Demillo (Ed.), *Cell to Cell Composition.* Cleveland: C.R.C. Press.

Twinning and Twins (MacGillivray, D. Campbell, M., & B. Thompson, Eds.). (1988). New York: John Wiley and Sons.

Ultrastructure of Human Gametogenesis and Early Embryogenesis (J. Van Blerkom, Ph.D. & P. M. Motta, M.D., Eds.). (1989). Boston: Kluwer Academic Publishers.

Van Blerkom, J., Manes, C., & Daniel, J., J.C. (1981). Development of Preimplantation Rabbit Embryos in Vivo et in Vitro. I. An Ultrastructural Comparison. *Developmental Biology, 35,* 262.

Wade, S., Francis C. (1975). Potentiality in the Abortion Discussion. *Review of Metaphysics, 29,* 239–255.

Wallace, W. A. (1985, October). Nature as Animating: The Soul in the Human Sciences. *The Thomist, 49*(4), 612–648.

Wallace, W. A. (1989). Nature and Human Nature as the Norm in Medical Ethics. In E. D. Pellegrino (Ed.), *Catholic Perspectives on Medical Morals* (pp. 23–53). Boston: Kluwer Academic Publishers.

Warnock, M. (1987). Do Human Cells Have Rights. *Bioethics, 1,* 2.

Warshaw, J. E. (1983). *The Biological Basis of Reproductive and Developmental Medicine.* New York: Elsevier Biomedical.

Wiggins, D. (1976). Locke, Butler and the Stream of Consciousness: and Men as a Natural Kind. *Philosophy, 51,* 131–1588.

Wimmers, M., & Merwe Van der, J. (1988). Chromosome Studies on Early Human Embryos Fertilized in Vitro. *Human Reproduction, 7,* 894–900.

Wreen, M. (1989). Whatever Happened to Baby Jane?. *Nous, 23,* 690–696.

NOTE ADDED IN PROOF

To identify a structure as being the organ of central control does not mean that it exercises its integrating function with total independence of other factors. Rather it means that the organ of central control *integrates* the other influencing factors (intra- and extra-organismic factors such as cytoplasmic proteins and the uterus) in such a manner that the entity is an organism; it is and functions as a unit. During the development of a multicellular organism the integrating center itself undergoes change in such a manner that its structure and function are proportionate in complexity to the organism which it unifies to make it an organism and not merely a random collection of cells and tissues. (In the born human and starting around the seventh month the brain appears to be that integrating center, while in the earliest stages of human embryogenesis some cells in the primitve streak may have that integrating function). A chimeric mouse (resulting from the fusion of two mouse embryos of different strains) is still *one* mouse albeit that it may have cells with different genomes.

Chapter 4

FETAL TISSUE TRANSPLANTATION AND MORAL COMPLICITY WITH INDUCED ABORTION

James Bopp, Jr.[1]

Editors' Summary: The author contends that transplantation therapy using fetal tissues from induced abortions is morally objectionable because it is unavoidably tainted by the immorality of elective abortions. Is the practice of harvesting fetal tissue from induced abortions separable from the induced abortion itself? In response, the author reviews the practice of tissue retrieval and describes briefly one published procedure. Because of the requirement that the fetal tissue be fresh, alive, and of a certain quality to meet the specific needs of the tissue

[1]The author expresses his appreciation to Richard E. Coleson, J.D., for research and writing assistance in preparing this article.

researcher, some degree of close cooperation between the abortionist and the researcher is required.

Complicity with past *abortions arises because of ethical principles articulated in connection with the Nuremberg War Crimes Trial. The Tribunal condemned the defendants for their actions in conducting the medical experiments as well as having taken "a consenting part" in such atrocities. A parallel with fetal tissue collection from induced abortions exists here as Bopp asserts. Even if an intermediary collector/processor is introduced, he does not break the chain of ethical responsibility.*

Complicity with future *abortions represents another ethically troubling situation. If fetal tissue transplantation becomes successful, this would be one more reason for undergoing an elective abortion. Studies have shown that in deciding about abortions women do take the perceived needs of others into consideration, often as a determinative factor. Financial gain is another factor even if it may be indirect. The 1.5 million abortions performed in 1985 generated some $282 million of revenue. Although the 1984 National Organ Transplant Act does outlaw the sale of human tissues, it does permit a "processing fee" that currently ranges from $25 to $175 per fetus. In addition, tissue banks pay clinics a "rental fee" of up to one thousand dollars a month in order to keep processors on site to quickly retrieve fetuses. These various financial incentives would tend to increase the pressure clinic personnel would place on women to abort and donate fetal tissues.*

Finally, these various factors collectively tend to erode respect for human life which in turn would further aggravate the gradual dehumanization of our culture.

The debate surrounding the use of fetal tissue from *induced* abortion has focused primarily on whether the transplantation procedure can be separated both practically and morally from the moral objections to the induced abortions which make the tissue available for transplantation. This article will argue that it cannot. If transplantation from fetal tissue from induced abortion becomes efficacious, transplant therapy will unavoidably be tainted by its association with and effect on the practice of elective abortion. Since induced abortion is a moral evil, transplantation therapy using such tissue is also morally objectionable.

THE PRACTICE OF FETAL TISSUE TRANSPLANTATION USING TISSUE FROM INDUCED ABORTIONS

The initial inquiry is whether the harvesting of fetal tissue from induced abortion as a practical matter is separated from the induced abortion itself. If it cannot be or is not it is inextricably intertwined with the morality of the abortion itself.

In regard to the fetal tissue collection process, the requirement that the fetal tissue must be fresh and alive tends to influence transplantation practices and has resulted in a combination of the abortion and collection techniques. One group of researchers described such a procedure in the *Archives of Neurology* (Madrazo et al., 1990).

Prior to the tissue collection, the pregnant women were given several blood tests, including one for human immunodeficiency virus (HIV). The fetuses whose brain tissue was to be harvested were all nine to eleven weeks in gestational age. An ultrasound test, coupled with later examination of fetal body parts after vacuum aspiration abortions were performed, was used to verify the gestational ages of the fetuses.

For the fetal tissue collection, the women were placed under general anesthesia or given sedation and a paracervical blockade, unlike the simpler and safer local anesthesia routinely employed in abortions. The collection took place while the human fetus was yet in the womb and alive, the collection technique actually being the agent ending the life of the fetus.

The women were first cervically dilated. Then a syringe (60-ml) attached to a plastic cannula (a tube 10-mm [ca. 3/8″] in outer diameter) was inserted into the uterus. The researchers used ultrasound to guide the open end of the tube to the head of the human fetus where suction was applied from the syringe to slowly aspirate the brain of the human fetus, along with whatever other tissue came along. Alternatively, a low-suction pump with a metal cannula was used without ultrasound guidance.

Great care was taken by the researchers to prevent bacterial contamination of the human fetal brain tissue. This concern, and doubtless the concern for tissue freshness, apparently dictated the removal of the tissue from the human fetus while it was yet living. To avoid contamination, the researchers removed the human fetal brain tissue from the rear opening of the cannula.

Although it was not mentioned, presumably routine high-suction vacuum aspiration or dilatation and curettage was used to complete the abortion of the now-dead fetuses and placentas.

After processing, the human fetal brain tissue was injected, by means of a cannula through a hole drilled in the recipient's skull, into targeted portions of the brain. The recipient received local anesthesia for the procedure.

It is evident from this description that the abortion and the collection procedure had become one. First, the fetal tissue collection technique itself became the means by which the destruction of the fetus was accomplished, but in a way designed to procure usable fetal brain tissue for transplantation. With this practical intertwining of fetal tissue collection and fetal destruction, the propriety of the transplantation is inextricably intertwined with the justification for the destruction of the fetus.

But fetal tissue transplantation collection techniques need not be so intertwined, on a practical level, as the one described above. In such a case, the more complex problems of complicity arise. However, it is apparent that, even if the induced abortion and the transplantation process at a practical level are separate, transplantation from induced abortion is still morally tainted. This is so because of the complicity of transplants with past, ongoing, and future abortion, the complicity with the abortion industry and the effect of such practices on the respect for human life.

1. COMPLICITY WITH PAST ABORTIONS

Complicity with past abortions arises because of ethical principles articulated in connection with the Nuremberg War Crimes Trial of "The Medical Case," which considered the guilt of German physicians who experimented on prisoners and their remains obtained from Nazi death camps. The Tribunal condemned the defendants for their actions in conducting medical experiments as well as for having "taken a consenting part" in such atrocities (Bopp and Burtchaell, 1988). The degree of one's having "taken a consenting part" is measured by attendance upon, acceptance of benefit from, and participation in an ongoing moral evil. Surely receiving a benefit—such as a heart for transplantation—from a person murdered without one's foreknowledge or passive witnessing of the murder bears a lesser degree of ethical culpability than where one knows that a murder is to occur and attends the event in order to obtain the heart as soon as possible after the death. In the former case, no complicity exists. In the latter case, severe ethical problems arise with regard to complicity.

The latter case is closely akin to what happened in the first fetal tissue transplant for Parkinson's disease by Dr. Curt Freed of the University of Colorado in November of 1988. Freed spent four days "drinking coffee all day and looking at tissue that was unacceptable" before he found what he wanted (Maugh, 1988). While at the clinic, Freed spent his time examining and reassembling fetal remains to be sure abortions were complete, a task normally performed by clinic personnel (Bond, 1988). In such a case, acquiescence and participation in the abortion activity is clear. The usual claim that the collection/processing will be done by third parties—and so researchers are ethically removed and immune from complicity—is unavailing.

Nor is the notion that an intermediary collector/processor creates a break in the chain of ethical responsibility convincing. If one would bear ethical complicity by being present at abortions, and even participating in the process, as Freed did, then the mere fact that some third party does the collecting/processing for you does not avoid ethical complicity. For example, if one hires a "hit man" to kill someone rather than killing in person, moral and legal complicity attach to the person paying to have the killing done. Thus, one can be liable for actions done, even if one doesn't do them personally. As regards an intermediary who collects and provides the fetal tissue, it is clear that the intermediary is acting as the agent of the researcher to collect the fetal tissue and the researchers are providing the financial incentive for the intermediary to engage in it. Therefore, the researcher is not shielded by the intermediary collector/processor and is involved in ethical complicity with the abortions performed.

Nor is it convincing to say that the sort of complicity described above should not be considered complicity because the web of complicity could be extended ad infinitum, e.g., "The grocer who sells food to the physician who performs abortions enables the physician to continue his work and the grocer is paid with the proceeds from previous abortions" (Robertson, 1988). The distinction lies in the degree of proximity to the wrongful act. This notion of *proximate* cause has long been part of the law, i.e., causation which is too remote cannot bring about liability. If remote causation is to be considered morally relevant, why should the parallel stop with the grocer? Why not blame the grocer's suppliers, or the grocer's grandmother, or the grocer's grandmother's ancestors who came to this country?

Applying the doctrine of proximate cause, the action of the grocer in accepting the abortionist's money for groceries, as the grocer accepts everyone else's money, does not provide specific motivation to the abortionist to engage in unethical activity. By contrast, the researcher/transplanter using fetal tissue from induced abortions is logically proximate to the abortionist and the woman deciding whether to choose abortion.

Moreover, the grocer argument would only be apt if the facts of the grocer analogy were more closely parallel to the abortionist's situation. A more parallel example would be where a mobster makes illegal moonshine, which he sells to a middle-man, who in turn sells it to the grocer, who has full knowledge of the illicit source of this beverage and sells it in his business. In such a situation, complicity in a wrong attaches to the grocer.

Fetal tissue transplantation research supporters argue that no complicity with induced abortion occurs during this process because the researchers and their transplant patients have nothing to do with the abortion (Robertson, 1988). The abortion, they assert, was the result of the mother's decision and would have occurred regardless of the research project. John Robertson uses the analogy of murder. Robertson argues that organ tissues retrieved from murder victims may be used without complicity in the murder; therefore, the source of the tissue should not make a difference in the morality of using tissue obtained after a wrong (Robertson, 1988).

However, Robertson's analogy to murder is too simplistic, as is his parallel analogy to victims of auto accidents. As Kathleen Nolan (1990) has noted:

> [O]ne of the most widely used arguments in favor of [fetal tissue transplantation] with tissue from electively aborted fetuses is that such transplantations are precisely analogous to transplantation from victims of auto accidents. It is claimed, moreover, that rates of elective abortion . . . will not be influenced by fetal tissue transplantation, just as use of adult organs has not led to diminished safety standards on the highways or to the repeal of motorcycle helmet laws. . . . [T]he proposed analogy obviously fails to take into account the differences between intentional and accidental death. . . . Nor is transplantation from an electively aborted fetus analogous to transplantation from a homicide victim; here death is also intentional, but someone other than the agent of death authorizes organ retrieval (p. 1028–29).

Moreover, the above example of Freed (who participated in the abortion clinic's program during extended waiting for tissue meeting his criteria) and the example given in the opening paragraphs of this chapter (describing researchers acting as agents of death by withdrawing the brain from a living fetus prior to the abortion procedure) shows how the analogy to murder is inaccurate. Murder is ordinarily a somewhat random, unpredictable occurrence in society. However, what if the murder is not the usual rather random variety, but is part of a systematic pattern, so that one could expect a murder to occur at a certain time and place and could, therefore, set up a processing center to collect and process cadavers? What if the murderer were known, and an intermediary rented space in a building owned by the murderer in order to more efficiently collect and process human tissue? What if the intermediary paid a processing fee to the murderer for the tissue? And what if the murder were systematically practiced on certain members of an identifiable class of human beings? Imagine further, that collectors and processors of human tissue accompanied the murderers to their deeds.

66

Imagine that the collectors and processors advised the murderers how best to kill the victims so as to make their tissue useful. And what if some collectors and processors even advised the murderers about when would be the best time to kill the victims for research purposes, e.g., letting young children get a little older so their tissue would be more suitable? Would not complicity be apparent?

One could even imagine a scenario where the systematic murder might be perfectly legal, to the point where it would not even be defined as murder by those dictating the laws of society, despite the fact that those disapproving of the practice could point to traditional elements of homicide in the practice, such as the intentional, pre-meditated taking of an innocent human life. There might even be a vigorous dissent to the practice, but with those dissenting powerless to change the situation because the controlling elite had decreed the practice to be legal. Imagine in this scenario that the number of murders is large and continuous. Would the fact that the practice is not proscribed by law make it justifiable? What if the law was in a state of flux, and this mass killing had been illegal for a long period of time but a particular regime had made it legal? Would mere assertion of legality make it moral? And what if this regime were in the process of being removed, and laws were again being passed to prevent the killing in some places. Would mere non-criminality in certain quarters remove the matter from legitimate moral debate in those places? In these situations, the ethical propriety of using the human tissue of these murder victims would clearly be questionable—indeed it would be clearly unethical—because of the problem of complicity in a moral, if not a legal, wrong.

The more extended analogies above reveal certain flaws in the argument of supporters of research using human fetal tissue from induced abortions. When the murder analogy is described so that it reflects the reality of abortion practice in the United States, the complicity argument takes on greater weight. This expanded analogy also looks more like the Holocaust, so that the convictions at Nuremberg becomes more evidently apt.

A few words are in order here about the reaction in certain quarters to any comparisons between complicity with abortion practice and the complicity of Nazi doctors with the Holocaust. Some, like Robertson, glibly dismiss such analogies. Robertson (1988) declares:

> If the complicity claim is doubtful when the underlying immorality of the act is clear, as with Nazi-produced data or transplants from murder victims, it is considerably weakened when the act making the benefit possible is legal and its immorality is vigorously debated, as is the case with abortion (p. 453).

However, this is no answer at all, for to the Nazi regime the morality of its actions was indisputable. And the acts were perfectly legal. Under the regime of legal positivism, what is legal is simply what the prevailing possessors of power say is legal. The Nazis' notion of racial hygiene made their actions in eliminating unwanted or undesirable persons perfectly moral in their view and therefore legal. The immorality of the Nazi Holocaust was "vigorously debated"—and still is—by supporters of social eugenics, anti-Semitic factions, and the like. It is simply no answer at all to assert legality, as is continually done in the present dialogue, without going to the underlying morality. And every regime in power believes in the morality of what it does. The immorality of the Nazi regime of unconsented experimentation and genocide is "clear"—as Robertson asserts—only to those who are not Nazis, supporters of eugenics, or anti-Semitic. It is a tragedy of human nature that what history later judges to be a grave immorality—for example slavery, genocide, infanticide, gladiatorial mortal combat, human sacrifice, capital punishment for minor offenses, torture, and euthanasia —seems perfectly moral to those engaged in the activity at the time.

While some glibly dismiss the Nazi analogy, others decry analogies from the Holocaust, claiming outrage that someone should use the lessons of the Holocaust to question something that they favor. Dr. Moscona (1988), for example, accuses the NIH Panel dissenters, including this author, as follows:

> The attempt to bracket transplantation research in one context with the Nazi dictatorship's crusade to exterminate a people because of religion or creed is even more shockingly misleading: it closes its eyes to the "ideological" dogmas that, by denying human rights to one class of citizens, unlocked oppression and provided the warrant for genocide; and it exploits deeply lacerated memories and emotions in the service of an extremist position. The Holocaust was not a medical research project to help Parkinson patients and rescue infants from fatal diseases. . . . The experimental "cruelties" [of the Third Reich] were not a main objective of the annihilation enterprise; they were just an incidental, opportunistic sideline of an obsessive "ideology" that denied human freedom and enslaved it to medieval hatreds in the name of world conquest. . . . This "ideology," above all the unspeakable deeds which followed, is the never-again-to-be-forgotten lesson and legacy of the Holocaust. . . . [E]quating freely surrendered abortus cells with tormented people poisoned with lethal insecticides defies reason and outrages morality. Is it negligence or a different frame of

68

priorities that inspire such analogies? . . . Is the Holocaust to be taken hostage in an assault on transplantation research? This is not constructive dissent. This might only feed ignorance, inflame passions, and inspire intolerance and extremism. . . . [I]n attempting to stigmatize the panel with "moral complicity," have they not strayed and lost sight of ethical and societal responsibilities (p. 27–28)?

Such a statement asserts an almost possessory interest in the lessons of the Holocaust, as if to say that these are the official lessons of the Holocaust and other applications violate the memory of those who died. However, the memory of the Holocaust and its unfortunate victims is held sacred in the minds of many, both Jew and Gentile. While it is true that some have a special interest because their ethnic, religious, ideological, or geographical class was thought undesirable by the Third Reich and suffered grievous wrong, the Holocaust in many ways affects us all so that we all have a moral obligation to learn from it.

In the process of learning from the Holocaust and applying its meaning, there may be differing views about what its lessons are. However, the proper response to views differing from one's own is to join debate on the lessons themselves. Righteous indignation over use of the Holocaust when one disagrees with the interpretation or application of the lessons of the Holocaust by another is no substitute for this debate.

Surely one of the lessons of the Holocaust is that it must never happen again. The beginnings of the mindset which led to the Holocaust are well documented (Lifton, 1986). It was a mindset that cheapened the value of life, which made people disposable, which rejected any inherent worth in persons, and which treated them as means to ends. Long before the Holocaust reached the "final" solution, there were "partial" solutions as society ridded itself of the unwanted. These were legal. Their morality was vigorously asserted. But they were wrong. And they led to even greater wrong. Thus, "the never-again-to-be-forgotten lesson and legacy of the Holocaust" is not just that the Nazi "ideology . . . denied human freedom and enslaved it to medieval hatreds in the name of world conquest" but that the Nazi ideology rejected the inherent value of individual human life. It is this willingness to treat people as means to an end which made possible conquest of neighbor nations, extermination of mental incompetents, gassing of aged and infirm persons, annihilation of gypsies, socialists, and other undesirables, and the eventual effort at genocide of an entire race. This utilitarian view of human life is at the core of the meaning of the Holocaust. Because the Holocaust must never happen again, the mindset which led to it must be recognized and rejected.

Many within the pro-life movement are deeply moved by the Holocaust and are devoted to seeing that it shall never happen again, to Jews or anyone. Thus, they object to any tendency to treat humans as disposable or as means rather than ends. Those who truly honor the Holocaust should welcome such reverence for the event and such resolve flowing from it.

On a more specific level, there are some logical flaws in Moscona's argument. In the passage quoted above, Moscona asserts that "[t]he Holocaust was not a medical research project to help Parkinson patients and rescue infants from fatal diseases." However, in the minds of those who engaged in the Holocaust, it was designed to achieve similar beneficent results for society by racial hygienics. "The Holocaust victims did not board trains out of free will and choice," it is asserted. Of course, but neither do aborted human fetuses go to their death out of free will and choice. The fact that women may abort out of freedom and choice has nothing to do with the propriety of abortion, for those who took lives in the Third Reich also did so out of freedom and choice. Moscona slips back and forth between the victim and the victimizer without remaining within the analogy he purports to refute. This logical error continues throughout the argument.

In addition, Moscona asserts that "[t]he 'experimental' cruelties were not a main objective of the annihilation enterprise; they were just an incidental, opportunistic sideline of an obsessive 'ideology. . . .'" While this is true, it proves nothing. No one argues that transplant research on fetal tissue from induced abortion is the main objective of our abortion-on-demand regime. The research is asserted to be precisely an "opportunistic sideline of an obsessive 'ideology' "—one which treats human life as expendable to attain good for society. The argument is that just as the world judged the Nazi doctors harshly for their complicity by experimentation on victims of the Nazis—in the immoral ideology which treated human life as inherently valueless and systematically killed innocent humans—so complicity by research on the victims of induced abortion is wrong.

Moscona further argues that "[e]quating freely surrendered abortus cells with tormented people poisoned with lethal insecticides defies reason and outrages morality." However, no one but Moscona has made this equation. No one can seriously argue that an aborted human fetus ever "freely surrendered" her "abortus cells." The analogy properly stated would compare "tormented" people—born and unborn—"poisoned with lethal" substances. Surely, no one can dispute that both victims of the Nazi Holocaust and victims of abortion die from substances designed to kill them.

Finally, a minor point about Moscona's description of Hitler's genocide program must be clarified. Moscona speaks of "the Nazi dictatorship's crusade to exterminate a people because of religion and creed." It is clear that religious belief was not the basis of Nazi extermination of Jews because ethnic Jews subscribing to both Judaism and Christianity were executed. Hitler thought them all unfit to live—clearly not on a sanctity of life basis but based on a variant of the quality of life position.

In sum, the lesson of history and the neutral application of ethical principles reveals that human fetal tissue research and transplantation with tissue obtained from induced abortions constitutes complicity with the ongoing moral wrong of abortion. It is a complicity by association and by tacit approval with an ongoing evil which is not at all comparable to the unpredictable, random, or unintentional deaths from suicide, homicide, or accident.

2. COMPLICITY WITH ONGOING AND FUTURE ABORTIONS

Complicity with future abortions is also a real and ethically troubling problem. If abortion is an ethical wrong, and one acts in such a way as to promote abortion, then one is guilty of complicity. Abortion is especially capable of promotion because, unlike the murder analogy of Robertson and others, there are currently few laws to discourage promoting abortion, although there are many laws which discourage promoting the murder of born human beings. These legal restraints against murder discourage collectors and processors of tissue and the researchers who use the tissue of murder victims from promoting murder to obtain their tissue.

However, because abortion is yet legal in many quarters, and has been since *Roe v. Wade* (1973), there are no comparable legal restraints. This makes the moral wrong of abortion susceptible to promotion (Rankin, 1990).

Thus, the notion that abortion is legal does not solve the moral problem of complicity by promotion of future abortions. Rather, the lack of legal restraints exacerbates the problem, making complicity by promotion of abortion possible and more likely.

Moreover, Kathleen Nolan (1990) has noted another logical impasse into which supporters of fetal tissue transplantation using tissue from induced abortions often fall:

Proponents of using tissue from electively aborted fetuses may object that the capital punishment example [quoted *supra*] is invalid because the fetus does not have the same moral status as children and adults who are full members of the human community. But if the fetus is not seen as having protectable interests akin to those of live-born humans, what is to prevent their usefulness in transplantation from changing attitudes toward [elective abortions]? That is, one cannot argue that the fetus is analogous to other transplant "donors" and thus is unlikely to be exploited as a source of tissue, and *simultaneously* claim that the fetus has a different moral status from other sources of tissue and thus deserves less protection. If fetuses are viewed as more expendable than live-born individuals, then the usefulness of using their tissues in such pursuits a[s] transplantation may very well encourage a more relaxed attitude toward [elective abortion] (emphasis in original) (p. 1028–29).

Thus, the evidence indicates that an increase in the number of abortions would in fact occur if fetal tissue transplantation became successful. Wide-spread knowledge of fetal tissue transplantation will add one more reason for women to have an abortion. While it is true that this knowledge will not provoke every woman who is intent on having her child to abort it simply for altruistic reasons, it will in all probability have an effect on the majority of women who are considering abortion. Studies have shown that most women are ambivalent about abortion, and from one-fourth to one-third consider the decision difficult to make (Kerenyi et al., 1973; Bracken, 1975). A large percentage of women end up changing their minds at least once, with five percent doing so after making the abortion appointment (Editor's Note, *Obset. Gynecol.*, 1977). Women vacillate on their abortion decision because it is normally based upon a number of evenly-weighed and often conflicting factors (Torres and Forrest, 1988; Bracken et al., 1978). Knowledge of the possible utility of aborted fetal tissue can only tip the balance in one direction. Even if this knowledge helps a woman to rationalize the decision as a noble act for humanity, this knowledge may skew her perspective and prevent her from considering all of the facts before making a sound decision.

Kathleen Nolan (1990) has explained the potential for affecting a woman's decision process as follows:

Since studies of women's decisionmaking about [elective abortion] (most notably Carol Gilligan's [1982]) show that women do take the perceived needs of others into account, as a major and often determinative factor, the potential for influence on individual [elective abortion] decisions is real, and it in no way demeans women to acknowledge this fact (p. 1028–29).

A concrete example of how knowledge about fetal tissue donation potential affects an abortion decision—and just from information given in the media—is given by James Childress. Childress (1990) reports that after he had defended human fetal tissue transplantation research on a national television program he received a call from a professor in another state. The professor indicated that he and his wife wished to procure an abortion, "but they also wanted to donate fetal tissue in order 'to reduce their troublesome thoughts about abortion.'" Childress referred the couple to others "who could help" and did not know what became of the matter. Clearly, however, the availability of human fetal tissue transplantation possibilities affected this couple's decisionmaking about abortion.

Fetal tissue research advocates, however, assert that any decision-making impact can be limited by not asking the woman for consent to donate the fetus until after she has made the decision to abort. If research and transplantation become successful, however, widespread media attention will assure that women know of the donation option before learning of it from the clinic personnel (Nolan, 1988). Thus, the use of fetal tissue for transplantation would be considered by the woman in making up her mind about abortion, even though her consent to the use of the tissue would come later. And "[a] pregnant woman considering elective abortion could have a vested interest in pursuing transplantation—if not for money, then to relieve guilt."

The widespread dissemination of information about fetal tissue transplantation research is evidenced by the appearance of articles on the subject in popular periodicals. One of these, a cover story published in the June 17, 1991, issue of *Time* magazine was entitled *When One Body Can Save Another* (Morrow, 1991). This article also includes a Yankelovich poll revealing public attitudes on the morality of fetal tissue transplantation: 47% did not believe it was morally acceptable to "[u]se fetal tissue to treat diseases" (36% thought it acceptable); 71% did not believe it was morally acceptable to "[c]onceive and intentionally abort a fetus so the tissue can be used to save another life" (18% thought it acceptable); and 78% did not believe it was morally acceptable to "[a]bort a fetus if the fetal tissue is not compatible for a transplant" (11% thought it acceptable).

Redbook magazine conducted a poll of its readers in September of 1990, gathering opinions about fetal tissue research (Kolata, 1990). Nearly 1300 readers responded and the results were printed in the December 1990 issue. A majority (61%) of those who responded stated that they believe this type of research is wrong. Fifty-eight percent felt that "some women who are ambivalent about abortion would be swayed to do so if they knew that they could donate the tissue." Another clear majority, 73%, believed that "publicizing the benefits of fetal tissue research would lead to a black market in aborted fetuses."

Glamour magazine ran the same type of poll and reported the results in the June 1989 issue. A significant number of readers reported concerns about fetal research. Twenty-three percent indicated that using fetal tissue in medical research will lead to more abortions. Ninety-five percent felt that women should not be allowed to profit from the sale of their aborted fetuses, although a majority still favored the use of the tissue for research. Even though in the minority, it is significant that a full 29% were against this type of research, and 26% were either unsure or thought that they would be more likely to have an abortion after gaining this knowledge.

As Kathleen Nolan stated above, women often make abortion decisions on the basis of the perceived needs of others (Nolan, 1990). Studies also show that some women electing abortion do not give the decision adequate reflection. David Reardon conducted a survey of 252 women in 42 states who had experienced difficulties following their abortion, and reported his results in *Aborted Women: Silent No More* (1987). Seventy-four percent felt that their decision was "not at all" thought out, while 88% reported that they were "not at all" informed with sufficient information to make the abortion decision. Fifty-four percent reported that "they felt very much" forced to have the abortion by outside forces, while only 26% believed themselves to be pressured "very little" or "somewhat." "Outside pressures" would certainly include key abortion clinic personnel, who not only have financial incentive to encourage abortion but will also have much to gain if women donate their fetuses.

Carol Everett, a former owner of two Texas abortion clinics, spoke of counseling offered by clinics: "Yes, we offered counseling, but that was for one thing, for our abortion business. The other services were just a sales technique. Everything we offered was geared toward selling abortion" (Litvan and Cooper, 1989).

Clinics operate for financial gain, and they do this by performing abortions. In 1985, over 1.5 million abortions were performed in this country, generating $282 million of revenue (Litvan and Cooper, 1989). The majority of this revenue is earned by abortion clinics, which have begun to dominate the industry as hospitals withdraw from this controversial operation. These clinics are projected to increase their revenue by 57% if aborted fetal tissue is routinely used for transplantation research (Hillebrecht, 1989). This is true even though the 1984 National Organ Transplant Act outlawed the sale of human organs or tissues because the law allows a "processing fee" which currently ranges from $25 to $175 per fetus (Hillebrecht, 1989).

Technically the fees are charged to cover the "expenses" of preparing and storing the fetal remains. Sometimes the tissue banks pay clinics a "rental fee" of up to one thousand dollars a month, in order to keep processors on site to quickly retrieve the valuable fetuses ("Fetal Flaw," 1990). This substantial financial incentive can only increase the pressure which abortion personnel place on women to abort and to donate fetal tissue.

Along with the psychological pressure to abort and donate will come financial inducements as well. Even if clinics do not directly pay women for their fetal tissue, they may indirectly transfer some of their new-found profits to clients by lowering the cost of the abortion and creating another incentive to abort. Clinics will try to encourage abortions and donations because the supply will not begin to meet demand if fetal tissue transplantation proves successful (Kolata, 1990).

Janice Raymond, Professor of Women's Studies and Medical Ethics at University of Massachusetts and Associate Director of Massachusetts Institute of Technology, warns that only 90,000 of the 1.5 million abortions performed in this country every year yield usable fetal parts (Kotata, 1990). Much of this tissue, however, may not be suitable for transplantation because of microbial contamination occurring during the abortion, which could infect as much as 85% of the tissue collected (Rice et al., 1993). This amount of usable fetal tissue would not even begin to satisfy the demand for the 1.5 million Parkinson's disease patients, let alone the 2.5 to 3 million Alzheimer sufferers, 6 million diabetics, and hundreds of thousands of accident victims (Kolata, 1990).

The shortage of fetal tissue could be exacerbated by new "do it yourself" abortion prescriptions which are being introduced into our country as a "birth control" device (Regelson, 1988). If a substantial number of women abort outside of a clinic setting, the supply of readily available fetal tissue from induced abortions would dwindle.

Lori Andrews, of the American Bar Foundation, suggests that this shortage of a valuable commodity be solved by conducting "free trade" in fetal tissue, and human body parts in general (Andrews, 1987; Sherman, 1987). Andrews believes that this is the best solution for all involved; the patient gets a needed transplant, and the mother or organ donor gets a financial benefit. Others, with perhaps a more personal motive will try to "solve" the shortage by soliciting foreign donors, establishing an "organ mafia," and setting up off-shore establishments that will provide fetal parts for a fee (Regelson, 1988b; Trucco, 1989). A cash commerce in fetuses seems impossible to avoid, encouraging some women to intentionally become pregnant in order to donate the fetus and receive a payment. Women's procreative ability could be exploited by ailing relatives who pressure them into conceiving and donating the tissue for their benefit (Hillebrecht, 1989).

Finally, women may be exposed to greater risks during the abortion process as some doctors use more dangerous techniques to assure that the fetus is of "marketable" quality. James S. Bardsley, President of the International Institute for the Advancement of Medicine, the nation's largest supplier of fetal tissue, admits that he advertises for doctors who use certain abortion methods which produce "intact" fetuses (Kolata, 1989). During the first trimester, he wants fetuses which are aborted with suction methods. During the second, dilatation and evacuation (d & e) or hysterotomy (in which the fetus is pulled out of the anesthetized woman alive) are preferred over more commonly used saline infusion methods, because they provide "fresher" tissue. One Florida doctor has announced that he has discovered a special suction technique which leaves the fetus intact 80% of the time. This procedure takes 15 to 25 minutes to perform, instead of the standard 5 to 7 minutes, and therefore may increase the woman's anxiety, discomfort, or risk of infection (Kolata, 1989).

An even greater risk arises if doctors attempt to delay an abortion until after the ninth week of gestation, when the pancreas, one of the fetus' most valuable possessions, is at the right stage of development for transplantation (Kolata, 1990). Proponents of this research suggest that prolonging gestation is comparable to maintaining the vital functions of a cadaver donor through medical support (Fine, 1988). However, there is a distinction, for women face greater medical risks when abortions are performed at these later stages, and the fetus itself is continually developing as the doctor prolongs the harvest, possibly to the point of feeling the pain of being sucked out of its mother (Fine, 1988).

Some would argue that this problem may be alleviated by procedural devices, such as not asking the aborted woman how she would like to dispose of her fetal tissue until after the abortion. As discussed above, however, this will not work because fetal tissue transplantation will become common knowledge if it becomes successful, so that women choosing abortion could be influenced by the possibility of tissue donation, even absent prior discussion of disposition of the tissue.

It is ironic, however, that nowhere in the discussions of when to ask a woman how she wants to dispose of her fetal tissue—to a lab or to an incinerator or trash can—do the concerns raised by abortion supporters arise in response to fetal disposal statutes. Abortion supporters have argued, in response to statutes designed to prevent the mindless dumping of human fetal remains in dumpsters, that having to make any decision about disposal places too great a burden on a woman seeking an abortion. For example, in *Leigh v. Olson* (1980), a federal district court agreed

76

with abortion clinic plaintiffs that a statute which required a woman to choose a method of disposal for the fetus violated her constitutional right to privacy declared by *Roe v. Wade* (1973). The court found that, even though one of the woman's choices was to let someone else decide about disposition of the remains, this was too great a burden on the woman's privacy right. It is inconsistent to say that asking a woman about disposal is now permissible because one of the options is donation to fetal tissue experimenters.

3. LEGITIMATING THE ABORTION INDUSTRY

The use of aborted fetal tissue will also increase the number of abortions in the U.S. in a more indirect yet pervasive way. If this research proceeds, the abortion industry will gain a new legitimacy and respectability through the symbiotic relationship which would be established between it, the medical community, the federal government, and the recipients of the tissue transplants (Doerflinger, 1989).

These relationships would occur because the acquisition of the tissue must be integrated into the procedures of the abortion clinic, due to the need for fresh tissue. When tied with such "humanitarian" research directives, abortion will gain a more positive and altruistic image, becoming an optional form of birth control for many who are now opposed to it.

4. ERODING RESPECT FOR HUMAN LIFE

Keith Crutcher, Ph.D., Department of Neurosurgery, University of Cincinnati Medical Center, wonders why advocates of a utilitarian approach to fetal research do not take their argument to its next logical extreme? If it would be immoral not to use aborted fetal tissue for all possible benefits, why not utilize it to solve the world's most serious problem, i.e., hunger. Crutcher argues, "It is not obvious what moral or legal difference, if any, exists between the maintenance of health and life through human tissue transplantation as opposed to its direct consumption" (Crutcher, 1989).

Why does this thought so totally repulse and shock our senses? It is not just that the thought of eating human flesh offends the tastes of many, because presumably the food engineers could suitably disguise the substance with a palatable color, texture, and flavor (perhaps disguising it as a high protein confection) before shipping it under a palatable pseudonym to third world countries where it would be distributed. Rather, we are shocked because the thought of cannibalizing a human body that has been born does the same thing. While we tell ourselves that an unborn baby is not truly human, our instinctive respect for the human corpse will not let us rationally treat its remains as just a piece of meat (Will, 1985). Pope Pius XII once commented that a "spiritual dimension of the human being gives residual dignity to the corpse, as does its eternal destiny" (Medical-Moral Newsletter, 1987). We recognize that a deceased human body is more than just tissue or waste. It is instead a physical connection with the being that left it behind, and it gives us a moral sense of mankind as a whole. These feelings have resulted in statutes and standards of scientific behavior which regulate the treatment of human cadavers.

The notion of setting up processing plants in abortion clinics to process the remains of innocent members of the human family for their use by others—no matter how valuable the contribution—erodes societal respect for human life. In a world where such respect is already in short supply, any depletion of the fund is both tragic and dangerous.

CONCLUSION

Thus, transplantation with fetal tissue from induced abortion is tainted by its association with induced abortion. It is morally compromised because it benefits from and promotes a moral evil, induced abortion. This moral compromise is inherent in the practice and renders transplantation therapy with tissue from induced abortion unacceptable.

References

Andrews, L. (1986, October). My Body, My Property. *Hastings Center Report*, pp. 28–38.

Bond, L. (1988, December). First U.S. Fetal Brain Tissue Transplant Performed. *National Right to Life News*.

Bopp, J., & Burtchael, J. (1988). *Report of the Human Fetal Tissue Transplantation Research Panel*. Washington, D.C.: National Institute of Health.

Bracken, M. (1975). *Research on the Fetus: Appendix*. Washington, D.C.: U.S. Department of Health, Education and Welfare.

Bracken, M., & Klerman, L. (1978). Abortion, Adoption, or Motherhood: An Empirical Study of Decision-Making During Pregnancy. *American Journal of Obstetrics & Gynecology, 130*, 256–57.

Childress, J. (1990). Disassociation From Evil: The Case of Fetal Tissue Transplantation Research. *Social Responsibility: Business, Journalism, Law, Medicine, 16*, 32–49.

Doerflinger, R. (1989, 20 August). Abortion Complicity Unavoidable. *Palm Beach Post*, p. 1E.

Editor's Note. (1977). *Obstetrics & Gynecological Survey*, 97.

Fetal Flaw. (1990, 1 January). *New Republic*, p. 1.

Fetal Tissue Research: Right or Wrong? (1990, December). *Redbook*, p. 170.

Fine, A. (1988, June/July). The Ethics of Fetal Tissue Transplants. *Hastings Center Report*, pp. 5–8.

Gilligan, C. (1982). *In a Different Voice: Psychological Theory and Women's Development*. Cambridge: Harvard University Press.

Hillebrecht, J. (1989). Regulating the Clinical Uses of Fetal Tissue: A Proposal for Legislation. *Journal of Legal Medicine, 10*, 269–322.

Kerenyi, T., Glascock, E., & Horowitz, M. (1973). Reasons for Delayed Abortion: Results of Four Hundred Interviews. *American Journal of Obstetrics & Gynecology, 117*, 307.

Kolata, G. (1989, 19 November). More U.S. Curbs Urged in Use of Fetal Tissue. *New York Times National*, p. 1, col 1.

Kolata, G. (1990, September). Miracle or Menance?, *216 Redbook*, pp. 174–176.

Lifton, R. (1986). *The Nazi Doctors*. New York: Basic Books.

Litvan, L., & Cooper, S. (1989, 12 June). Court Could Do Major Damage to $282 Million Abortion Industry. *Washington Post*, p. A1.

Madrazo, I., et al. (1990). Fetal Homotransplants (Ventral Mesencephalon and Adrenal Tissue) to the Striatum of Parkinsonian Subjects. *Archives of Neurology, 47*, 1281–2.

Maugh II, T. (1988, 21 November). Doctor Who Broke Restriction on Fetal Tests Under Attack. *Los Angeles Times*, p. 1/3.

Medical-Moral Newsletter. (1987), *24*, 25–28.

Morrow, L. (1991, 17 June). When One Body Can Save Another. *Time*, pp. 54–58.

Moscona, A. (1988). *Human Fetal Tissue Transplantation Research*. Washington, D.C.: National Institutes of Health.

Nolan, K. (1988, December). Genug Ist Genug: A Fetus Is Not a Kidney. *Hastings Center Report*, pp. 13–19.

Nolan, K. (1990). The Use of Embryo or Fetus in Transplantation: What There Is to Lose. *Transplantation Proceedings, 22*, 1028–29.

Rankin, J. (1990, March/April). Letter to Editor. *Hastings Center Report*, p. 50.

Reardon, D. (1987). *Aborted Women: Silent No More*. Chicago: Loyola U. Press.

Regelson, W. (1988, 14 November). A Wise Fetal Tissue Policy. *New York Times*, p. A19.

Rice, H., et al. (1993). Bacterial and Fungal Contamination of the Human Fetal Liver Collected Transvaginally for Hematopoletic Stem Cell Transplantation. *Fetal Diagnosis and Therapy, 8.*

Robertson, J. (1988). Fetal Tissue Transplants. *Washington University Law Quarterly, 66*, 443–493.

Sherman, R. (1987, 7 December). Uproar Grows Over Selling of Fetal Parts. *National Law Journal*, p. 1.

Sixty-Nine Percent Favor Using Fetal Tissue for Medical Research. (1989, June). *Glamour*, p. 56.

Torres, A., & Forrest, J. (1988, June). Why Do Women Have Abortions? *Family Planning Perspectives*, p. 175.

Trucco, T. (1989, 1 August). Sales of Kidneys Prompt New Laws and Debate. *New York Times*, p. C8.

Will, G. (1985, 3 October). Respecting the Human Body. *Washington Post*, p. A23.

Chapter 5

THE PRINCIPLES OF COOPERATION
IN CATHOLIC THOUGHT

The Reverend Russell E. Smith

Editors' Summary: Father Russell Smith provides an explanation of the various parts of the principle of cooperation and applies the principle to the ethical issue of using human fetal tissue. The chapter begins by showing that the obligation to avoid evil is based both on the revealed moral law and the natural moral law. However, physical and moral evil must be avoided even while being related to it in some way. The theological tradition of the Church has developed several moral principles for judging the ethical permissibility of actions which relate to evil, including the principle of cooperation. The historical development of the principle of cooperation is noted together with an explanation of the three classic examples of cooperation and the two types of cooperation, formal and material. The second half of the chapter begins with a review of the critical moral principles of Donum vitae (Instruction on Respect for Human Life in its Origin and on the Dignity of Procreation) *by the Congregation for the Doctrine of the Faith which are pertinent to the question of cooperation in induced abortion through the use of human fetal tissues from that source. Father Smith's analysis concludes that the use of human fetal tissue from induced abortions is proximate, mediate, contingent, material cooperation in abortion, and that it is not ethically justifiable since the benefit derived from cooperation is disproportionate to the value of innocent human life, to the value of the research, and to the scandal which would result from such cooperation.*

INTRODUCTION

The doctrine of Christ, and therefore the doctrine of the Church, has an ethical component. Far from teaching the mere avoidance of evil action, Christ taught that one must be perfect as our heavenly Father is perfect (cf. Mt. 5:48). Essentially, the moral aspect of the teaching of Christ requires serious asceticism involving prayer, fasting and the cultivation of the virtues.

The practice of Christian faith has always forbidden the deliberate performance of evil acts. Evil acts, called sins, involve the violation of the law of God revealed in holy Scripture or in one's "heart" or conscience (cf. Rom. 1:20–32). The Christian religion strictly forbids the performance of evil action even if good can come from it (cf. Rom. 3:8).

This teaching, that the end does not justify the means, is not confined to the moral law of revealed doctrine. It is part of the patrimony of philosophical ethics. Socrates is the outstanding teacher of moral philosophy and this conviction is a cornerstone of his own ethics (cf. Plato's *Crito*). Socrates also taught that the performance of evil, the lack of morality, is itself the greatest ill one can suffer (cf. Plato's *Gorgias*). A line from Aristotle (the pupil of Plato) eulogizing Socrates concisely summarizes the role and goal of philosophical ethics: "This is the man whom evil men do not even have the right to praise, who taught us to be happy while being good."

Three moral concepts have been formulated and refined to deal with the ethical permissibility of actions which relate to either physical evil or the moral evil of other agents. These are known as (1) the principle of the double effect; (2) the choice of the "lesser evil"; and (3) the principles of cooperation. These concepts have been taught and reflected upon, and with the exception of (2), they have enjoyed unquestioned acceptance in philosophical ethics and Catholic moral theology. The precise formulations of these principles has varied from one school to another.

It must be said that within Catholic moral theology since the early and mid-1960s, all three concepts have been the subject of intense scrutiny, occasionally drastic modification and even rarely total rejection.

This results largely, but not entirely from currents of theological thought that must honestly be regarded as laxist.

Underlying the tradition's formulations of these principles is unquestioned acceptance of an objective moral order and the conviction that some actions are "intrinsically evil," that is, are never justifiable regardless of the circumstances of the act. Revisionist theology in general rejects both of these underlying presuppositions which necessitate the formation of the principles to begin with. The bulk of revisionist theology relies on "proportionalism," which is the theological version of utilitarianism or consequentialism in philosophical writings of the modern and contemporary periods.

Revisionist theology and its rejection or radical modification of the principles of double effect and cooperation is not acceptable as a basis of institutional protocol because its practical conclusions are generally in dissent from the teaching of the Church and are contrary to the clear teachings of Christ. Therefore, it is incumbent upon Catholic healthcare facilities and medical schools to evaluate procedures, protocols and projects which concern physical and moral evil in light of the applicability of the principles of double effect and cooperation.

The precise question here is: What are the principles of cooperation and what bearing do they have on fetal tissue research and organ transplantation in Catholic healthcare facilities?

WHAT ARE THE PRINCIPLES OF COOPERATION?

The name of St. Alphonsus de Liguori is most often associated with the theological refinement of the principles of cooperation.[1] It was this theologian who in fact gave an acceptable interpretation to these principles which avoided the extremes of rigorism and laxism. It was actually the Jesuit moralist Thomas Sanchez who had posed the question of scandal and cooperation in his work, *Moral Handbook on the Precepts of the Decalogue* (Sanchez, 1613). On March 2, 1679, the Holy Office of the Universal and Roman Inquisition issued a condemnation of sixty-five theses which were considered to be too lax. In one of these theses, the Holy Office condemned the view that a servant who assisted his master rape a virgin by accompanying his master to the window and assisting him in gaining entrance to the room by holding a ladder or opening a

---

[1]See Roy (1968: 377–435). This is a classic article which exhaustively reviews the development of this doctrine from Thomas Sanchez to St. Alphonsus.

door or something similar, if this assistance were done out of fear of punishment or reprisal, was not seriously sinful.[2] St. Alphonsus made the principles of cooperation acceptable by introducing the distinction between formal and material cooperation (the former never acceptable and the latter possibly acceptable) and by a consideration of scandal as a serious invitation to sin. The Alphonsian distinctions are described below. It should be noted, however, that since his time, many different moralists have made refinements and distinctions of their own, but the basic teaching derives from that of St. Alphonsus.

Cooperation in the ethically significant sense is defined as the participation of one agent in the activity of another agent to produce a particular effect or joint activity. This becomes ethically problematical when the action of the primary agent is morally wrong.

There are three basic examples of cooperation on the part of individuals: the hostage, the taxpayer and the accomplice. The participation or cooperation of these individuals in the morally questionable acts of the principal agent is quite distinct one from another.

The hostage is forced to comply with the evil act of another person with threats. Fear on the part of the cooperator more or less compels him to cooperate. This diminishes the culpability of the hostage and in some cases diminishes it completely.

The accomplice may perform the same act as the hostage. But culpability is imputed fully in the case of the accomplice because cooperation in this instance is free and willed (directly intended.)

The taxpayer is an example of one who cooperates with a principal agent (the government) in an important, in fact essential, mission (societal governance.) Nevertheless, it is possible that the government sponsors activities which are immoral. The taxpayer contributes in some way to this immoral activity.

It is obvious at this point that the theological development of the principles of cooperation have considered the actions of *individuals* which cooperate with the evil actions of others. Contemporary theological considerations are not so insular. There are questions about "corpo-

---

[2]See Denzinger and Schönmetzer (1973). The decree in question concerns the opinion of Thomas Tamburini, S.J., found in his *Explicatio decalogi* (Ludg. 1659) lib. V. cap. 1, #4, nr. 19. The decree of the Holy Office of the Universal and Roman Inquisition, entitled "Errores doctrinae moralis laxioris" is of 2 March 1679, confirmed by His Holiness Pope Innocent XI as *Propositiones LXV damnatae*. Proposition #51 [DS 2151] reads as follows: "Famulus, qui submissis humeris scienter adiuvat herum suum ascendere per fenestras ad stuprandam virginem, et multoties eidem subservit deferendo scalam, aperiendo ianuam, aut quid simile cooperando, non peccat mortaliter, si id faciat metu notabilis detrimenti, puta ne a domino male tractetur, ne torvis oculis aspiciatur, ne domo expellatur."

rate actions" of cooperation, such as joint ventures between healthcare institutions in which the joint venture may be morally questionable because the philosophy and action of one of the partner institutions may be repugnant to the other cooperative institution.

This naturally leads to a consideration of the morality of "toleration." Toleration may be defined as "a reaction of mind that permits, for some proportionate good reason, an evil or improper situation or person. In the practical order the evil is generally a vice, in the intellectual order it is an error which is allowed to exist without positive approval" (Palazzini: 1236). For present purposes, toleration is considered to be in the practical or political order. "It would be inaccurate to hold that the State must always eliminate, if possible, all moral and religious errors on the grounds that their tolerance is itself immoral. The duty to restrain moral and religious error is not itself an ultimate end of action" (Palazzini: 1237) nor of the State.[3] In other words, it is not the goal of the State, nor precisely the goal of (civic) law to make citizens virtuous but to promote the common good.

A consideration of toleration is not applicable to this study of the ethical aspects of the collection of fetal tissue for research and transplantation, inasmuch as toleration is a passive acceptance of an error of the intellectual or practical order and cooperation is an active participation of one agent either directly with or parallel to the action of another.[4]

Clearly, there is a sharp distinction between the hostage and the accomplice, even though the specific action performed by both may be identical. The involvement of the former is called *material* cooperation, that of the latter is called *formal* cooperation. The distinction is determined by the will (intention) of the cooperator. The formal cooperator has the same intention as that of the principal agent. Therefore, the culpability of the formal cooperator is identical with that of the principal agent.

Formal cooperation in the morally evil activity of another is not morally permitted. Such cooperation is itself immoral since the cooperator intends that the evil action should occur.

Material cooperation admits of a spectrum of degrees which is the subject of important ethical distinction. The basic teaching is presented in the Pope John Center's *A Moral Evaluation of Contraception and Steril-*

---

[3]Cf. St. Augustine, *De ordine* II, 4, 12. St. Thomas Aquinas, *De regimine principum* IV, 14; *Summa theologiae* I–II, 96, 2; 101,1 ad 2; II–II 10, 11.
[4]The theme of "toleration" is an extremely important line of theological development and research. For a fuller examination of this topic see Keenan (1989).

ization (Atkinson and Moraczewski, 1979). The following articulation is largely a paraphrase of the authors' work.

Traditionally, the principles of cooperation have made use of a number of distinctions, the major four of which are:

1. between *formal* and *material* cooperation
2. between *immediate* and *mediate* material cooperation
3. between *proximate* and *remote* mediate material cooperation
4. between *necessary* and *contingent* material cooperation

Atkinson and Moraczewski continue:

'Cooperation' here will be taken to mean any assistance of or concurrence with another person in an act that is an objective violation of God's law (i.e., an objectively sinful act.) *Formal cooperation* is understood as any cooperation that directly intends the sinful act of the principal agent: the sinful act is directly desired by the cooperator either as an end in itself or as a means to something else. *Material cooperation* is any form of concurrence in which the cooperator desires neither the sinful act for itself nor as a means to anything else, but rather permits the sinful act to occur. *Immediate material cooperation* is cooperation in the sinful act itself, whereas *mediate material cooperation* is cooperation in one or more of the circumstances leading up to the act. Forms of mediate material cooperation are distinguished as *proximate* or *remote*, depending on how closely the circumstances about which there is cooperation are associated with the sinful act itself. *Necessary cooperation* is cooperation without which the sinful act could not occur; *contingent* (or *free*) cooperation is cooperation not necessary for the occurrence of the sinful act. Driving a getaway car for a bank robber would be a form of formal cooperation if the driver was part of the gang; but if the driver were an innocent bystander who had been kidnapped by the gang to assist in the robbery, then such cooperation under coercion would only be material. Joining in a friend's lie for the sake of the friendship would be an instance of immediate material cooperation, providing that the cooperator did not himself desire that the lie be told, whereas publishing a book written by someone else which one knew contained lies would be an instance of mediate material cooperation. Selling pornographic books would be an instance of proximate material cooperation, whereas working as a janitor in the bookstore would be more remote material cooperation. Opening a bank vault for a would-be robber is necessary cooperation if the robber has no explosive; but it is contingent or free if the robber could blow open the vault.

The traditional teaching of material cooperation may be summed up under three principles:

1. formal cooperation is never permissible because the desire that the sinful act occur is itself an objective violation of God's law.

2. immediate material cooperation is never possible because by cooperating in the sinful act itself one is also violating God's law even though he cooperates for some other reason; and

3. mediate material cooperation may be permissible, providing that the action of the cooperator is not itself a violation of God's law and providing that the cooperation is done for a proportionately serious reason.

In deciding this last point, various factors must be balanced against one another: (a) the more serious the harm of the sin, the more significant must be the good sought to justify cooperation; (b) the more proximate or indispensable the cooperation, the more significant must be the good sought. Thus, to take examples from the cases already cited, there is nothing *per se* objectionable about publishing or selling books or sweeping floors; but whether these activities are justifiable in the circumstances mentioned will depend on how significant are the goods at stake, how much harm the libelous or pornographic books will do, how closely connected with the sinful action are the circumstances in which there is cooperation, and how indispensable is the cooperation for the sinful action to occur (Atkinson and Moraczewski, 1979: 78–80).[5]

COOPERATION AND FETAL TISSUE RESEARCH

It must first of all be acknowledged that research and experimentation on fetal tissue, while not immoral in itself, is nevertheless subject to ethical scrutiny. The general ethical "landscape" of fetal tissue research and experimentation was delineated in the 1987 "Instruction" issued by the Congregation for the Doctrine of the Faith (CDF) entitled

---

[5]As stated above, there are as many refinements to the principles of cooperation as there are moralists writing on the subject. This presentation, however, is the most concise and lucid for the purposes of this essay.

Donum vitae. While fully acknowledging the goodness of scientific research as an aspect of responsible stewardship, the Church teaches and human reason discerns that action in this sphere is more than a matter of technique and skill. There is an ethical component to this research, reflection upon which must precede and accompany any research or experiment proposal. The entire first section of the *Instruction* deals with the respect that must be accorded each human being.

There are five fundamental points made about the general ethical aspects of fetal research and experimentation. They are enumerated in the following question and answer form:

1. "What respect is due the human embryo, taking into account his nature and identity? . . . The human being must be respected—as a person—from the very first instant of his existence."[6]

2. "Is prenatal diagnosis morally licit? . . . If prenatal diagnosis respects the life and integrity of the embryo and the human foetus and is directed towards its safeguarding or healing as an individual, then the answer is affirmative."

3. "Are therapeutic procedures carried out on the human embryo licit? . . . As with all medical interventions on patients, one must uphold as licit procedures carried out on the human embryo which respect the life and integrity of the embryo and do not involve disproportionate risks for it but are directed towards its healing, the improvement of its condition of health, or its individual survival."

4. "How is one to evaluate morally research and experimentation on human embryos and foetuses?[7] . . . Medical research must refrain

---

[6]The document continues with this interesting paragraph: "This Congregation is aware of the current debates concerning the beginning of human life, concerning the individuality of the human being and concerning the identity of the human person. The Congregation recalls the teaching found in the *Declaration on Procured Abortion:* 'From the time that the ovum is fertilized, a new life is begun which is neither that of the father nor of the mother; it is rather the life of a new human being with his own growth. It would never be made human if it were not human already. To this perpetual evidence . . . modern genetic science brings valuable confirmation. It has demonstrated that, from the first instant, the programme is fixed as to what this living being will be: a man, this individual-man with his characteristic aspects already well determined. Right from fertilization is begun the adventure of a human life, and each of its great capacities requires time . . . to find its place and to be in a position to act' [12–13, *AAS* 66 (1974) 738]. This teaching remains valid and is further confirmed, if confirmation were needed, by recent findings of human biological science which recognize that in the zygote resulting from fertilization the biological identity of a new human individual is already constituted."

[7]There is an internal reference in the text of *Donum vitae* (n. 28) which distinguishes between research and experimentation: "By *research* is meant any inductive-deductive process which aims at promoting the systematic observation of a given phenomenon in the

from operations on live embryos, unless there is a moral certainty of not causing harm to the life or integrity of the unborn child and the mother, and on condition that the parents have given their free and informed consent to the procedure. It follows that all research, even when limited to the simple observation of the embryo, would become illicit were it to involve risk to the embryo's physical integrity or life by reason of the methods used or the effects induced . . . If the embryos are living, whether viable or not, they must be respected just like any other human person; experimentation on embryos which is not directly therapeutic is illicit . . . The corpses of human embryos and foetuses, whether they have been deliberately aborted or not, must be respected just as the remains of other human beings" (CDF, 1987: I).[8]

---

human field or at verifying a hypothesis arising from previous observations . . . By *experimentation* is meant any research in which the human being (in the various stages of his existence: embryo, foetus, child or adult) represents the object through which or upon which one intends to verify the effect, at present unknown or not sufficiently known, of a given treatment (e.g. pharmacological, teratogenic, surgical, etc.)" (CDF, 1987: I).

[8]There is no directive either from Canon Law (1917 or 1983) nor from the current *Ethical and Religious Directives for Catholic Health Facilities* regulating the disposal of human tissue. One is therefore free to dispose of this material in whatever way is most convenient and respectful. In the contemporary hospital setting of the USA, this is usually cremation (or disposal at sea).

This precise question was presented to the Holy Office of the Universal and Roman Inquisition in 1897 by the Superior General of the Sisters of the Sorrowful Mother, a community of hospital Sisters. She explained that the practice followed in their hospitals involved occasionally burying the excisions and amputations in unblessed ground adjoining the hospital or burning them. The Superior General explained that burial of the amputated members in a cemetery would often be morally impossible and sometimes even physically impossible" (McFadden, 1967: 294).

The Holy Office's response was very careful and compassionate: "With regard to the amputated members of non-Catholics, the Sisters may safely continue their present practice. They should try to have the amputated member of Catholics buried in blessed ground; but if serious difficulties stand in the way of such burial, the Sisters need not be disturbed about their present practice. As for the burning of the members, if the physicians demand this, the Sisters may keep a tactful silence and carry out their orders. Moreover, it is the mind of the Sacred Congregation that, if it can be done, a small part of the hospital garden should be blessed and set aside for the burial of the amputated members of Catholics." This reply of the Holy Office was dated 3 August 1897 and received the official approval of Pope Leo XIII three days later.

This was reiterated in a slightly mitigated form in the *Ethical and Religious Directives* which were in force *until* 1971. The directive (#59) read as follows: "Major parts of the body should be buried in a cemetery when it is reasonably possible to do so. Moreover, the members of Catholics should, if possible, be buried in blessed ground. When burial is not reasonably possible, the burning of such members is permissible." This directive has been omitted in both the 1971 and 1975 revisions of the *Directives*. Father Charles McFadden,

89

5. Finally, there is a question that can be applied to the discussion at hand, even though the crafting of the question by the CDF is aimed at the document's primary concern, namely *in vitro* fertilization: "How is one to evaluate morally the use for research purposes of embryos obtained by fertilization 'in vitro?' . . . Human embryos obtained *in vitro* are human beings and subjects with rights: their dignity and right to life must be respected from the first moment of their existence. It is immoral to produce human embryos destined to be exploited as disposable 'biological material.' . . . It is a duty to condemn the particular gravity of the voluntary destruction of human embryos obtained 'in vitro' for the sole purpose of research, either by means of artificial insemination or by means of 'twin fission' " (CDF, 1987: I) There is direct applicability to the scenario in which one may conceive and abort a child for research purposes.

APPLICATION AND ETHICAL CONCLUSIONS

The ethical question of cooperation vis-a-vis fetal tissue research and experimentation revolves around the moral evil of abortion.

Assuming that elective abortion is morally wrong, is it morally permissible to obtain fetal tissues and organs from electively aborted fetuses?

The first distinction to be determined in answering this question is whether such cooperation is formal or material. Can the intention of the researchers be separated from the intention to abort the fetuses?

It seems to me that the answer to this question is "yes, the intentions *can* be distinct." On the one hand, the researchers are only interested in research. Their research on fetal tissue does not absolutely depend on the performance of an abortion. Abortion itself is a metaphysically con-

---

O.S.A., considered to be a rather strict moralist, made the following commentary in his *Medical Ethics*, a standard text in Catholic schools in the 1960s and early 1970s: "It must be acknowledged that some recommendations of the Holy Office are not always possible of fulfillment in this country . . . [M]any of our large city hospitals do not have any garden and, even if they did, it is likely that the sanitary codes of the state or community would not permit such a burial, [and for the hospitals and families of patients] the constant repetition of the formalities for numerous amputations would constitute an excessive drain on time and personnel" (McFadden, 1967: 295).

tingent circumstance attaching to the fetal tissue upon which research is being done. In fact, for acceptable fetal tissue to be available from the abortion industry, it would be necessary to radically modify the way abortions are performed. Saline injection and suction destroy the viability of the tissue structures.

This moves the proposed cooperation between research and abortion into the realm of *material cooperation*. It is then necessary to determine where this would be located within the spectrum of material cooperation.

Here, it would seem to be *proximate mediate material cooperation*. *This cooperation would also be contingent*.

It is *material* cooperation because the intention of the researcher can (at least logically) be distinct from that of those who intend the abortions. It would be *mediate* cooperation because there is not direct involvement in the sinful act of abortion itself and it would be *contingent* because the absence of research would not bring an end to the abortion industry. That is to say, the abortion industry exists in society apart from any research project. However, it must also be noted that the possibility of fetal tissue research benefits *may* increase the number of abortions by associating the choice of abortion with some potentially beneficial societal progress. This is a serious ethical concern. Finally, this material cooperation would be *proximate* for several reasons: the volume of fetal tissue that would become available for research and the industrial changes that would be incumbent upon the sites of abortions because of the surgical modifications and protocols necessary to link abortion clinics with research procurement agencies. (See chapter 4 of this volume.)

Finally, the factors that must be balanced for the justification of material cooperation are:

1. the value of innocent human life (sacrificed in abortion).
2. the value of the research being performed.
3. the scandal involved in such proposed cooperation.

Scandal is more than a public relations problem. It would arise from the almost insurmountable impression of being formal cooperation (which in some instances it may well be). The value of the lives aborted would be further denigrated by making the victims mere instruments of medical progress. In other words, the humanity of fetal life would be further cheapened by rendering it to be a merely instrumental good rather than a basic, inalienable and inviolable good. The value of the research is not enhanced by utilizing electively aborted tissue. It is not clear that such a great volume of tissue is necessary to fill research needs and it seems very possible that adequate amounts and adequate quality of tissue can be obtained in ways that do not depend on morally objectionable sources. For these reasons, material cooperation would not be justified in the instance. However, the issue is quite different when the tissue is obtained from miscarriages, as this volume brings out.

References

Aquinas, Saint Thomas. *De Regimine Principum*.

Aquinas, Saint Thomas. *Summa Theologiae*.

Atkinson, G. and Moraczewski, A. (1979). *A Moral Evaluation of Contraception and Sterilization: A Dialogical Study*. St. Louis: Pope John XXIII Medical-Moral Research and Education Center.

Augustine, Saint. *De Ordine*.

Congregation for the Doctrine of the Faith. (1987). *Donum Vitae*.

Congregation for the Doctrine of the Faith. (1974). *Declaration on Procured Abortion*.

Enchiridion Symbolorum Definitionum et Declarationum de Rebus Fidei et Morum (H. Denzinger & A. Schönmetzer, Eds.). (1973). Rome: Herder.

Innocent XI. (1679). *Propositiones LXV Damnatae*.

Keenan, James, S.J. (1989). Prophylactics, Toleration, and Cooperation: Contemporary Problems and Traditional Principles. *International Philosophical Quarterly, 29*(2), 205–220.

McFadden, C. J. (1967). *Medical Ethics*. Philadelphia:. F.A. Davis Co.

National Conference Catholic Bishops. (1973). *Ethical and Religious Directives for Catholic Health Facilities*.

Palazzini, P. (1962). *Dictionary of Moral Theology*. Baltimore: The Newman Press.

Roy, R. (1968). La Cooperation Selon Saint Alphonse de Liguori. *Studia Moralia, VI*.

Sanchez, T. (1613). *Opus Morale in Praecepta Decalogi*.

Tamburini, T. (1659). *Explicatio Decalogi*.

Selected Bibliography

These selected sources represent a general review of the literature for those interested in the topic of this chapter. In no way should one have the impression that this represents an exhaustive listing of articles on the topic of cooperation.

Ashley, B. M., & O'Rourke, K. D. (1989). *Healthcare Ethics: A Theological Analysis* (third ed.). St. Louis: The Catholic Health Association of the United States.

Curran, C. (1975). Cooperation in a Pluralistic Society. In *Ongoing Revision in Moral Theology*. Notre Dame: Notre Dame University Press.

Fitzpatrick, F. (1988). *Ethics in the Practice of Nursing*. London: The Linacre Centre.

Haering, B. (1961). *The Law of Christ* (Vol. 1, pp. 289–291). Newman, Westminster.

McFadden, C. J. (1967). *Medical Ethics* (pp. 357–371). Philadelphia: F.A. Davis Co.

Riccius, D. (1881). *Casus Theologiae Moralis Universae*.

Rie, M. A. (1991). Defining the Limits of Institutional Moral Agency in Health Care: A Response to Kevin Wildes. *The Journal of Medicine and Philosophy, 16*, 221–224.

Roy, R. (1968). La Cooperation Selon Saint Alphonse de Liguori. *Studia Moralia, 6*, 377–435.

Ulshafer, T. R. (1992, May). On the Morality of Legislative Compromise: Some Historical Underpinnings. *Linacre Quarterly, 59*(2), 10–23.

Wildes, K. W. (1991). Institutional Integrity: Approval, Toleration and Holy War of Always True to you in My Fashion. *Journal of Medicine and Philosophy, 16*, 221–220.

Chapter 6

THE DETERMINATION OF FETAL DEATH IN MISCARRIAGE: ITS ETHICAL SIGNIFANCE FOR FETAL TISSUE TRANSPLANTATION

Peter J. Cataldo
Thomas Murphy Goodwin

Editors' Summary: The question of when the human fetus, whose tissues will be procured for use, is dead is a critical one for a proper ethical evaluation of the use of human fetal tissues from miscarriages. Cataldo and Goodwin explain that meeting the two goals of treating certain diseases with human fetal tissue and preserving the inviolability of human life pivot on the accurate determination of fetal death. Given these parameters of the issue, the authors first present medical data on the determination of fetal death at the gestational ages pertinent to the use of fetal tissues for transplantation. The ethical analysis of the chapter begins with an account of how the moral goods of the inviolability of life and the conservation of life are fulfilled only through a truly virtuous compassion toward both the fetal donor and the recipient of fetal tissues. A consideration of the conceptual distinc-

tion between defining death and determining death is then made with a view to-
ward critically analyzing various theories about fetal death which may be used as
the basis for justifying the use of tissues from live human fetuses. These are theories
which view the human fetus as either being dead before it is alive, a human or-
ganism but not a human being, or available for tissue procurement if it is non-
viable. Each of these theories is rejected and the criteria for diagnosing fetal death
examined earlier in the chapter are presented as necessary for jointly fulfilling the
goods of the inviolability of human life and the conservation of human life in the
use of human fetal tissue.

Chapter Procedure

Our procedure in this chapter is to begin with an account of how a
determination of the death of the miscarried human fetus is made, particularly as it relates to fetal tissue transplantation. Not only is this necessary for a genuine ethical evaluation of the issue, but this particular
medical aspect of the issue is also in need of study as a medical phenomenon. The second step in our procedure is to show how the fundamental
obligations not to kill innocent human life and to conserve human life,
explained in the Introduction of this volume, will not allow for a pseudo-
compassionate response to the needs of potential tissue recipients.
Thirdly, an analysis of the Pope's critical question (cited in the Introduction), "What is death?" as it applies to the issue is provided. Our conclusion brings together the various medical and ethical factors examined
in the previous sections and summarizes the reasons why it is not morally permissible to procure tissue from the human fetus unless that preborn child is certainly dead according to biological criteria.

I. THE DETERMINATION OR DIAGNOSIS
OF FETAL DEATH

Human fetal tissue for research and transplantation may be obtained from several sources. Tissues may be obtained following an elective abortion. This is the source which has been used in most research
centers in North America and Europe (Lindval, et al., 1988: 3–4). Tissue
may also be obtained following naturally occurring pregnancy losses:
miscarriage or surgical removal of an extra uterine pregnancy (Madrazo,
et al., 1990: 1–5). The technical feasibility and experience of using fetal
tissue from naturally occurring losses is discussed elsewhere in this volume. An important aspect of the possible use of fetal tissue from naturally occurring losses is the determination of fetal death.

Traditionally, death has been determined on the basis of the irreversible loss of certain "vital signs," in particular spontaneous functioning of heartbeat and respiration (National Commission, 1975: 111; ACOG. 1992: 254). This standard has been applied in practice to the diagnosis of fetal death *in utero* and after expulsion or removal of the fetus from the uterus (or other site of implantation in the case of extra uterine gestation). Alternative approaches to the diagnosis of fetal death have been offered in which the loss of vital signs are not viewed as central. These are reviewed below. The following discussion deals first with the practical aspects of the determination of fetal death as they are encountered in clinical practice. Attention is directed to the gestational age range before 20 weeks when fetal tissue most suitable for transplantation is likely to be obtained.

FETAL DEATH DIAGNOSED IN UTERO

The standard for the diagnosis of fetal death *in utero* is the absence of cardiac activity on 2 dimensional real time ultrasound (ACOG, 1992: 254). If cardiac activity has been observed previously but is not observed on a subsequent ultrasound examination, fetal death is certain. Similarly, if the fetus is of a size consistent with 9 weeks gestation (from the last menstrual period) or older and cardiac activity is not observed, fetal death is established. If cardiac activity has not been previously observed and the fetus is too small (ultrasound size consistent with approximately 9 weeks gestation or less) to allow clear identification of the area of the fetal chest, a repeat examination may be required to be certain that fetal death has occurred. Serial hormone determinations may aid in the determination of fetal death in such doubtful cases.

Other findings on ultrasound such as lack of fetal movement, compression of the fetal parts and overlapping of the skull bones are supportive of the diagnosis but not specific. Criteria based on findings other than ultrasound (such as absence of fetal heart tones on auscultation) are not sufficient for the diagnosis of fetal death *in utero*.

THE DIAGNOSIS OF FETAL DEATH AFTER MISCARRIAGE WITH OR WITHOUT SURGICALLY ASSISTED REMOVAL OF THE FETUS

Miscarriage is most commonly defined as the expulsion from the uterus during the first half of gestation (20 weeks or less), of a fetus weighing less than 500 grams, or measuring less than 25 cm. The diagnosis of death after expulsion of the fetus from the uterus is established with certainty when such a fetus "exhibits neither heart beat, spontaneous respiratory activity, spontaneous movement of voluntary muscles or pulsation of the umbilical cord" (National Commission, 1975: 111). According to the *Guidelines for Perinatal Care* of the American College of Obstetricians and Gynecologists (ACOG, 1992: 254) the fetus in whom any of the above listed vital signs are present should be reported as a live birth, regardless of gestational age, weight or size. The same guidelines note that "heartbeats are to be distinguished from transient cardiac contractions; respirations are to be distinguished from fleeting respiratory efforts or gasps." However, no specific criteria for making such distinctions are provided.

In practice, once the process of miscarriage is felt to be irreversible (inevitable or incomplete abortion), unless spontaneous completion of the miscarriage is felt to be near at hand, it is common to remove the fetus and placenta or assist spontaneous partial expulsion in order to diminish blood loss and reduce the risk of infection. Prior to 14 weeks gestation this is usually accomplished by suction or sharp curettage of the uterus. After 14 weeks gestation it is usually accomplished by prostaglandin augmentation of uterine contractility or, less commonly, by dilation and evacuation. Before 14 weeks gestation, surgical completion of the miscarriage is frequently undertaken without determining whether the fetus is still alive or not. After 14 weeks gestation and as the size of the fetus approaches the current limit of viability *ex utero*, it is more common to ascertain whether the fetus is alive prior to assisting in the removal of the fetus and placenta. This is so because in certain rare circumstances the fetus may survive to viability with either expectant management (as in the case of spontaneous rupture of membranes) or surgical management (as in the case of cervical incompetence).

Virtually all fetuses removed from the uterus by current surgical techniques (suction or sharp curettage or dilatation and evacuation) will lack vital signs after removal even if the fetus was alive prior to the procedure. Fetuses expelled spontaneously or after induction or augmentation of uterine contractility (usually with prostaglandins or oxytocin) may, however, demonstrate some or all of the above listed vital signs. Since expelled fetuses who are born alive will constitute the best tissue source for transplantation careful attention must be paid to this group.

The precise proportion of fetuses who will demonstrate vital signs after expulsion at any given gestational age is unknown. Between 14 and 16 weeks gestation some fetuses who are expelled from the uterus intact will exhibit vital signs. We have seen the fetal heartbeat persist several hours in a fetus of less than 150 grams (corresponding to approximately 15 weeks gestation). As the length of gestation approaches the limit of viability *ex utero* (around 23–24 weeks gestation) the proportion of fetuses delivering who demonstrate vital signs increases.

96

The natural history of these vital signs which may be present after expulsion of the fetus prior to "viability" has not been well-described. The fetal heartbeat has been seen to persist beyond all other signs of life, in some cases being present after more than 12 hours. In our experience, several hours persistence is not uncommon, especially if the fetus is maintained in a cold environment. Generally speaking, prolonged persistence of the fetal heartbeat is most commonly noted near the limit of *ex utero* viability and is less commonly encountered as gestational age decreases from that point. This phenomenon and its relationship to the ambient temperature has been described in various animal species by Dawes (Dawes, 1968: 141–159).

It is unclear whether adhering to the standard definition of death will result in difficulties for transplantation of fetal tissue. In many institutions, the reporting of a live birth means that the fetus is not treated as a surgical specimen but as human remains from which tissue may be obtained only during a formal autopsy. Even if this is not the case, there may be a delay of several hours in obtaining tissue due simply to the persistence of vital signs as noted above. The practical effect of this possible delay will depend in part on the tissue that is sought. In the gestational age period thought to be most suitable for obtaining neuroblasts (9–11 weeks), for example, the question would rarely arise, since virtually all fetuses expelled from the uterus would fulfill the standard criteria for death, even if they had been recently alive.

At later gestational ages, more difficulties may be encountered. Between 16 and 10 weeks gestation, it is likely that delaying procurement of tissue for several hours until death can be established would reduce the suitability of tissue from some organs for subsequent transplantation. On the other hand, there is preliminary evidence that viable bone marrow stem cells, for example, can be recovered under these conditions.[1] Alternatives to the standard definition of death have been proposed by certain authors. Such proposals, which would have the effect of allowing procurement of fetal tissue even in the presence of vital signs are reviewed critically later in this chapter.

THE DIAGNOSIS OF FETAL DEATH IN EXTRA UTERINE GESTATIONS

The natural history of extra uterine gestation and the circumstances of the termination are such that few fetuses may be expected to

---

[1]Unpublished observations: Maria Michejda, M.D. and T. Murphy Goodwin, M.D.

yield tissue suitable for transplantation. Nevertheless, there are occasions when a fetal heartbeat is seen prior to surgery and the fetus may be indirectly removed intact. In the vast majority of cases, the fetus is less than 12 weeks in gestation and separation of the fetus from the placental circulation results in prompt cessation of the heartbeat. In the relatively rare circumstance of an extra uterine gestation of more advanced gestational age, criteria for the diagnosis of fetal death would be approached in a similar fashion to that presented above.

There has been little ethical discussion regarding the practice of removal of the still living fetus after the diagnosis of inevitable or incomplete miscarriage especially at less than 14–16 weeks gestation. In these cases, there is no chance of survival regardless of the management. After 16 weeks gestation, ethical justification for assisting in removal of the still living fetus under the circumstances described, at least by medical means, might possible on the basis of several moral principles, including the principle of the double effect. Augmentation of uterine contractility may be undertaken in order to remove the diseased organ, usually the infected or bleeding placenta and/or membranes. However, it is beyond the scope of this chapter to deal with the ethics of this specific question.

II. FULFILLING MORAL OBLIGATIONS TOWARD THE LIVES OF THE DONOR AND RECIPIENT WITH TRUE COMPASSION

The moral duties we have toward the human fetus outlined in the Introduction—the duty not to kill directly and the duty to conserve life—are the same duties we have toward the recipients of human fetal tissue, such as the Parkinson's or Alzheimer's patient: "The debilitating physical or psycho-social conditions of the Parkinson's and Alzheimer's patient do not take precedence over the sacredness of their lives as being created in the image of God; nor can these conditions snuff out the primordial inclination to conserve life, and, therefore, the corresponding natural law obligation we have on their behalf" (see Introduction).

The sacredness and goodness of human life are not contingent upon the individual condition of human life. The intelligibility of these goods is not determined by, nor dependent upon, the mutable, involuntary circumstances of an individual life. Such circumstances do not determine moral good as such; rather, our acts of fulfilling moral goods must be proportionate to the circumstances under which we act. The "quality of life" argument which would morally justify a euthanasia solution (i.e., a direct killing) for Parkinson or Alzheimer patients on the basis that their lives, at a certain point, have no meaning, confuses the role of circumstances in moral evaluation. This "quality of life" argument erroneously makes the good of conserving human life itself proportionate to circumstances, rather than understanding *the acts* in fulfillment of this good as being proportionate to circumstances. Laboring under a confused concept of the role of circumstances in moral judgment, a false notion of compassion arises, which would on the one hand justify euthanasia for patients who might otherwise benefit from fetal tissue transplantation, and on the other justify cooperation with abortion for the purpose of fetal tissue transplantation. It is this pseudo-compassion to which we will now briefly turn our attention.

The pursuit of, and commitment to, the good of conserving human life as an integral component of compassion is certainly true for the Christian.[2] "In authentic Christian Belief," write Benedict Ashley, O.P. and Kevin O'Rourke, O.P., "every individual has a responsibility to choose life and to fight for it. Christians must fight for a full and abundant life and must accept disease and death only as inevitable incidents in the battle, but not as its final outcome" (Ashley and O'Rourke, 1989: 48). Pope John Paul II writes in his encyclical *Salvifici doloris* that the New Testament parable of the Good Samaritan answers the perennial question, "Who is my neighbor?" The answer to this question also answers the question "what the relationship of each of us must be towards our suffering neighbor" (John Paul II, 1984: 49).

We learn from the parable, John Paul II explains, that our relationship is one of stopping beside the suffering neighbor. This stopping is a twofold unleashing of love in the human person in the forms of compassion and help (John Paul II, 1984: 48–52). The Good Samaritan does not indifferently pass by his neighbor. In the name of both "fundamental human solidarity" and "love of neighbor" he stops and shows compassion by making himself available and by expressing a sensitivity of heart toward the sufferings and misfortune of others (John Paul II, 1984: 51). John Paul II rightly points out that "the Good Samaritan of Christ's parable does not stop at sympathy and compassion alone. They become for him an incentive to actions aimed at bringing help to the injured man" (John Paul II, 1984: 49). This is a help in which no material means are spared and which is effective to the extent possible.

In 1949 at the Fourth International Congress of Catholic Doctors, Pope Pius XII spoke on the vocation of the physician and advancement in medicine: "Careful as he is lest some advantage of such progress escape his attention, the physician is continually on the look-out for all which brings healing, or at least alleviates man's suffering and sickness"

---

[2]See Ashley and O'Rourke (1989: 44–49).

(Pius XII, 1979a ed.: 115). For both Pius the XII and John Paul II true compassion does not succumb to fears either within the care giver or within the patient, degenerating into sentimentality and a rationalizing of "fatal practices" (Pius XII, 1979b ed.: 90).[3] For example, compassion could never rightfully justify an act of euthanasia against a Parkinson's or Alzheimer's patient.[4] It is irrational indeed to believe that the cure or medical treatment for some diseases is to kill the afflicted patient.[5] Nor could cooperation with a direct abortion to cure these same patients be justified in the name of compassion. Such deadly compassion does not come from the virtue of compassion, but arises from an irrational emotion.[6]

Thomas Aquinas rightly argues that the motive of compassion is the desire to correct a defect in someone who suffers unhappiness from corruptive or distressing evils (Aquinas, 1952 ed.: II–II, q. 30). But Aquinas also recognizes that the wish for happiness is not a wish for true happiness or true good unless the wish is just, i.e., unless it is a wish in accordance with the fulfillment of our human nature. That element which safeguards this justice, which regulates the movement of the heart toward the distress of another, is reason.[7] The regulation by reason of the passionate response to one who suffers is what constitutes compassion as a virtue. However, a pseudo-compassion which moves someone to kill directly is contrary to the virtue of compassion, since it is opposed to the natural law desire for self-preservation. Moreover, rather than correcting a defect, pseudo-compassion actually causes a defect in the individual (and at that, the ultimate defect of death). It is also ironic that pseudo-compassion is justified on the grounds that it is a non-paternalistic, autonomy-respecting response to the wishes of the patient. This is argued to the point of eliminating any distinctions relevant to the

---

[3]See also John Paul II (1990): "The need of the heart commands us to overcome fear. . ." (p. 7). Lawrence Blum (1980) rightly explains that compassion ". . . does not involve an identity confusion in which the compassionate person fails to distinguish his feelings and situation from the other person's. Such a pathological condition actually precludes genuine compassion because it blurs the distinction between subject and object" (p. 231). This describes well what we have called pseudo-compassion.

[4]For prominent examples of the characterization and description of direct killing as a compassionate response see Quill (1991); Quill, Cassel, & Meier (1992); and Brody (1992).

[5]Monsignor James J. Mulligan has described those who hold this position in the context of prenatal diagnosis: "Seeing a disease, and having no cure, they decide simply to forge ahead and banish the disease by killing the person who has it" (Mulligan, 1991: 115).

[6]On the emotivistic character of the human fetal tissue transplantation debate see Bopp & Burtchaell (1988: 50).

[7]Reason is not used here in the sense of logic or argument.

wishes of care-giver and patient. In fact, pseudo-compassion is a terrible abuse of the stature of the one who responds to the suffering person. Even pseudo-compassion cannot escape the fact that in the relationship of compassion one person has "more" than the other relative to what they suffer. Pseudo-compassion is a cruel irony and deception in light of this undeniable relationship for pseudo-compassion turns this relationship into one of dominance over the person who suffers.[8] Yet it is precisely this relationship of inequality which demands a just assuagement of suffering and makes the virtue of compassion the greatest of the social virtues for Aquinas:

> But of all the virtues which relate to our neighbor, mercy is the greatest, even as its act surpasses all others, since it belongs to one who is higher and better to supply the defect of another, in so far as the latter is deficient (Aquinas, 1952 ed.: II–II, q. 30, 4).

The truth about pseudo-compassion is that it maintains the inequality of this relationship by causing the person to have even less than what they already lack; in fact it causes the person to have nothing.

Thus, it is only out of a duty to care for one's own health and that of others, fulfilled in and through the virtue of compassion, that we may turn to the use of human fetal tissue. Given these moral demands, we must be certain of the fetus' death prior to procurement of tissue. Knowing whether a particular human fetus is dead presupposes that we are able to define death. However, as soon as we pose the question, "What is death?" we find it necessary to distinguish between defining death and making a determination of death. That is, we must distinguish the state of affairs called death from the judgment of that state in the individual case. What this distinction is and how it applies to human fetal tissue transplantation will now be explored in the next two sections.

III. DEFINING AND DETERMINING DEATH

Germain Grisez and Joseph Boyle outline the task of defining death according to an ordering of three types of definitions:

> A definition of death in theoretical terms will tell what happens when an organism dies when this matter is considered within

---

[8]See Dyck (1992).

the framework of a general theory of life. A definition of death in factual terms will tell what observable or inferable state of affairs obtains if the theoretical concept of death is satisfied. A definition of death in operational terms will tell how to establish that the factual state of affairs obtains (Grisez and Boyle, 1979: 63).

Grisez and Boyle have outlined what could otherwise be described as the definition of death proper or *per se*, the observable signs of death so defined and the specific means by which the signs of death are verified. The distinctness of all three related aspects of the issue of defining death must be preserved. Robert Veatch was one of the first to point out the serious conceptual mistakes which can arise from confusing the various categories used to define death.[9] The categories for determining the fact of death can be confused with the definition of death itself, which is to beg the question about what death is.[10] We will attempt to answer the question of what death specifically is as it relates to fetal tissue transplantation by first examining the concepts of death as such, death as observable, and death as verified.

From a strictly physical point of view, death, in its broadest terms, is the cessation of life. The life of the human being is an integrated activity, each part of the human organism existing for the maintenance of the whole. If the integration of the whole irreversibly ceases, the individual dies. If each part is fully intelligible only in relation to the whole, then it is the unity of the human organism which defines its life and the absence of that unity its death. Traditionally, self-motion or self-change has been identified as the unique characteristic of the integrated unity of life. The living being is not passive but self-active, as is evident in its four activities of growth, metabolism, irritability, and reproduction.[11] Thus, the ab-

---

[9]See Veatch (1989: 16–17). However, for Veatch to describe the traditional view of the soul in terms of being "an independent nonphysical entity that is necessary and sufficient for a person to be considered alive," which is "a relic from the era of dichotomized anthropologies" (p. 29) is a gross error. Moreover, to state that not since the day of Descartes has the question of the locus of the soul been "dealt with definitively," not even mentioning the prior work of Thomas Aquinas on the question, is an inexcusable historical oversight (see p. 33).

[10]Interestingly, Grisez & Boyle (1979: 74) show that Veatch commits the same fallacy of begging the question in the treatment of his own formal definition of death.

[11]See Moraczewski & Showalter (1982: 16–17). This tradition goes back to Aristotle and his definition of nature: ". . . nature is a source or cause of being moved and of being at rest in that to which it belongs primarily, in virtue of itself and not in virtue of a concomitant

sence of this self-initiated activity indicates the absence of the organism, i.e., an absence of the whole by which and for which various activities were caused.

If death has occurred, certain things may be observable about it. Those organs and activities critical to the integrated unity of the organism will either be destroyed or cease to function spontaneously, i.e., will cease to function with the self-initiation of an organism. This aspect of death comes under the category of the determination of death, specifically death as observable. Given the definition of death as the cessation of the organism as a whole, what is observed about death can be characterized as an event rather than a process. There is a fixed point in time at which the integrated unity of the organism exists no longer, even though what were once individual parts of the whole may continue to exist for a time.[12] Albert S. Moraczewski, O.P., and J. Stuart Showalter, J.D., have stated this distinction in the following way: "Because the human organism is made of cells, tissues, and organs that are living parts, death of the organism as a whole is not the same as death of the whole organism. In the former instance, the human being has lost its fundamental unity; it is no longer an organism. . . . In the latter case—death of the whole organism—the implication is that every organ and cell has died" (Moraczewski and Showalter, 1982: 11–12). The distinction is meant to point up the essential difference between the unity of the organism and the disunity of what remains after the death of the organism. An organism is by definition a whole; but if the whole no longer exists, there is no organism whose death, after a process, may be identified as the "death of the whole organism." There are, rather, discrete cells and tissues of the former organism which continue to exist in an individualized dying process. It is their death which must be distinguished from the death of the organism as a whole.

The distinction between the death of the organism as a whole and the individual death of the remains of the former organism has always

---

attribute" (Aristotle, II, 1, 192b 20). However, Aristotle wrongly predicated self-motion to inanimate things.

[12]On the question of death as process or event, one of the early debates between Robert S. Morison and Leon Kass is still helpful (see Morison, 1971 and Kass, 1971). Morison argued that since, in his estimation, death is essentially a process, then making a determination of death is essentially a value judgment. Kass countered, and rightly, that Morison did not even consider the human organism as a whole entity and failed to make other critical distinctions as well, such as between ignorance about the moment of death due to technological obstructions and the fact of this moment in nature. Ultimately, a position like Morison's which assumes a reductionist biology begs the question on defining and determining death.

been observed in the irreversible cessation of certain bodily functions. Traditionally, death was determined on the basis of the irreversible loss of the spontaneous functioning of heartbeat and respiration. This remains a sufficient standard in a great many cases.[13] However, for many cases in which the use of life-support systems maintains the functions of heartbeat and respiration, the death of the brain must be the basis for determining death of the person. All of the organ systems of the human body are coordinated by the brain as the integrating center. If this physical cause of the integrated unity of the human organism has been destroyed—forebrain, midbrain, and brainstem—then the person has died.[14] The distinction between the death of the organism as a whole and the death of the remains of the former organism is paralleled in the distinction between the loss of integrated function and the loss of structure. The irreversible loss of integrated function is not necessarily also the loss of structure, as has been explained by Vincent J. Collins, M.D.: ". . . you can have a loss of function without the loss of structure and that is important, because it is on the basis of the loss of functions, not on the loss of structure, that we make the determination and the diagnosis of death. When spontaneous function is irreversibly lost, structure may not be destroyed, but death exists" (Collins, 1980: 11). Collins makes a helpful three-fold distinction for understanding the deterioration of functions. There are, he explains, three types of loss of function which occur in a sequential manner: "One is the absence of *spontaneous* function; two

---

[13]This view in both the classical and Christian traditions presumes that the individual human being is a composite unity of the principles of matter and form, who is identified with neither but is the composite unity of both. Matter is the principle by which the individual has the potency to become this particular human being, and form the principle by which the individual is a human being, rather than some other kind of being. It is the rational soul which acts as the formal principle of the human being. The person's act of existence, then, is dependent upon the composite unity of the two principles. If that unity is destroyed, the person no longer exists in the ordinary sense. This is the position which we assume. It is important to note it here for the present context as well as for our critique of other positions below.

[14]It is interesting to note that the notion of a single organ being the integrating center of the functions of the body finds a parallel in the thought of Thomas Aquinas. For Aquinas, the heart performed the integrating function which modern science now knows to be the brain. In its function as form, the soul, according to Aquinas, was united to the body without an intermediary. However, as a moving cause of the bodily operations, the soul was united to the body through the heart. Thus it was ultimately by the soul, through the medium of the heart, that the operation of the other parts of the body took place (see Aquinas, 1949 ed.: 9 c.; ad. 4; ad. 13). We find no special difficulty in substituting modern scientific knowledge about the integrating function of the brain for the role which Aquinas gave to the heart in relation to the human soul. See also Chapter 3 on this point.

is the loss of the *integration* of function; and three is the loss of *reversibility* of dysfunction" (Collins, 1980: 116). It is possible to restore the loss of spontaneous function. Once, however, the integration of function is lost, i.e., once the entire brain is dead, the loss of function is irreversible. It is a "loss of reversibility of dysfunction." Thus, the loss of spontaneous function is significant as a sign of the other two types of losses.

The President's Commission for the Study of Ethical Problems in Medicine and Biomedical and Behavioral Research treats the sort of account given here as a distinction between the integrated function view and the whole brain view of death. They rightly describe the human organism as a system whose elements "are mutually interdependent, so that the loss of any part leads to the breakdown of the whole and, eventually, to the cessation of functions in every part. . . . On this view, death is that moment at which the body's physiological system ceases to constitute an integrated whole" (President's Commission, 1981: 32–33). The Commission also recognizes in this integrated function view the reduced significance of continued oxygenation and metabolism for some cells or organs, and of continued respiration and heartbeat (President's Commission, 1981: 33). In the whole-brain view of death, the Commission explains that ". . . the heart and lungs are not important as basic prerequisites to continued life but rather because the irreversible cessation of their functions shows that the brain had ceased functioning" (President's Commission, 1981: 34). While the Commission admits that the integrating function of the brain is important to both positions, it does not seem that the Commission needed to make a logical distinction between them. Both views are actually two mutually dependent aspects of one and the same view of the determination of death. The significance of the death of the whole brain is that the brain serves as the integrating center for the organ systems of the body, and its irreversible loss is the loss of that unity. On the other hand, the irreversible absence of integrated function is not possible without the destruction of the whole brain upon which that function depends.

The second aspect of determining death concerns the criteria for establishing or verifying that death has occurred. The President's Commission formulated the Uniform Determination of Death Act (UDDA) which has been the model law for "definition of death statutes" in all fifty states:

An individual who has sustained either (1) irreversible cessation of circulatory and respiratory functions, or (2) irreversible cessation of all functions of the entire brain, including the brain stem, is dead. A determination of death must be made in accordance with accepted medical standards (President's Commission, 1981: 73).

The wording of UDDA should actually be interpreted as reflecting the two aspects of the determination of death rather than being a "definition of death." Its first sentence describes what is observable about death. The second sentence refers to the criteria to be used for verification of what is observed. The Commission found that the criteria for verifying death developed by an ad hoc committee of the Harvard Medical School in 1968 (the "Harvard Criteria") are reliable. The criteria are, as cited by the Commission: "1. unreceptivity and unresponsitivity; 2. no movements or breathing; 3. no reflexes; [4.] . . . a flat electroencephalogram (EEG) . . . as a confirmatory test. . . . All tests were to be repeated at least 24 hours later without showing change" (President's Commission, 1981: 25). In addition to the Harvard Criteria, the Commission recognized the validity of other criteria developed later in response to some of the deficiencies of the Harvard Criteria (President's Commission, 1981: 25–30).

IV. PROCURING TISSUE FROM LIVE HUMAN FETUSES: REDEFINING LIFE AND DEATH

The analysis thus far has been based upon the premise that it is not morally permissible to procure tissue from a live human fetus. However, the modification of abortion techniques which would keep the fetus alive according to heart and lung criteria, and the modification of techniques to obtain tissue prior to abortion, have run parallel with arguments justifying the use of tissue from live human fetuses.[15] The Center for Biomedical Ethics in its *The Use of Human Fetal Tissue: Scientific, Ethical, and Policy Concerns* has categorized these arguments as attempts either to: (1) change the current definitions of death according to a higher-brain definition of death (which would classify the preborn child as dead); (2) change the current definition of life according to a whole-brain definition of life (which would classify the preborn child up to a certain gestational age as a human organism but not a person); or (3) justify the procurement of tissue on the basis of the nonviability of the living human fetus (Vawter, et al., 1990). Each set of arguments will now be given a response as they are represented by certain proponents.

---

[15]For an example of the modification of abortion techniques to facilitate fetal tissue procurement, see Olson et. al. (1987: 164, 173).

106

Karen Gervais in her *Redefining Death* argues that the declaration that something exists or not must be based upon a knowledge of what kind of thing it is (Gervais, 1986: 109). For Gervais the human being is identified essentially as "a personal existence," the necessary condition for which is consciousness (Gervais, 1986: 169; 44–45). Thus, according to Gervais, the permanent absence of consciousness is a sufficient condition to declare the death of the person and that human life is no longer present (Gervais, 1986: 69). Gervais makes an application of this position to the case of the anencephalic infant which is directly relevant to our analysis.

It follows from what she calls her "ontological" definition of death, which uses an upper-brain-death criterion to determine death, that "the anencephalic infant is neither actually nor potentially a living person. Where the condition of personal identity [a functioning upper-brain] is not fulfilled in a human being's case, that individual is dead. . ." (Gervais, 1986: 138). Hence, Gervais draws this conclusion from the fact that the anencephalic infant lacks what is otherwise called the "substrate of consciousness." Gervais argues for this conclusion as the only consistent one with respect to the anencephalic child, contrary to the conclusion reached by Michael Green and Daniel Wikler, whose upper-brain-death criterion she analyzes (Green and Wikler, 1980). Gervais gives a concise summary of their "ontological argument" in which upper-brain death is equivalent to the death of the person:

> . . . Green and Wikler characterize their own theory as an individual essentialism, claiming that the essence of the individual rests on his continued possession of a particular psychological continuity or history. On the basis of this claim about the essence of the individual, they make the following claims: when personal identity is lost, a person has ceased to be; when the person has ceased to be, she has died; brain death (specifically upper-brain death) is the death of the substrate that supports functions essential to the retention of personal identity; and therefore the death of a person's upper brain is that person's death. (Gervais, 1986: 112)[16]

---

[16]Apparently, Gervais does not find that Green and Wikler adequately justify why the redefinition of death ought to focus on persons rather than organisms in the first place, even though they show to her satisfaction that the death of the upper-brain is the death of the

Gervais criticizes Green and Wikler for making an inconsistent application of their ontological argument to the case of the anencephalic infant.

Green and Wikler argue that the anencephalic must be identified as a living human being since the only possible condition for identifying the "life and existence" of the anencephalic is the condition of having a human body, not the condition of being a person since the infant permanently lacks the substrate of consciousness. Gervais claims that their argument creates a new identity criterion which contradicts the criterion of using the upper-brain as the substrate of consciousness (Gervais, 1986: 138). Even if Green's and Wikler's argument about anencephalics is found consistent, Gervais still maintains that there ". . . is no good reason to maintain existence, life will end anyway, and the anencephalic infant will never have a conscious life. . . . It is confusing to speak of alive bodies and dead persons, since a similar distinction could be drawn across the board, even in brain-death cases" (Gervais, 1986: 139). However, while Green and Wikler may be wrong on other grounds, contrary to Gervais, their point is precisely that the anencephalic cannot be considered a dead person by their account in the same way that other individuals would be considered dead under their theory who lack the same substrate of consciousness. Green and Wikler's conclusion about anencephalic infants can only be based upon real potentialities, but the potential for personal identity does not even exist in the case of the anencephalic infant according to Green and Wikler. Thus, given their view of personal identity, they conclude that the criterion for determining an anencephalic's death must necessarily be different than the one used for other human individuals.

What is instructive for our purposes about Gervais' analysis of Green and Wikler is that an infant without a "substrate of consciousness" is considered dead by Gervais. The anencephalic under her view would be dead. However, the lack of a substrate of consciousness as the definition of death would, presumably, entail that all preborn human beings are dead until such time that they have a substrate of consciousness. Using the data from the brain-based definition of life examined below, this transition point from death to life would take place at the 20th week of gestation. We are then left with the conclusion that all non-anencephalic preborn human beings are dead before they are alive. There would not

person (see, e.g., Gervais, 1986: 156–158). Gervais attempts to supply the missing reasons for defining death in terms of the human as person. Defining death as the death of the person is justified by Gervais on the basis that it allows for a better, contractarian public policy of dealing with the death of certain kinds of individuals, such as those in PVS, which is not possible under an organismic definition of death.

be any reason on the basis of Gervais' view which would invalidate the procurement of fetal tissue for transplantation during this pre-life period of death. There would not seem to be any obstacle to donating tissues in the same way that tissues and organs would be donated from a human being declared to be dead according to Gervais' upper-brain criterion. Even if the pre-life individual were considered a potentially living person by Gervais, this fact could not consistently allow for the impermissibility of tissue procurement since such an individual would still lack the substrate of consciousness necessary for personal identity. The potentiality for personhood notwithstanding, the implication of Gervais' theory is that the preborn individual is for a time in a condition of death.

Why is it that a theory like Gervais' entails the rather incongruous result that death precedes life, that what she would consider potentially living persons progress through a pre-life period of being dead? The central reason for this incongruity lies within Gervais' "individual-essentialism" or personal identity theory of human existence. Her theory is a reductionism which reduces personal identity to only one part of human existence, namely, to consciousness. Moreover, there is a further reduction of consciousness to the functions of the neocortex of the brain. Her theory at the minimum implies that the physical functions of the upper-brain are sufficient to account for consciousness, and excludes any immaterial causes which would also be an essential component of personal identity. Our objection is not with the claim that consciousness depends in some way upon a functioning neocortex, since every indication shows that it does, but with the assumption that personal identity can be sufficiently defined by material factors.

The necessity of a pre-life period of death also posits a radical discontinuity within human life which is both biologically and philosophically erroneous. As will be shown below in our analysis of the whole-brain definition of life, the identification of personal identity with the development of the physical substrate for consciousness at a certain point in time is impossible, since at any given point a more primary substrate to the previous substrate may be identified. To use the presence of a "substrate" as a criterion is, therefore, self-defeating since the existence of successive substrata reveals not a radical shift from death to life but rather a continuum of "substrata" retrogressing back to a truly original point.[17] The referent of the "substrate of consciousness" would properly be that original point which is the substrate of all that follows.

---

[17]See Moraczewski (1990).

Even according to Gervais' language of the "potentially living person" a continuum is recognized. To possess the real potential for something (as opposed to the possibility for something) is in a certain sense already to be that very thing for which there is a potential.

In the end Gervais' theory presents a dualistic view of human existence—the very quality for which she criticizes others. This dualism is observed in her accounts of the beginning and end of human life and in her dichotomous way of presenting the debate about defining death. In her theory the person is essentially independent from the totality of the body. For Gervais, the person does not even have a contingent dependence upon the body as a whole, according to which view the person is not the same thing as the body but is also not other than the total body while the body lives. To identify the person as a personal existence, the condition for which is the biological substrate of consciousness, is to exclude any essential role of bodily existence in that identification. Moreover, Gervais' intellectual perspective on the issue itself reflects her dualistic view of human life and death. She understands the debate only in terms of "organismic" theories of human existence and "personal" theories.[18] This is a false dichotomy since there is a third view which understands the human being to be a composite unity, neither simply "organismic" nor simply "personal," and in which the capacity for life is neither disjunctively nor conjunctively related to the human being. All such views of the human being identify its existence with some one particular principle, and emphasize either the capacity of this principle to be disjoined from organic life at a certain point, or its accidental conjunction with organic life.[19]

THE 1ST AND 2ND TRIMESTER HUMAN FETUS: A HUMAN ORGANISM BUT NOT A HUMAN BEING

The dualism of a theory like Gervais' is brought to its logical fulfillment in a position like that of Julius Korein, M.D. Korein has argued that the recognition of brain death as the death of the individual entails that the beginning of an individual human life ought to be equated with the onset of brain life (Korein, 1990). Korein states that the death of the entire brain is considered "equivalent to" the death of the individual (Korein, 1990: 982). However, he points out that the recent recognition

---

[18]See for example, Gervais (1986: 20, 45, 77, 160, 164–165, and 169).
[19]See Gervais (1986: 164).

110

of persistent vegetative states has shown that the life of the human being, individual, or person is actually equivalent to what he calls the "critical system of the brain (CSB)." This is so since in the absence of the CSB, the organism "could no longer be described by the term 'human being' (or inivual [sic] or person)" (Korein, 1990: 982). Korein defines the CSB in this way: "This is the cerebral-reticular complex which is the substrate for such functions as sentience, mentation, emotions, memory, self-awareness, learning, attention, and other forms of complex information processing including storage and analysis. It is the CSB that is *invariant* in those states that may be referred to as the *human being*" (Korein, 1990: 982). The human being, individual, or person is biologically defined by the substrate of the CSB which, after its onset, is said to remain invariant throughout various stages of the human being. In addition, the "human organism" must be distinguished from the "human being" which is defined, according to Korein, by the invariant substrate of its DNA. The human organism is a member of the species *homo sapiens* whose DNA is the substrate for its life cycle periods "including the gametes, the zygote, pre-embryo, embryo, early, mid and late fetal stages, birth, infancy, adolescence, and adulthood" (Korein, 1990: 982). Thus, for Korein, the human organism is present whenever DNA is present, but the human being is present only after the 20th week of gestation, since not until this time are the incipient stages of the CSB detectable. "Therefore," Korein concludes from the evidence he presents, "as a lower limit, brain life cannot begin earlier than the twentieth week. It is after this time that we have the major changes that are relevant to the onset of brain life—life of the human being" (Korein, 1990: 983).

Korein claims that the argument for the onset of the human being is an objective one because it is "independent of economic, political, religious, and legal considerations," and is independent of the changes in technology affecting viability limits (Korein: 1990: 982). He believes that this objectivity in turn permits the argument to be applied to "biomedical ethical problems" (Korein, 1990: 982). Korein leaves the reader to draw his or her own specific conclusions concerning "fetal rights, abortion, fetal transplants, and anencephaly," which may be derived from his premise that the human being is defined by the CSB, and his or her existence is contemporaneous with the onset of the CSB (Korein, 1990: 983).

Korein's thesis is seriously flawed on several counts. The argument fails both because of internal inconsistencies, and because of some suppressed assumptions that make the thesis a question-begging proposition. First, the human entity must, according to Korein's descriptions, be two different biological individuals at the same time, i.e., to be a full human entity is to be two essentially different things defined by two dif-

111

ferent substrata. To be fully human means to have the two substrata that make one both a human organism and a human being. That these substrata are indeed independent according to Korein is evidenced by the fact that to be a human organism is not necessarily to be fully human, since for at least the first 20 weeks of organic life the human organism cannot be called a human being; nor can a human organism in a persistent vegetative state be considered a human being on Korein's thesis. Therefore, to be fully human is to be two different biological individuals at the same time: a "human organism" and a "human being." However, it is impossible for two different individuals to be identified as one. If Korein is to treat the human entity as one unified being, there would need to be some third substrate underlying both the "human organism" and the "human being" as two stages of a unified life; but identifying the life and death of the human entity would then be determined on the basis of this third substrate, not the CSB.

Second, the CSB cannot truly be a substrate, given Korein's own description of the onset of the CSB. He refers to both the human's DNA and the CSB respectfully as the "invariants" of the human organism and the human being. Presumably, the DNA and CSB are considered substrata precisely because they are unchanging aspects of the human entity which provide continuity through the various changes and stages of the human entity. However, Korein shows quite clearly that the CSB itself, even after its onset at the 20th week of gestation, undergoes a considerable amount of change for the remainder of prenatal life and beyond (Korein, 1990: 983). Korein's developmental explanation of the CSB as an invariant substrate is not even consistent with the way in which he uses the terms "invariant substrate" to refer to the DNA. At least the DNA, by Korein's own admission, is in itself unchanged and present from the very beginning.

If the CSB is itself in process, then it must have some substrate underlying it. Since in Korein's scheme, the DNA is the only other substrate within the human entity, the DNA would have to be the substrate for the CSB. In fact, as he explains, the "human organism" (as defined by the DNA) is present through the very same stages which include the development of the CSB.[20] By Korein's own account, this fact would ne-

---

[20]It is a puzzlement that the human organism is said to be present throughout various life cycles one of which is the gamete stage: "The invariant of the human organism will be considered to be the species defined by its DNA. Thus, homo sapiens, like any other animal species, may be considered as a dynamic organism which undergoes changes through a life cycle. The stages of the cycle are composed of several periods, including the gametes. . ." (Korein, 1990: 982). How can a human organism be said to be present in the

112

cessitate that the DNA be the substrate of the CSB. Korein's definition of the "human being" would then collapse into the definition of the "human organism," because, for him, biological substrata are the bases for defining individuals. If the only true biological substrate of the human entity is its DNA, then the human individual must be said to be the human organism, which is a conclusion in direct contradiction with what Korein sets out to prove.

Third, Korein's interpretation of brain death, from which he argues to the CSB definition of the human being, contains a suppressed assumption. However, this assumption is the very thing in need of proof. Korein wrongly assumes that the determination of death according to neurological criteria is, by itself, equivalent to the death of the "individual" as he puts it, i.e., the death of human being as person. In fact, as was shown above, the determination of brain death presumes no more and no less than the death of the human organism as organism, i.e., as a unified whole. Therefore, the only legitimate equivalency about human life which might be granted on the basis of brain death is that the life of the "human individual" is equivalent to the life of the human organism as a whole. Once again it is the precise opposite of what Korein concludes which comes closer to reality; namely, it is his concept of the human organism and not the CSB which is more consistent with the concept of "brain death" as the determinant of death.

Fourth, Korein gratuitously assumes, and gives no evidence to prove, that the substrate for the sensory and intellectual functions of the human being, including the functions themselves, are explained in their totality by material factors. In effect, he is arguing that the human being does not begin until the development of a certain biological system, because it is already assumed that the human being is defined by its materiality. However, that the human being is simply and only a material being is one of the very things in question.

Fifth, and finally, another suppressed assumption within Korein's position is that only actual characteristics and functions can be the identifiers of what kind of life a thing has.[21] Ultimately, it is an assumption that the identification of what is real must be exclusive of the potential. Korein simply asserts that a "human organism" which is in a persistent vegetative state "could no longer be described by the term 'human be-

---

form of a gamete? A gamete does not of itself, i.e., prior to fusion, represent the beginning of a separate human organism. This obvious mistake is indicative of Korein's inability to grasp the unity which human entities possess.
[21] This is a common mistake made by many writers on the subject of the beginning of life. See for example, Ivan (1988: 20–21; 24).

ing'," and likewise he asserts that the human being is defined by an actual CSB, which is the substrate for actual functions. But why must the real only include the actual and exclude the potential? In fact, actual and potential are mutually relative terms used to explain the real. To understand one is to understand the other. Thus, it could be argued (against Korein's assumption) that the actuality of a real individual human zygote cannot rightly be comprehended without its potency for an actual CSB. While it is true that the actual human zygote does not have an actual CSB, it is also true that the reality of the zygote includes its potency to its CSB. Therefore, to identify the reality of what it means to be human is to include both human actuality and potentiality. To mark the beginning of the "human individual" with the onset of an actual biological system is to arbitrarily exclude an essential element of that individual's real existence—its potency to act. But to include the element of potency necessitates that one mark the beginning of the "human individual" at conception. As was shown above, one and the same human individual cannot be divided into discrete actualities. The human being is a unity, a unity of act and potency; to mark its beginning is necessarily to mark the reality of both.

THE HUMAN FETUS: AVAILABLE IF NONVIABLE

Mary B. Mahowald, Jerry Silver, and Robert A. Ratcheson have argued that it would be morally permissible to procure fetal tissue from nonviable living fetuses (Mahowald, Silver, and Ratcheson, 1987: 11–12).[22] Presumably, "nonviable living fetuses" would include fetuses both *in utero* and *ex utero*. "Nonviability," they state, is a term which applies "not only to anencephalic infants, but also to fetuses or individuals whose imminent death is unavoidable" (Mahowald, Silver, and Ratcheson, 1987: 13). Apparently, in addition to the nonviability of anencephalic infants, the nonviability of "fetuses" refers to fetuses with other conditions *in utero*, and the nonviability of "individuals" refers to fetuses with other conditions *ex utero*, including the condition of a live aborted fetus.[23]

---

[22]They have also implied that transplantation from viable fetuses in utero might have justification since they are less likely to be counted as uncontroversial persons compared with the viable abortus; see Mahawold, Silver, and Ratcheson (1987: 12).

[23]In Mahowald (1993) Mahowald concludes that ". . . nonviable fetuses and abortuses are those unable to survive even with assistance. Nonviability thus implies that an entity is alive but dying" (p. 150). This statement would certainly be true of life *ex utero*, but it is not true of the life of nonviable fetuses *in utero*. Her failure to specify the meaning of nonviability

The authors give an analysis comparing organ transplantation from live donors and from cadavers with transplantation of fetal tissue, and also compare surrogate motherhood to fetal tissue transplantation. From this analysis they are able to formulate several moral requirements for the use of fetal tissue. Mahowald, Silver, and Ratcheson apply all but one moral condition to fetal tissue transplantation from the other three procedures. The three conditions they apply are: "consent of a proxy; a significant research or therapeutic goal; and ascertainment that other (less problematic) means of obtaining the goal are not available" (Mahowald, Silver, and Ratcheson, 1987: 12). The one condition which is inconsistently excluded from application to fetal tissue transplantation they describe as: "the burden to the donor (including loss of an organ or tissue, risk, and possible pain of the procedure) proportionate to its expected benefit to another or others" (Mahowald, Silver, and Ratcheson, 1987: 11). The authors specify what they would consider a disproportionate burden: ". . . we believe that the . . . condition is not met if the procedure entails direct termination of the donor's life, as would occur in whole brain or heart transplantation from a living donor" (Mahowald, Silver, and Ratcheson, 1987: 11).[24] The authors make no explicit recognition of the fact, nor provide a specific explanation why they have omitted the condition that the procedure not directly result in the death of the donor of fetal tissue. This omission cannot be due to the fact they do not consider the fetus a donor, because in several places they either explicitly refer to the fetus as the donor or indirectly recognize its donor status by the need for a proxy (Mahowald, Silver and Ratcheson, 1987: 12, 14).

By a process of elimination one can only presume that the omission of the vital organ prohibition from the other conditions as they are applied to fetal tissue transplantation is because the nonviable fetus will not survive. If the fetus's condition is incompatible with life, and is irreversible, then directly taking its life would be a burden proportionate to the therapeutic good of transplantation. Somehow the nonsurvivability of the fetus would make the burden proportionate. However, apart from the lack of merit to the argument itself, the reason of nonsurvivability is simply inconsistent with the authors' prohibition against direct termina-

---

relative to both life *ex utero* and life *in utero* results in an ambiguity about the term "nonviability" similar to that which is utilized in the position of Mahowald, Silver, and Ratcheson (1987) analyzed above.

[24]This condition is also repeated with specific reference to fetal tissue transplantation in the same section on transplantation from live donors; see Mahowald, Silver, and Ratcheson (1987: 12).

tion of life in their section on "Transplantation from live donors." The authors have shown through their acceptance of this prohibition that the nonsurvivability of adult live donors is not a circumstance justifying direct termination of life for the sake of transplantation. If the circumstance of nonsurvivability is not an exception to the prohibition, why would it be an exception in the case of fetal tissue transplantation?

The authors state that the "retrieval of essential organs and tissue from dead fetuses is more acceptable than their retrieval from nonviable living abortuses" (Mahowald, Silver and Ratcheson, 1987: 12). The fact that they did not include the prohibition against direct termination of life allows them the moral latitude expressed by the words "more acceptable." It is a latitude which is then manipulated in this way: "We believe, however, that use of essential organs or tissue from nonviable fetuses is morally defensible if dead fetuses are not available or are not conducive to successful transplants" (Mahowald, Silver, and Ratcheson, 1987: 12).[25] As was explained above, this conclusion assumes that the nonsurvivability of the fetus makes the burden of directly terminating its life proportionate to the good of transplantation. However, it is never explained by Mahowald et al. how a particular circumstance of individual life, viz., its survivability, may be regarded as a substitute for the life itself and thereby become the basis for judgment about the direct taking of that life. Their position hinges on this suppressed assumption, that a circumstance of an individual life may substitute for the life itself as the referent of moral judgment. Yet, this assumption is the very thing which needs proof. The nonsurvivability of life is morally decisive against life only if one has already assumed that a particular circumstance of life can be equivalent to the good of life itself and can be morally decisive for our actions toward life as such.[26]

The various attempts to redefine the concepts of life and death such that the human fetus would be classified as either dead, or not fully alive as a human being, and implicitly to define the life of fetus as subhuman because of its nonviability, are all attempts which fail and collapse by the weight of their own internal contradictions and inconsistencies. Once the

---

[25]Mahowald has apparently modified this view to exclude living fetuses as sources of tissue in Mahowald (1993: 161), although this is not entirely clear from her language and reasons.

[26]Paul Ramsey makes an analogous point with respect to experimentation with living fetuses who are doomed to abortion or miscarriage: "The proposal is to do damaging or highly risky experiments upon the dying, i.e. the still-living nonviable fetus, precisely in order to make rapid medical progress. *Incidentally*, abortion makes these dying available. No one's views on the morality of abortion alters or can remove the offensiveness of such research practiced on the dying" (Ramsey, 1975: 40).

116

lack of intrinsic merit to these arguments is recognized, they may be seen as so many utilitarian attempts to marginalize the preborn child for the purpose of satisfying a particular medical need.[27]

Conclusion

Answering the question, what is death, posed by John Paul II at the beginning of this volume, is critical not for the utilitarian purposes of meeting the medical need for organs and tissues or reducing the burden on society of unwanted people. Rather, finding the answer is of critical importance only in relation to the moral goods of the inviolability of human life and the conservation of human life. It is because these goods are absolute realities, and in relation to them, that the definition and determination of death receive their moral significance. In accordance with these goods we cannot treat a living human being as if he or she were dead, since to do so would be a direct act of killing.

The problem of determining the death of the human fetus cannot be solved by redefining the concepts life and death as such. The human fetus, as Chapter 3 has shown, is fully human, made in the image of God. This child does not progress through a pre-life period of death, nor a period of being a human organism but not a human being, nor is it subhuman because of life-denying anomalies or because it is doomed to abortion. True compassion for those who would benefit by the transplantation of tissues from the preborn child dictates that such an action be first reconciled with respect for life according to its inviolability and its conservation—a life which is fully human beginning with fertilization. Given these facts, the preborn child must be certainly dead by the most reliable criteria which are: the absence or irreversible cessation of any vital signs including respirations, heart beat, or movement of voluntary muscles. The donation of human fetal tissues cannot be morally good and permissible if these medical criteria of determining death are not applied.

References

American College of Obstetricians and Gynecologists (1992). *American Academy of Pediatrics: Guidelines for Perinatal Care*. 2nd ed. American Academy of Pediatrics and the American College of Obstetricians and Gynecologists.

---

[27]See how the authors examined cite the specifically utilitarian value of their positions: Gervais (1986: 22–23, 152, 166–177); Korein (1990: 983); Mahowald, Silver, and Ratcheson (1987: 12).

American College of Obstetricians and Gynecologists Technical Bulletin (1993). No. 176.

Aquinas, Saint Thomas. (1949). *De Anima* (J. P. Rowan, Trans.). St. Louis: B. Herder Book Co.

Aquinas, Saint Thomas (1952). *Summa Theologica* (Fathers of the English Dominican Province, & Sullivan Daniel J., Trans.). Chicago: Encyclopaedia Britannica, Inc.

Aristotle. (1941). *Physics*. In *The Basic Works of Aristotle* (R. McKeon, Ed.) (R. Hardie & R. Gaye, Trans.). New York: Random House.

Ashley, B. M., O.P., & O'Rourke, K. D., O.P. (1989). *Healthcare Ethics: A Theological Analysis*. St. Louis: The Catholic Health Association of the United States.

Blum, L. (1980). Compassion. In A. O. Rorty (Ed.), *Explaining Emotions* (pp. 507–18). Berkeley: University of California Press.

Bopp, J., Jr., & Burtchaell, J. T., C.S.C. (1988). Human Fetal Tissue Transplantation Research Panel: Statement of Dissent. In *Report of the human fetal tissue transplantation panel National Institutes of Health* (p. 50).

Brody, H., M.D. Ph.D. (1992, 5 November). Assisted Death—A Compassionate Response to A Medical Failure. *The New England Journal of Medicine*, pp. 1384–1388.

Collins, V. J., M.D. (1980). Definition of Death. In *The New Technologies of Birth and Death: Medical, Legal and Moral Dimensions* (pp. 115–119). St. Louis: Pope John Center.

Congregation for the Doctrine of the Faith. (1974). *Declaration on Procured Abortion*. Boston: Daughters of St. Paul.

Dawes, G. (1968). Birth Asphyxia, Resuscitation, and Brain Damage. In *Fetal and Neonatal Physiology: A Comparative Study of the Changes at Birth* (pp. 141–159). Chicago: Year Book Medical Publishers.

Defining Death: Medical, Legal and Ethical Issues in the Determination of Death. (1981). Washington, D.C.: President's Commission for the Study of Ethical Problems in Medicine and Biomedical and Behavioral Research.

Dyck, A. J., Ph.D. (1992, Winter). Physician-Assisted Suicide: Is It Ethical? *Trends in Health Care, Law & Ethics*, pp. 19–22.

Gervais, K. G. (1986). *Redefining Death*. New Haven: Yale University Press.

Green, M., & Wikler, D. (1980, Winter). Brain Death and Personal Identity. *Philosophy and Public Affairs*, pp. 105–133.

Grisez, G., & Boyle, J. M., Jr. (1979). *Life and Death with Liberty and Justice: A Contribution to the Euthanasia Debate*. Notre Dame: University of Notre Dame Press.

Ivan, L. (1988, August). Brain Death in the Infant and What Constitutes Life. *Transplantion Proceedings*, pp. 17–25.

John Paul II. (1990, 11 January). Address to the Pontifical Academy of Sciences, December 14, 1989. *Origins*, pp. 523–525.

John Paul II. (1984). *Salvifici doloris*. Boston: St. Paul Editions.

Kass, L. (1971, 20 August). Death as an Event: A Commentary on Robert Morison. *Science*, pp. 698–173.

Korein, J. (1990, June). Ontogenesis of the Fetal Nervous System: The Onset of Brain Life. *Transplantation Proceedings*, pp. 982–983.

Lindval O., e. a. (1988). Fetal Dopamine-Rich Mesencephalic Grafts in Parkinson's Disease. *Lancet, 2*, pp. 1483–1484.

Madrazo I., e. a. (1990). Fetal Homotransplants (Ventral Mesencephalon and Adrenal Tissue) to the Striatum of Parkinsonian Subjects. *Arch Neurol, 47*, pp. 1281–1285.

Mahowald, M. B. (1993). *Women and Children in Health Care: An Unequal Majority*. NY: Oxford University Press.

Mahowald, M. B., Siver, J., & Ratcheson, R. A. (1987, February). The Ethical Options in Transplanting Fetal Tissue. *Hastings Center Report*, pp. 9–15.

118

Moraczewski, A. S., O.P., & Showalter, J. S., J.D. (1982). *Determination of Death: Theological, Medical, Ethical, and Legal Issues*. St. Louis: The Catholic Health Association of the United States.

Moraczewski, A. S., O.P. (1990). Personhood: Entry and Exist. In *The Twenty-Fifth Anniversary of Vatican II: A Look Back and A Look Ahead* (pp. 78–101). Braintree: The Pope John Center.

Morison, R. S. (1971, 20 August). Death: Process or Event. *Science*, pp. 694–698.

Mulligan, J. J. (1991). *Choose Life*. Braintree: The Pope John Center.

National Commission for the Protection of Human Subjects of Biomedical and Behavioral Research, Report and Recommendation: Research on the Fetus. (1975). DHEW Publications. No. (05).

Olson, L. e. a. (1987). Human Fetal Tissues Grafted to Rodent Hosts: Structural and Functionaal Observations of Brain, Adrenal and Heart Tissues In Oculo. *Experimental Brain Research, 164*(173), 164, 173.

Pius XII. (1979a). Allocution to Delegates at the Fourth International Congress of Catholic Doctors, September 29, 1949. In *The Human Body* (pp. 114–119). Boston: St. Paul Editions.

Pius XII. (1979b). Allocution to the Delegates of the International Union of Catholic Women's Leagues, September 11, 1947. In *The Human Body* (pp. 90–91). Boston: St. Paul Editions.

Quill, T. E., M.D. (1991, 7 March). Death and Dignity: A Case of Individualized Decision Making. *The New England Journal of Medicine*, pp. 691–694.

Quill, T. E., M.D., Christine K.Cassel, M., & Diane E. Meier, M. (1992, 5 November). Care of the Hopelessly Ill: Proposed Clinical Criteria for Physician-Assisted Suicide. *The New England Journal of Medicine*, pp. 1380–1384.

Ramsey, P. (1975). *The Ethics of Fetal Research*. New Haven: Yale University Press.

Veatch, R. M. (1989). *Death, Dying and the Biological Revolution: Our Last Quest for Responsibility*. New Haven: Yale University Press.

Chapter 7

THE MANAGEMENT OF ECTOPIC
PREGNANCIES: A MORAL ANALYSIS[1]

William E. May

Editors' Summary: This chapter first presents important up-to-date accounts of the condition of ectopic pregnancy, methods of treatment for it, and a comprehensive analysis of the ethics of treating ectopic pregnancy which includes implications for the use of fetal tissue from such pregnancies. William May's ethical analysis of the various methods of treatment begins with the foundational work of theologian T. Lincoln Bouscaren. The surgical procedure of salpingectomy, or segmenting that portion of the Fallopian tube which is pathological, and the

[1]Many people have helped me in preparing this paper, which has been repeatedly revised. John T. Bruchalski, M.D., William Hogan, M.D., and William Colliton, M.D. answered many of my questions concerning the medical procedures discussed. Dr. Bruchalski in particular was of great help in providing me with relevant medical literature. Dr. Colliton kindly sent me a written commentary, of great value, raising questions about some of the

method of expectant therapy, are found to be ethically permissible according to the tradition of Catholic teaching. The treatment using methotrexate, a drug which kills rapidly dividing cells, is found to be morally unacceptable because in the author's estimation this method attacks cells which are part of the embryo proper, rather than non-embryonic cells. The majority of the chapter focuses on salpingo(s)tomy, the procedure in which the embryo is removed from the Fallopian tube without removing the tube. May critiques an earlier argument of his which attempted to justify salpingo(s)tomy and which used the thought of Germain Grisez. May had argued that since what one does in a human act is determined by what one has chosen to do, the extraction of the embryo in order to remove it from a lethal environment and save the life of the mother does not constitute a direct abortion, because the latter is not what is chosen. May had earlier argued that the foreseeable death of the embryo is an unintended, indirect effect of the direct life-preserving choice. One has chosen to preserve life, and so that is what is done. However, May's final conclusion is that salpingo(s)tomy cannot be justified on his earlier held grounds. Unlike the ethically justified use of hysterectomy to treat a pregnant cancerous uterus, salpingo(s)tomy is a direct act of killing against the child and not an act directed toward the mother. Therefore, this procedure is not morally acceptable. Additionally, expectant therapy and salpingectomy are found to be ethically justified, but not, as stated above, the use of methotrexate. May's analysis takes the reader into a discussion of the question of the role of the object of the human act, and provides an extended analysis of analogies made between killing in self-defence, craniotomy, and salpingo(s)tomy.

Chapter Procedure

Here I will (1) describe ectopic pregnancies and their frequency, (2) summarize current medical procedures advocated for their management, (3) note relevant teaching of the magisterium, and (4) offer a moral evaluation of the methods proposed for managing ectopic pregnancies. At the conclusion I will comment briefly on the feasibility and

positions taken in earlier drafts. John Finnis and Germain Grisez offered excellent criticisms of the first draft, and Professor Grisez carefully examined later versions, generously commenting on them and offering suggestions. Ronald Lawler, O.F.M. Cap. raised serious objections to some of the positions I took in one of the drafts and helped me, through his written critique, to understand some matters of crucial importance more clearly, leading me to revise some views I had espoused. Hannah Klaus, M.D., with whom I discussed the paper, called my attention to some relevant medical literature I had failed to note. Finally, Kevin Flannery, S.J., offered very excellent criticism of the penultimate draft of this essay. I am very grateful to all these persons for the help they have given me. The final paper, of course, with the positions it takes, is my responsibility.

122

morality of using fetal tissue obtained from ectopic pregnancies for medical research and therapy.

ECTOPIC PREGNANCIES AND THEIR FREQUENCY

An ectopic ("out of place," from the Greek **ek,** out of, and **topos,** place) pregnancy occurs when a developing new human being does not implant in the uterus, where it belongs, but in some other place, usually in the fallopian tube or, more rarely, in the ovary, the cornua, the abdomen, or the cervix. Such pregnancies pose serious risks to the mother's life because of the danger of hemorrhage.

During the past two decades there has been an alarming increase in the incidence of ectopic, particularly tubal, pregnancies.[2] The principal factors responsible for this include the increasing number of sexuality transmitted diseases, especially pelvic inflammatory disease, tubal sterilization, the use of intrauterine devices and progesterone contraceptive pills, and *in vitro* fertilization.[3]

MEDICAL PROCEDURES FOR MANAGING ECTOPIC PREGNANCIES

1. TUBAL ECTOPIC PREGNANCIES

John A. Rock describes four treatment procedures for managing tubal ectopic pregnancies: (1) "expectant" therapy, (2) drug therapy through use of methotrexate (MTX), (3) conservative surgical treatment through linear salpingotomy, salpingostomy, or segmental resection, and (4) radical surgical treatment through salpingectomy (Rock, 1992: 421–427).

(1) "Expectant" therapy simply means that nothing is done. Rock says that "the natural history of ectopic pregnancy suggests that a majority of these tubal pregnancies may resolve without treatment"; indeed, such spontaneous resolution may occur in as many as 64% of patients

---

[2] In 1970, 17,800 ectopic pregnancies were reported in women aged 15–44; by 1980 the figure had reached 52,000 women of these ages, and today it is estimated that approximately 1 pregnancy in every 60 is ectopic, and the rate is continuing to increase. For data see Rock (1992: 412, Table 18-1). See also Cannon and Jesionowska (1991: 1033); Leach and Ory (1987: 230); A.C.O.G. (1992).
[3] On this see Rock (1992: 412–414); Sultana, Easley, and Collins (1992: 285).

(Rock, 1992: 420).[4] Thus, in the majority of cases no medical intervention is needed to protect the mother's life, since there is a spontaneous abortion or miscarriage. Expectant therapy demands careful monitoring of the ectopic pregnancy, which today, thanks to remarkable developments in monitoring pregnancies, can be discovered at a much earlier time than previously. If the tubal pregnancy does not spontaneously resolve, then medical interventions are required to protect the mother's life.

(2) Methotrexate (MTX) is widely used today to cope with tubal pregnancies. MTX is a highly toxic drug whose use must be carefully monitored. MTX, recommended for "patients with small unruptured ectopic pregnancies or if there is evidence of persistent ectopic pregnancy after conservative surgery" (Rock, 1992: 421), interferes with the synthesis of DNA (dexoyribonucleic acid) and cell multiplication. It resolves tubal pregnancies chiefly by attacking the trophoblast,[5] i.e., the outer layer of cells produced by the growing baby, connecting it with its mother. The trophoblast is, in truth, a *vital organ* of the baby during gestation. Although it is discarded later on, it must be regarded as an integral part of the body of the unborn child (just as baby teeth, which are later discarded, are integral, although not vital, to growing children). Once the trophoblast has been dissolved by MTX, the unborn baby dies and is aborted.

(3) Two conservative surgical treatments currently recommended for tubal pregnancies are linear salpingotomy (or, at times, salpingostomy) and segmental resection. In salpingo(s)tomy an incision is made over the distended part of the tube and the unborn child is removed from it.[6] In segmental resection the portion of the fallopian tube affected by the ectopic pregnancy is removed and the remaining segments are then connected.[7]

---

[4] With a reference to the study of Fernandez, Rainhorn, and Papiernik et al. (1988: 171).

[5] "Actively proliferating trophoblastic tissue is exquisitely sensitive to this effect of MTX, which forms the rationale for its use in the treatment of EP ectopic pregnancies" (Cannon and Jesionowska 1991: 1034).

[6] Rock (1992) describes the procedure as follows: "gentle pressure is exerted from the opposite side of the tube [and] the products of gestation are gently expressed from the lumen [the cavity of the tube]. Because a certain amount of separation of the trophoblast has usually occurred, the conceptus generally can be easily removed from the lumen. Gentle traction by forceps without teeth or by suction may be used if necessary" (pp. 422–423).

[7] Use of MTX, linear salpingo(s)tomy, and segmental resection are advocated because these procedures do not require the excision of the entire fallopian tube and thus enhance the possibility that the woman may subsequently become pregnant. On this see Rock (1992: 421–425).

124

(4) The most radical surgical treatment of a tubal pregnancy is salpingectomy, or removal of the entire tube along with the unborn child. This is necessary "when a tubal pregnancy has ruptured, causing intraabdominal hemorrhage that must be quickly controlled" (Rock, 1992: 425).

2. OVARIAN ECTOPIC PREGNANCIES

Ovarian ectopic pregnancies, while rare, have recently increased in number because of the use of IUDs (Rock, 1992: 430). One author claims that many ovarian pregnancies go to term, but unfortunately provides no evidence to support his claim (O'Donnell, 1991: 167). The commonly recommended procedure to manage ovarian pregnancies is surgical resection of the ovary, i.e., removal of the section of the ovary affected by the pregnancy and reconnecting its remaining portions (Rock, 1992: 432).

3. ABDOMINAL ECTOPIC PREGNANCIES

These are quite rare and are of two types: primary and secondary. A primary abdominal pregnancy occurs when the baby implants originally in the abdomen; a secondary, which is more common, when a tubal pregnancy ruptures with subsequent implantation in the abdomen (Rock, 1992: 433–434). Ectopic pregnancies of this kind can usually be managed to allow the child to come to term and to be delivered by a laparotomy or incision in the abdomen.[8]

4. CERVICAL ECTOPIC PREGNANCIES

These are rare but highly dangerous ectopic pregnancies, completely incompatible with development of the unborn child to viability. The standard treatment is abdominal hysterectomy. Rock notes that it is possible to evacuate the pregnancy by a skillful D&C, but this procedure "is usually complicated by profuse hemorrhage, which generally necessitates an abdominal hysterectomy" (Rock, 1992: 433–434). These preg-

---

[8]Telephone conversation with John T. Bruchalski, M.D., on August 10, 1992.

nancies are also at times treated by administration of MTX, at times used to lessen blood loss in connection with hysterectomy (Rock, 1992: 433–434).

Relevant Teaching of the Magisterium

The Church teaches that every human life is of incalculable worth and that it is *always gravely immoral intentionally to kill innocent human beings.*[9] The Church's teaching on this matter is the basis for its teaching on the absolute immorality of directly intended abortion, which is well known and clearly set forth in many documents of the magisterium.[10] The magisterium has made it clear that what is condemned as absolutely immoral is *direct* abortion, as distinct from *indirect* abortion. Two passages from Pius XII are most important in understanding this distinction. In the first, in which he was explaining the meaning of the fifth commandment, "Thou shalt not kill," as this had been traditionally understood by the Church, he wrote: "So long as man commits no crime, his life is intangible, and therefore every action which tends directly toward its destruction is illicit, whether this destruction be the *end intended* or only a *means* to an end, whether this life is embryonic, or in full flower,

---

[9]On this see Grisez (1987: 291–313).

[10]On the immorality of directly intended abortion see the following documents of the magisterium: Sixtus V, *Constitution Effraenatam*, October 29, 1588, in *Enchiridion Familiae: Textos del Magisterio Pontificio y Conciliar sobre el Matrimonio y la Familia*, ed. A. Sarmiento and J. Escriva Ivars (Madrid: Ediciones Rialp, 1992) 1.191–199; Innocent XI, Decree of the Holy Office, March 2, 1969, in *Enchiridion Familiae*, 1.216–217; Pius XI, Encyclical *Casti connubii*, December 31, 1930, n. 64, in *Enchiridion Familiae*, 1.747–748; Pius XII, Address *La vostra presenza* to the Italian Medical Biological Union of St. Luke, November 12, 1944, in *Enchiridion Familiae*, 2.1306–1307; Pius XII, Address *Vegliare con sollecitudine* to the Italian Catholic Union of Midwives, October 29, 1951, in *Enchiridion Familiae*, 2.1429–1430; Pius XII, Address *Nell'ordine* to the National Congress of the "Family Front," November 26, 1951, in *Enchiridion Familiae*, 2.1468–1472; John XXIII, Encyclical *Mater et Magistra*, May 15, 1961, n. 190, in *Enchiridion Familiae*, 2.1755; Vatican Council II, Pastoral Constitution *Gaudium et spes*, nn. 27 and 51, in *Enchiridion Familiae*, 3.1827–1828, 1838–1839; Paul VI, Encyclical *Humanae vitae*, July 25, 1968, n. 14, in *Enchiridion Familiae*, 3. 1920; Paul VI, Address *Salutiamo con paterna effusione* to the XXIII National Congress of the Union of Italian Catholic Jurists, December 9, 1972, in *Enchiridion Familiae*, 3.2044–2048; Congregation for the Doctrine of the Faith, *Declaration on Procured Abortion*, November 18, 1974, in *Enchiridion Familiae*, 3.2071–2095; John Paul II, Homily during the Mass on Capitol Mall of Washington, D. C., October 7, 1979, in *Enchiridion Familiae*, 3.2380–2381; Congregation for the Doctrine of the Faith, *Instruction on Respect for Human Life in Its Origin and on the Dignity of Procreation*, February 22, 1987, in *Enchiridion Familiae*, 5.4608.

or already approaching its term" (Pius XII, 1944).[11] In a second text Pius XII said:

> We have on purpose always used the expression *direct attack on the life of the innocent," "direct killing."* For if, for instance, the safety of the mother-to-be, independently of her pregnant condition, should urgently require a surgical operation or other therapeutic treatment, which would have as a side-effect, in no way willed or intended, yet inevitable, the death of the fetus, then such an act could not any longer be called a *direct* attack on innocent life. With these conditions, the operation, like other similar medical interventions, can be allowable, always assuming that a good of great worth, such as life, is at stake, and that it is not possible to delay the operation until after the baby is born or to make use of some other effective remedy (Pius XII, 1951).

The magisterium of the Church has so firmly condemned as absolutely immoral every direct abortion that in my opinion, and in that of other theologians, we can conclude that the teaching of the magisterium on this matter has fulfilled the conditions set forth in Vatican Council II's Dogmatic Constitution *Lumen gentium* required if a teaching of the ordinary and universal magisterium is to be regarded as *infallibly proposed.*[12] This is an irrevocable, irreformable teaching of the Church.

Moreover, the magisterium has not only condemned direct abortion in the strongest terms, but it has also addressed specific issues pertinent to the question of ectopic pregnancies. It has done so in a series of decrees issued by the Holy Office (today called the Congregation for the Doctrine of the Faith) during the final years of the nineteenth century and the first years of the twentieth.[13]

---

[11]This text was cited by Paul VI, with reference to the immorality of abortion, in *Humanae vitae*, footnote 24 (in *Enchiridion Familiae*, 3.1920); by the Congregation for the Doctrine of the Faith in its *Declaration on Procured Abortion*, November 18, 1974, n. 7, footnote 15 (in *Enchiridion Familiae*, 3.2078); and by the Congregation for the Doctrine of the Faith in its *Instruction on Respect for Human Life in Its Origin and on the Dignity of Procreation (Donum Vitae)*, February 22, 1987, footnote 20 (in *Enchiridion Familiae*, 5.4608).

[12]For a brief presentation of the reasons why it is reasonable to hold that the core of Catholic moral teaching, including the teaching on the grave immorality of direct abortion has been infallibly proposed, see May (1991: 207–215).

[13]The relevant decrees are the following: (1) the Decree of the Holy Office of August 19, 1889 and confirmed by Leo XIII regarding the immorality of "craniotomies" and "any

Commenting on these decrees, T. Lincoln Bouscaren wrote as follows in his classic work on ectopic pregnancies: "The question is whether these decrees absolutely forbid *every removal* of an ectopic fetus before viability, or whether they apply only to such removals as are *directly death-dealing* to the child" (Bouscaren, 1944: 59).[14] After a painstaking study of the matter, which showed, on the basis of medical evidence then accessible, that a tubal pregnancy so damaged the fallopian tube that its removal was required in order to protect the life of the mother, Bouscaren concluded that the decrees of the Holy Office do not forbid *every removal* of a nonviable ectopic pregnancy, but only those that are *directly death-dealing*.[15] In short, Bouscaren held that the fallopian tube was so damaged by the ectopic pregnancy that it could be regarded as a patho-

---

other surgical operation which is a direct killing of the fetus or of the pregnant mother" (text in *Enchiridion Symbolorum Definitionum et Declarationum de Rebus Fidei et Morum*, ed. Henricus Denzinger and Adolphus Schoenmetzer [33rd ed.: Barcelona: Herder, 1975], n. 3258; hereafter referred to as DS]); (2) the Decree of the Holy Office of May 4, 1898, which stated that in cases of "urgent necessity, laparotomy for the removal of ectopic conceptions is possible for the lives of both the fetus and the mother," a decree also confirmed by Leo XIII (DS, nn. 3336–3338; see also *Enchiridion Familiae*, 1.576); and (3) the Decree of the Holy Office of March 5, 1902 (DS, n. 3358). This Decree was in answer to the question: "Whether it is sometimes licit to remove from the mother ectopic fetuses which are immature before the expiration of the sixth month after conception." The reply was: "In the negative, according to the Decree of May 4, 1898, which declares that as far as possible serious and opportune provision must be made for the lives of both the fetus and the mother. As regards the times, let the petitioner remember that according to the same decree no hastening of delivery is allowed unless it be done at a time and in a manner which are favorable to the lives of the mother and the child, according to ordinary contingencies." This decree lacked papal approbation.

[14]The second and revised edition of Bouscaren's work, a model of scholarship, was published in 1944. The first edition had been published in 1933, and that edition was a revision of his 1928 Latin dissertation on the subject, presented to the Faculty of Moral Theology of the Gregorian University in Rome in partial fulfillment of the requirements for the degree of Doctor of Sacred Theology (STD). When Bouscaren published the second edition of his work, he carefully integrated the latest medical literature on the subject. At that time, ectopic pregnancies could be discovered only at a relatively advanced stage of development, when the mother's fallopian tube was already badly damaged and in imminent danger of rupturing.

[15]"The removal of a pregnant fallopian tube containing a nonviable living fetus, even before the external rupture of the tube, can be done in such a way that the subsequent death of the fetus will be produced only indirectly. Such an operation may be licitly performed if all the circumstances are such that the necessity for the operation is, in moral estimation, proportionate to the evil effect which is permitted. In all such operations, if the fetus is probably alive, care must be taken to baptize the fetus immediately, at least conditionally" (Bouscaren, 1944: 147).

logical organ seriously endangering the mother's life. Its removal (by sal-pingectomy) had as a foreseen consequence the death of the unborn child, but this evil effect was not directly intended and was simply an un-avoidable concomitant of a medical procedure that was itself morally jus-tifiable as a life-saving intervention. The abortion of the unborn child was, consequently, not direct but indirect.

Bouscaren's thesis won the approval not only of the moral theolo-gians of his day but also of the bishops of the United States. Thus, both in their *Ethical and Religious Directives for Catholic Hospitals,* published in 1949, and in their 1971 revision of this document under the title *Ethical and Religious Directives for Catholic Health Care Facilities,* they accepted as morally justifiable the excision of a fallopian tube (a salpingectomy) con-taining a nonviable fetus. In the 1971 document they said:

> In extrauterine pregnancy the dangerously affected part of the mother (e.g., cervix, ovary, or fallopian tube) may be removed, even though fetal death is foreseen, provided that: (a) the af-fected part is presumed already to be so damaged and danger-ously affected as to warrant its removal, and that (b) the operation is not just a separation of the embryo or fetus from its site within the part (which would be a direct abortion from a uterine appendage), and that (c) the operation cannot be postponed without notably increasing the danger to the mother (NCCB, 1971).

From the above it is evident that salpingectomies can rightly be used as means of managing tubal pregnancies *when the condition of the tube is such that it poses a serious threat to the mother's life.* Here it should also be noted that Bouscaren explicitly rejected salpingo(s)tomies as immoral, on the grounds that they constitute direct abortion: "this method of op-erating, if the fetus is alive, is certainly a direct killing, and certainly in-defensible. It is one thing to remove the tube containing the fetus; it is another thing to remove the fetus directly. . . . It is necessary to empha-size the fact that only the first method of operating—the removal of the tube itself, without interfering directly with the fetus—is the only method which is in any way defended in this thesis" (Bouscaren, 1944: 101–102). Directive # 16 of the Bishops' *Ethical and Religious Directives* also repudiates salpingo(s)tomies as immoral, for, as we have seen, it ex-pressly states that a procedure can not be allowed if it is "just a separa-tion of the embryo or fetus from its site within the part," insofar as this "would be a direct abortion."

MORAL ANALYSIS

1. TUBAL ECTOPIC PREGNANCIES

A. Salpingectomy and Segmental Resection

From our review of relevant magisterial teaching (and of Bouscaren's work) it is evident that the removal of the entire fallopian tube by salpingectomy is morally licit when this is urgently required to protect the mother's life. If the medical facts are such that a salpingectomy is necessary for this purpose, the abortion is indirect, not direct. It seems likewise clear that segmental resection is morally justifiable for the same reasons and under the same conditions under which a salpingectomy is required. In this procedure the affected part of the fallopian tube (the pathological part) is removed with its contents, and as a foreseen but not directly intended result the unborn child will die. O'Donnell is correct in holding that the " 'Bouscaren approach' is legitimately applied in the microsurgical technique of removing the severely damaged segment of the tube with the fetus *in situ,* when this is indicated due to the extent of the damage of the maternal tissue" (O'Donnell, 1991: 165).

Currently, as we have seen, medical authorities regard salpingectomy as "radical surgical treatment," necessary only "when a tubal pregnancy has ruptured, causing intraabdominal hemorrhage that must be quickly controlled" (Rock, 1992: 425). But, as noted already, Bouscaren and the American bishops regarded the procedure as necessary even before the tube had ruptured, when there was danger that it would rupture unless a salpingectomy (or segmental resection) were done. Here we need to recall the fact that, in earlier years of this century, when Bouscaren was writing and even when the bishops of the United States revised their *Ethical and Religious Directives* in 1971, it was not possible to detect an ectopic pregnancy in its early stages, as can be done today.[16] In Bouscaren's day the possibility that a woman had a tubal pregnancy was not considered until she came to her doctor to complain of symptoms leading him to suspect that this was indeed the case. By this time the trophoblastic tissues of the unborn child were already firmly embedded in the fallopian tube and there was the imminent danger of tubal rup-

---

[16]For a description of the diagnostic procedures available today for detecting ectopic pregnancies early in their development, see Rock (1992: 414–420).

ture. Because of the changed medical picture, salpingectomies and segmental resections are now considered by the medical community as methods of last resort in managing tubal pregnancies. It is thus necessary to examine other methods currently proposed and to offer a moral analysis of them.

B. Expectant Therapy

Since nothing is done to bring harm to either the unborn child or to the mother if "expectant therapy" is employed, there are no moral objections to it as such. Nature, apparently, runs its course, and the unborn child who has implanted in the fallopian tube is spontaneously aborted (a miscarriage) or dies and is absorbed before there is any threat to the mother's life. Here the moral imperative seems to be to monitor the situation closely in order to protect the mother's life should there be no spontaneous "resolution" of the problem threatened by a pregnancy of this kind.

But, in the light of scientific evidence, I believe that a much more stringent moral obligation is incumbent upon doctors who discover tubal pregnancies at an early stage of development when "expectant" therapy is recommended. This is the imperative to seek to transplant the developing baby from the fallopian tube into the uterus where it belongs. I say that this is an obligation in the light of scientific evidence, and I will now look at this.

O'Donnell refers to a successful transplantation of an unborn child from the fallopian tube into the womb (O'Donnell, 1991: 166).[17] What is most remarkable is that the article to which O'Donnell refers, by Dr. C. J. Wallace, was written in 1917! In his article Wallace observed that at that time "early diagnosis of ectopic pregnancy is next to impossible unless it is accidentally discovered." But, he continued,

> when we do find an early case, where the tube is still in healthy condition, not too badly distended, and all things favorable, I think we should make a supreme effort to save the life of the growing child by opening the tube carefully and dissecting out the pregnancy intact and transplanting it into the uterus where nature intended it should go. It can be very quickly

---

[17]O'Donnell, to support this claim, refers to an article by Wallace (1917: 578–579).

done. It does not endanger the life of the mother. (Wallace, 1917: 578–579)[18]

Wallace then reported a case that occurred in 1915, when he operated on a woman on September 15 for fibroid tissue in the posterior wall of the uterus. When he opened her abdomen, he "found an ectopic gestation in the left tube. . . . The tube was very soft and healthy, enlarged to the size of a walnut but not distended." He then transplanted the child from the fallopian tube into the mother's uterus, and her pregnancy continued normally until a healthy boy was born on May 2, 1916. He then said , "I have not the least doubt that many such transplanted ectopic pregnancies will be reported in the near future" (Wallace, 1917: 579).

Wallace's hope, unfortunately, was not realized, for there is no report of a successful transplantation of a child from the fallopian tube into the womb until 1990, some seventy-three years after Wallace's article.[19]

But it seems to me that Wallace's hope is today quite realistic. Not only do we have available today the means for discovering tubal pregnancies early in their development (otherwise doctors would not recommend "expectant therapy"), but we also have much more knowledge about the particulars of transplantation and the technologies required in order to carry them out. Here it is worth noting that over 65% of tubal pregnancies "spontaneously resolve themselves" if "expectant therapy" is administered. Surely it is possible today to consider transplanting the unborn children whose existence is detected when this method is recommended. Since it is possible to save their lives in this way and at the same time care for their mothers, surely there is an obligation to attempt their transplantation from fallopian tube to womb.

C. MTX Therapy

The management of tubal ectopic pregnancies by the use of methotrexate (MTX) is the procedure recommended today when the pregnancy does not resolve spontaneously during the time that expectant

---

[18]Note that Wallace refers to the "growing child," not to an embryo or fetus. He thought it evident that a human child began to be at conception/fertilization.

[19]See Shettles (1990: 2026–2027), where he describes the successful transplantation in 1980 of a forty-day old infant from the mother's fallopian tube into her uterus, with subsequent safe delivery.

therapy is employed. The morality of this "treatment" procedure has not, so far as I know, been discussed as yet by Catholic moral theologians. As we have already seen, MTX "works" by attacking the tissues of the trophoblast, a vital organ of the developing unborn child. In short, it kills the unborn baby whose bodily remains are then able to pass through the fallopian tube. This seems to be its mode of operation. It therefore seems clear to me that its use constitutes direct abortion. Consequently, it ought not to be employed as a method of managing tubal pregnancies.

D. Salpingo(s)tomy

In reviewing relevant magisterial teaching we saw that Bouscaren, after examining decrees of the Holy Office relevant to the removal of ectopic fetuses from their mothers prior to viability concluded that these decrees did not condemn every removal of a nonviable ectopic unborn child but only those removals which are *directly death-dealing* to the child. We likewise saw that Bouscaren explicitly considered the morality of salpingo(s)tomy and concluded that this method constituted direct abortion and is therefore immoral. The Bishops of the United States, as we have seen, came to the same judgment. Both Bouscaren and the Bishops of the United States concluded that a salpingectomy (and, by analogy, segmental resection) are morally licit precisely because these procedures are used only when the fallopian tube itself is so damaged that it can be regarded as a pathological organ threatening the mother's life because of the imminent danger of hemorrhage. Its removal is warranted even though it is foreseen that the unborn baby within the tube will die as a result. Under these conditions the death of the unborn child can rightly be regarded as the unavoidable but unintended effect of a medical procedure that is itself life-saving and not death-dealing.

Some Catholic moral theologians who completely accept the teaching of the magisterium that every direct abortion is always gravely immoral believe that salpingo(s)tomy can also be morally justified. They think that abortion in this instance can be "indirect" and that the death of the unborn child, although foreseen, is neither intended as an end nor chosen as a means to the good end of saving the mother's life. Germain Grisez is the most prominent of these theologians. He first advanced this claim in his comprehensive study of abortion, published in 1970. After reviewing the position common to Catholic theologians after Bouscaren, he wrote:

> ... a simpler justification [than that commonly accepted] is
> possible. . . . The justification is simply that the very same hu-

man act, indivisible as to its behavioral process, has both the good effect of protecting human life and the bad effect of destroying it. The fact that the good effect is subsequent in time and in physical process to the evil one is irrelevant, because the entire process is indivisible by human choice and hence all aspects of it are equally present to the agent at the moment he makes his choice. (Grisez, 1970a: 340)

Continuing, Grisez put the matter as follows: "In principle, if the good effect (saving the mother's life) is attained in and through the same indivisible process which is initiated by the abortifacient procedure, then the abortion need not be intended" (Grisez, 1970a: 341).

As these citations show, at that time (1970) Grisez focused on factors such as the indivisibility of the process to support his claim that the death of the unborn child is not directly but only indirectly intended. In his 1970 work he also appealed to the moral principles operative in St. Thomas's discussion of the question whether a private individual can rightly "kill" another in defending himself from an unprovoked attack. In developing and clarifying his understanding of human action and of the moral reasoning underlying what has come to be known as the "principle of double effect"—a "principle" rooted in St. Thomas's analysis of self-defense—Grisez has made it clear that features such as the indivisibility of the process are *not* the decisive issues in determining whether something is "direct" or "indirect." The crucial issue is to identify correctly the moral object of the action, of one's choice. Grisez has therefore, in his later writings, made it clear that the object of the human act—*what one does*—is precisely what one chooses to do: it is the object of the inner act of the will, which St. Thomas calls the object of choice, of *electio*, the act of the *voluntas eligens.* It is, Grisez says,

what is sought for its own sake and/or included as a means in the proposal one adopts (see *S.t.*, 1–2, q. 1, a. 3; q. 19, a. 5). What one brings about, including all foreseen side effects, is far more extensive than what one chooses to do, and "does" in this strict sense. One determines oneself primarily in choosing. . . . One does not determine oneself in the same way with respect to foreseen side effects, which are neither sought for their own sake nor included in the proposal one adopts. (Grisez, 1983: 239–240)[20]

---

[20]See also footnote 12 (which is appended at the end of the quoted passage), p. 249, where other Thomistic texts are cited by Grisez to support his position.

As this passage shows, Grisez believes that his analysis of human action is supported by the thought of St. Thomas. He also thinks that it is compatible with the teaching of the magisterium as expressed by Pius XII in the Addresses in which Pius distinguished between "direct killing" and killing that is in no way intended or willed but follows as an inevitable side-effect of one's freely chosen act. Pius XII had clearly identified as *direct* what one wills either as the *end intended* or as the *means chosen* to the end.[21]

Since Grisez appeals to St. Thomas's analysis of the "killing" involved in an act of defending oneself from an unprovoked attack to support his position, it is important properly to understand Aquinas's thought on this matter.

According to St. Thomas a private individual would be doing something morally bad if, in defending himself from an unprovoked attack, his "intention" was to kill the individual attacking him, i.e., if either the precise object of his inner act of choice was to kill—i.e., if he was choosing to kill the assailant as the means of defending himself—or the end for whose sake he chose to defend himself was to kill the assailant. But, Aquinas argued, an individual can justly use appropriate force to stop an unprovoked attack when this is required to ward off an immediate threat to his own life. The force needed to stop the attack may be such that it will result in the assailant's death. Even if the person defending himself foresees that this will definitely result, the killing of the assailant need not enter into this person's "intention"; that is, the killing of the assailant need be neither the *means chosen* nor the end for whose sake the act of self-defense (i.e., the means) is chosen. When this is the case, the death of the assailant is not "intended" in the proper sense of that term. Rather, as Aquinas says, it is *praeter intentionem*, outside the scope of one's intention.[22]

If both Aquinas and Grisez are to be properly understood, it is absolutely essential to distinguish clearly, as St. Thomas does, between the *natural species* of an action and its *moral* species. *Killing an innocent person* and *killing an assailant* in an act truly describable morally as an act of *defending oneself from an unprovoked attack* by use of measured force are both, according to Aquinas, "acts of killing" in their "natural" species (*Summa theologiae*, 1–2, 1, 3, ad 3).[23] But they differ in their **moral** spe-

---

[21]See the passages from Pius XII cited above.

[22]See Aquinas (*Summa theologiae*, 2–2, 64, 7). See Grisez's analysis (1970a: 326–327) of this text. Grisez elsewhere gave a more extensive analysis of this text (Grisez, 1970b: 73–75).

[23]See Aquinas (*In II Sent.*, d. 40, q. 1, a. 2, ad 4.)

cies because the killing of an innocent person is an "act of killing" in the moral sense and as such is intrinsically (*secundum se*) evil (*Summa theologiae*, 2–2, 64, 6), whereas the killing involved in legitimate self-defense by the measured use of force against an unprovoked attack is a partial aspect of an action that is morally good. It is morally good because *it is morally specified by the object of the will's choice as an **act of self defense** and **not** as an **act of killing***. It is critically important to recognize that, if the *moral species* of an act can truly be said to be that of legitimate self-defense, the *killing of the assailant, even if this is reasonably foreseen, is **not** "intended*,*" i.e., it is neither the *means* chosen nor the *end* for sake of which the means is chosen (*Summa theologiae*, 2–2, 64, 6).[24] The *means* in legitimate self-defense is precisely an *act of self-defense*.

According to this analysis, therefore, a person who is attacked by another without provocation and whose life is in danger because of this attack can take a gun, aim it at the assailant's head, pull the trigger so that a bullet exits the gun and enters the assailant's head, blowing out his brains, and do so *without necessarily "intending" the assailant's death IF there is no alternate means of stopping the attack*. The *natural species* of the act is killing, but this is not its *moral species*. It is not its moral species because, as St. Thomas says, "moral acts receive their species according to what is intended [i.e., according to what is *chosen* as a means or aimed at an *end*], but not from what is outside the scope of intention (*praeter intentionem*)" (*Summa theologiae*, 2–2, 64, 7).[25] However, if the individual unjustly attacked proposes, either as the means chosen or the end aimed at, to kill the assailant, the moral species of the act is no longer that of self-defense but that of killing.

I think the issue can be made clearer if we express it in terms of intelligible proposals that one adopts by choice and executes. If the intelligible proposal adopted by choice is "to stop an unprovoked attack by shooting the assailant in the head because this is the only way to stop the attack," then the human act chosen and in this sense intended by the person can truly be called an act of legitimate self-defense and not an act of killing, even if the one defending himself foresees that by shooting the assailant in the head the assailant's brains will be blown out and the

---

[24]It is absolutely essential to recognize that, in this article, Thomas expressly states that if a private individual deliberately *intends* the death of the assailant, the *moral species* of the act changes from being an act of legitimate self-defense into an illicit act of killing. Its moral species is changed precisely because the *object* of the inner will act of choice is changed. The *object* of this act is no longer self-defense but *killing*.

[25]"morales autem actus recipiunt speciem secundum id quod intenditur, non autem ab eo quod est praeter intentionem."

assailant will die. But if the intelligible proposal adopted by choice is "to blow out the brains of the assailant," then the human act chosen and in this sense intended by the person can not truly be called an act of legitimate self-defense but must be recognized as an act of killing, chosen as the means of defending oneself. One can not, in other words, adopt by choice (=intending as a *means*) the proposal to blow out someone's brains without adopting by choice (=intending as a *means*) the proposal to kill that person. The object of one's choice (of one's intention) in the first instance is *stopping an unprovoked attack,* and this is the object giving the act its moral species. The object of one's choice (of one's intention) in the second instance is *killing the assailant,* and this is a moral object quite different from *stopping an unprovoked attack,* and it gives to the act a different moral species.

Grisez applied Aquinas's analysis of killing in self-defense to some sorts of procedures that Catholic moral theologians had regarded as *direct abortions* (e.g., salpingo(s)tomy). He explicitly acknowledged (and his way of acknowledging is, as will be seen later, most important) that his application of Aquinas's analysis to these procedures also diverges from the teaching of the magisterium as set forth in the decrees of the Holy Office. He thus did not propose the conclusions that he, as a philosopher, had reached as *practical norms* for believing Catholics to follow but rather as hypotheses to be critically examined in the light of faith. He fully accepts the teaching of the magisterium that every direct abortion is an intrinsically evil act, and indeed he considers this teaching as one that has been infallibly proposed.[26] Nonetheless, Grisez argues that the judgments of the Holy Office concerning craniotomies and the removal from the mother of immature ectopic pregnancies *may* have excluded procedures that need not be considered *direct* abortions. Here we should recall that Bouscaren, commenting on these decrees, concluded that they excluded removals that are *directly death-dealing* but that they did not exclude *every removal.* Although Bouscaren and other Catholic theologians (along with the magisterium) considered craniotomies and salpingo(s)tomies as *directly death-dealing,* Grisez is of the opinion that when these procedures are used, the death of the unborn child need be neither the *means chosen* nor the *end intended* and that, therefore, it is possible to regard them not as constituting direct abortion but rather as indirect abortion.

It is now necessary to offer a critical examination of Grisez's position by considering the objections that some theologians have raised regard-

---

[26]On this see Grisez (1987).

ing it and by presenting his analysis and the applications he and Joseph Boyle have made of it more fully.

First of all, some theologians think that Grisez tries, unsuccessfully, to justify as "indirect" some sorts of procedures previously regarded as "direct" abortion by extending analogously to these procedures St. Thomas's argument for the legitimacy of self-defensive actions foreseen to have lethal effects. They rightly note the *disanalogies* involved, in particular, the fact that the unborn child simply cannot be considered as the agent of an unprovoked attack on his or her mother.[27]

However, as we have seen, Grisez does not argue for his position by making an analogy between the procedures which he thinks are not "direct" abortions and legitimate self-defense. Rather, he argues that the *human* or *moral act*, as specified by the object of choice, is *not* to kill the unborn child but rather to remove it. The act of removing the unborn child, which is certainly intended by the agent, has two effects: one, which is intended, is the saving of the mother's life; the other, which is not intended, is the subsequent death of the unborn child. On Grisez's analysis a salpingo(s)tomy *could* be morally justified inasmuch as the death of the unborn child, which may be clearly foreseen, is neither the *means* one chooses (= the object of the inner will act of choice) to attain the good effect of saving the mother's life, nor is it the *end* for the sake of which this means is chosen. Rather, on his analysis, the means chosen to attain the good end of saving the mother's life is the removal of the unborn child from its site in the fallopian tube (where it cannot survive, if conditions warrant a salpingo(s)tomy—and it is only under such conditions that a salpingo(s)tomy could be morally justified). The chosen act of removing the unborn child has as its effects both the good end of saving the mother's life (the effect intended by the agent) and the bad effect of the unborn child's death (a foreseen but unintended effect). Thus, on Grisez's analysis, this procedure conforms to the *moral principles* underlying Thomas's analysis of killing in self defense and the requirements set forth by Pius XII to distinguish *direct* abortion from procedures in which the death of the unborn child is neither the means chosen nor the end intended, i.e., procedures that can truly be regarded as indirect abortions.

---

[27]Thus, for example, Marcellino Zalba, S.J., who himself accepts Grisez's analysis, notes that "multi verebuntur acceptare hypothesim huius scriptoris" for this reason. See Zalba (1976: 567). Unfortunately, Zalba does not identify any of the "many" who fear this. Zalba may have had in mind the kind of criticism brought against Grisez by John Finnis in Finnis (1972).

Grisez's analysis, when applied to salpingo(s)tomies, seems plausible. Indeed, Marcellino Zalba, S.J., recognized as a theologian who fully accepts the teaching of the magisterium, is in substantial agreement with Grisez, whom he calls a "docile disciple of St. Thomas."[28] Nonetheless, before examining the application of Grisez's analysis to salpingo(s)-tomies more closely, it will help to look at the application he and Joseph Boyle make of this analysis to craniotomies and to consider other criticisms made of Grisez's approach.

Grisez believes that his analysis can legitimately be applied to craniotomies and that such procedures need not be regarded, as the Holy Office and Catholic theologians faithful to the magisterium maintain, as *direct abortions.* Craniotomies were recommended in the past when the woman was in labor but could not deliver the baby because the child could not pass through her pelvic cavity. If the labor did not end, the woman would surely die, and the *only* way to end labor was to remove the unborn child by a craniotomy. But this requires the perforation of the baby's skull, the emptying out of its brain, and collapsing the skull. I think it not unreasonable to say that ordinary people would conclude that "removing" the unborn child in this way necessarily includes the willingness or "intention," however reluctant, to "kill" the unborn child. Yet Grisez, in his 1970 work on abortion, argued as follows:

> if it were impossible to prevent the mother's death (or worse, the death of both [mother and child]) except by cutting up and removing the child piecemeal, it seems to me that this death-dealing deed could be done without the killing itself coming within the scope of intention. The very deed which entails death also (by hypothesis) initiates a unified and humanly indivisible physical process which saves life. But if it is possible to save the mother's life without the death-dealing deed, then the intent to kill would enter the agent's act as its determining meaning (Grisez, 1970a: 341).

Later on, Joseph Boyle argued that in this sort of case "the death of the fetus in no way contributes to the continuance of labor and thus to

---

[28]Zalba (1976: 567–568) writes: "unicus actus secundum ordinem naturae . . . habetque duas significationes seu effectus in ordine humano et morali: est simul in seipso salituferus matri et mortiferus proli; quaeritur cum sufficienti motivo, et intenditur solus aspectus salituferus; praeter intentionem est, et dolenter acceptatur acceleratio positiva mortis infantis. In omni casu, in tantum huic ratiocinandi rationi favorem damus, in quantum ea non habeatur tanquam acceptatio abortus directi, cuius absolutam illeceitatem firmiter sustinemus."

saving the mother's life, and thus the bringing about of this effect just as such is not a means to these ends. . . . it is not the *killing* which removes the threat; the means here appears to be the craniotomy itself insofar as it alters the dimensions of the skull *in order* to allow labor to proceed. It is the dimensions of the baby's skull being altered and not its being dead which saves the mother's life" (Boyle, 1977: 309).

In short, according to Grisez and Boyle in procedures of this kind the *object* of choice (i.e., the object giving the act its *moral species*) is *not* the killing or the death of the unborn child, but rather the *craniotomy understood as **an act of altering the dimensions of the baby's skull***. According to Grisez and Boyle, choosing to do this (i.e., choosing to alter the dimensions of the baby's skull) is *not* the same as choosing to *kill an innocent human being*. The human or moral act chosen, in other words, is not an act of killing but rather the act of altering the dimensions of the baby's skull. This act has two effects: one good and directly intended, namely, the saving of the mother's life; the other bad, but not intended directly but only foreseen and accepted, i.e., the death of the unborn child. Most people, I believe, would reject this line of thinking and conclude that Grisez and Boyle are really *redescribing* the act in terms of its intended (in the sense of future, as distinct from *present* intentions) consequences. I will return to this. Now to look at some of the criticisms of Grisez's analysis made by other theologians.[29]

Joseph V. Dolan, S.J., commenting on the passage in which Grisez speaks of cutting the child up piecemeal and removing it, writes: "the good effect depends not just on the action as a physical cause but on the realization of a mediating evil effect of it," and that, consequently, "the 'cutting up and removing the child piecemeal' is in the proper sense mediative of the desired good effect and thus intended in a way the removal of an ectopic fetus along with removal of the pathological tube is not" (Dolan, 1972: 143). In addition, Dolan thinks that Grisez's contention that in a salpingo(s)tomy, for instance, the direct intent is simply the removal of the unborn child from its site and, if possible, the placement of it in an artificial womb where it could be brought to term is utterly

---

[29]Here I should note that Grisez's analysis has simply not received from theologians (both those faithful to the magisterium and those who are not) the serious attention it requires. In what follows I will consider the objections levelled in print by Joseph V. Dolan, S.J. (the only one, aside from John Finnis (1972) who offered somewhat cryptic criticisms, who, so far as I know, has explicitly taken up Grisez's application of his analysis to craniotomies in print) and in private communications by Ronald Lawler, O.F.M. Cap.

unrealistic.[30] Dolan thinks that Grisez's reasoning is overneat and that, for instance, "even the mugger who stabs his resisting prey through the heart is unlikely to intend cessation of life as such; he wants only non-resistance." "Are we to say," Dolan continues, "that death in this case is a mere result and that murder is not imputable. . . . ?" Dolan's point is that

> in these circumstances of unjust aggression, "killing" in the moral sense occurs with the placing of an action known to be death-dealing, not with extirpation of the victim perhaps several hours later. Similarly, a directly intended "removal" of a fetus from the only environment in which it can in fact survive (whatever the imagined abstract possibilities) is in moral terms itself an intended "killing." Removal is identically the lethal invasion of the physical integrity to which an innocent person has an inviolable right" (Dolan, 1972: 143).

Ronald Lawler, O.F.M. Cap., while rejecting the view (rejected also by Grisez) that "physical forms of behavior of themselves always necessitate the conduct being that of a single kind," e.g., killing, nonetheless argues that when someone understands that the act he is choosing to do is one which of its very nature kills a person, then he is engaging in an act of killing. By this Lawler means that if, for example, "in defending myself I intend to kill the person, or *if my act is an act which I grasp as an act of killing the person*, then I am in the wrong."[31] By this he means that if, for instance, the proposal that I am adopting by choice (= what I am presently intending to do = object of my act of choice) is *to cut off a person's head* or *to blow out someone's brains*, then I can not reasonably claim that I did not intend, i.e., choose, to kill that person and that I can not reasonably say that I was adopting by choice a proposal *to stop an unprovoked attack*, i.e., to defend myself by an act of measured force. Similarly, he argues, if I adopt by choice the proposal *to crush the skull and brain of an infant* I simply can not truly claim that I am only adopting by choice a proposal *to remove the infant* or *to change the dimensions of its skull*, simply because I cannot adopt a proposal this kind by choice and *not intend the*

---

[30]Grisez had suggested, in support of his analysis, that we imagine the possibility that the unborn child "removed" from the fallopian tube could be brought to term with the help of an artificial womb. See Grisez (1970a: 340–341).

[31]Ronald L. Lawler, O.F.M.Cap., personal communication; emphasis added.

141

baby's death. Thus in his judgment, Grisez and Boyle are not correct in identifying the object of human choice (of one's intention) in their way of analyzing what is at stake in a procedure such as a craniotomy.

I agree with Lawler's critique and thus think that the application made by Grisez and Boyle of the principles concerning the determination of the *moral species* of a human act to procedures such as craniotomies is incorrect. In other words, if the means one chooses to "remove" the unborn child from the mother's body can be realistically understood only as the adoption by choice of a proposal to crush the baby's skull or to cut it up piecemeal, then it is not true to say that *what one is choosing to do* (= the intelligible proposal that one is adopting by choice) is *to remove the baby,* merely foreseeing its death and intending only its removal and the subsequent effect of saving its mother's life. I therefore do not agree with the claim, made by Grisez and Boyle, that procedures such as craniotomies can be truly considered only *indirect abortion* and not *direct abortion.*

Moreover, in a very important recent article Kevin Flannery, S.J., has mounted what I believe is a very convincing argument against the Grisez-Boyle position regarding craniotomy by contrasting the logical structure of a craniotomy with that of a hysterectomy required when a pregnant woman is suffering from cancer of the uterus—a situation in which Catholic moralists agree that the hysterectomy is justified and that the abortion and death of the unborn child is not directly intended. In the hysterectomy case, first of all, the operation is performed *on the woman,* whereas the craniotomy (or what Grisez and Boyle prefer to call a "cranium-narrowing" operation) is performed *on the unborn child.* Secondly, in the hysterectomy case no "redescription" of the action is necessary in order to show that the death of the unborn child is "outside the means directed toward the health of the woman." But in the craniotomy case it is necessary to "redescribe" the action by calling it a "cranium-narrowing" operation undertaken to change the measurements of the baby's skull. He concludes by saying:

> that there is a difference of logical structure between the two cases is a fact. . . . But does this fact have moral relevance? We have strong reason to believe so, for the difference in logical structure between the two cases involves the good (or ill) done to the subject who is operated upon. The practice of medicine has as its sole legitimate object, so it seems to me, the health of the individuals it turns its attention to. But in the craniotomy case this is not its object: the fetus, who is clearly the object of the operation, is killed. In this instance, medicine has not been

142

practiced in a reputable manner. This is morally relevant (Flannery, 1993: 511–512).

In earlier drafts of this essay, I went on at this point to defend sal-
pingo(s)tomy by applying the Grisez-Boyle analysis to this procedure. I
argued that in a salpingo(s)tomy the *object of one's choice* can properly be
described as **the removal of a nonviable unborn baby from a site where
both its own life and the life of its mother are imperiled.** It is not, I
argued, what one of the critics (Ronald Lawler, O.F.M.Cap.) of earlier
drafts of this paper contended, namely a choice to **expel the unborn
baby from the place where it lives, and where alone it can live for some
time,** nor is it a choice, as Lawler maintained, **to thrust it toward certain
and prompt death.**[32] The object of one's choice, I argued, is therefore
not to abort the unborn child. Its abortion, i.e., **its expulsion toward
certain and prompt death,** is rather unintended side-effect of its re-
**moval from a site where both its own life and that of its mother are
imperiled,** and its removal causes both its death (the unintended effect
of its removal) and the saving of the mother's life (the intended effect of
its removal). It is true that the mother's life can be saved by salpingectomy or segmental resection. But in both these procedures, regarded as
morally justifiable, the unborn child *is removed* from the mother's body
with its consequent death inevitably foreseen.

In the earlier drafts of this paper, then, I defended the following
thesis: **removing an unborn child from a fallopian tube, damaged to
such an extent that the lives of both mother and child are imperiled,
need not be considered direct abortion.** But I now believe that Flannery's critique of the Grisez-Boyle argument to justify craniotomy seriously challenges the attempt I had made to justify salpingo(s)tomy.
Flannery himself compares a *salpingectomy* with a hysterectomy in dis-
cussing the difference in the "logical structure" between a hysterectomy
and a craniotomy. "It might not," he writes, "be a hysterectomy which is
required but the removal of a fallopian tube [salpingectomy] which has
become infected as a consequence of an ectopic pregnancy. As long as
the operation is performed upon the woman, for her health, and there
is required no artificial redescription of the act in order to separate off
the death of the fetus from the means, the act is of the same logical form
as the hysterectomy case" (Flannery, 1993: 512).

In a salpingo(s)tomy, the operation is performed both on the
woman *and* on the unborn child. An incision is made in the woman's fal-

---

[32]Ronald Lawler, O.F.M. Cap., personal communication of February 9, 1993.

lopian tube (the operation on the woman); this operation, however, does not, of itself, protect the woman's life. The unborn child is then removed or separated from the fallopian tube. This operation, performed on the child, is undertaken in order to save the mother's life, it is true, but it is not done for the good of the child (unless there is the possibility of transplanting the unborn child into the womb). If this is the proper way of describing what is going on in a salpingo(s)tomy, then it seems to me that the procedure is directly abortifacient and that the reasoning I had used to justify it is faulty. I had sought to justify the procedure by describing it as the "removal of an unborn child from a fallopian tube, damaged to such an extent that the lives of both mother and child are imperiled." I now believe that this way of describing procedure is not adequate. The removal is done, not to protect the child from the certain death that it faces in this site, but to protect the mother's life and, moreover, *to preserve her fallopian tube.* In the light of Flannery's analysis of the logical differences between craniotomy and hysterectomy and his comments regarding the legitimacy of salpingectomy, I now conclude that salpingo(s)tomy amounts to direct abortion and hence ought not to be used in the management of ectopic pregnancies.

Before concluding this section, I think it important to draw attention to a most important point made by Grisez at the end of his argument to justify craniotomy (and salpingo(s)tomy). Grisez explicitly stated that he did not propose his conclusion *"as a practical norm of conduct for my fellow believers."* He proposed it, rather, as an hypothesis to be examined in the light of faith. He then said:

> Those who really believe that there exists on this earth a community whose leaders are appointed and continuously assisted by God to guide those who accept their authority would be foolish to direct their lives by some frail fabrication of mere reason instead of conforming to a guidance system designed and maintained by divine wisdom (Grisez, 1970a: 345–346).

The attitude embodied in these lines, which Grisez wrote in 1970, is the attitude that the magisterium itself wants fostered in Catholic scholars engaged in philosophical and theological study. In the 1990 *Instruction on the Ecclesial Vocation of the Theologian (Donum Veritatis)*, the Congregation for the Doctrine of the Faith had this to say:

> The willingness to submit loyally to the teaching of the Magisterium on matters *per se* not irreformable must be the rule. It can happen, however, that a theologian may, according to the case, raise questions regarding the timeliness, the form, and

even the contents [emphasis added] of magisterial interventions (CDF, 1990: n. 14).

Thus, even if the argument advanced in earlier drafts of this paper to justify the use of salpingo(s)tomy in cases of ectopic pregnancy is plausible, it ought not to be adopted as a practical norm. It was originally proposed as a hypothesis to be tested, and in my own opinion it does not seem to pass a critical test posed by Flannery.

2. OVARIAN ECTOPIC PREGNANCIES

Pregnancies of this kind, as we saw in our review of the medical literature, are usually handled by an ovarian resection—removing the hemorrhaging part of the ovary (which contains the unborn child)—and resecting its remaining portions. This procedure seems to be analogous to segmental resection of the fallopian tube when this is required to protect the mother's life. In this procedure the abortion is not directly intended. Although O'Donnell claims that "a considerable portion of ovarian pregnancies have gone to term," he gives no evidence to support his contention (O'Donnell, 1991: 67). Obviously, if this can be done without endangering the mother's life, it must be done.

3. ABDOMINAL ECTOPIC PREGNANCY

This kind of ectopic pregnancy is apparently the kind in which the unborn child can develop to viability without endangering the life of the mother. If the membranes rupture, the unborn child dies within the peritoneal cavity. If the baby develops to viability it can be delivered and the procedures outlined by Rock—clamping the cord and leaving the placenta in situ, with the possible use of MTX to hasten the degeneration of remaining segments of the trophoblast—are surely morally permissible.

4. CERVICAL ECTOPIC PREGNANCIES

As already noted, these pregnancies usually require abdominal hysterectomy. If a hysterectomy is performed, this seems morally justifiable as indirect abortion. At times a D&C is recommended. Use of a D&C, unless it is known that the unborn child has already died, would in my judgment constitute direct abortion and would thus be immoral.

145

CONCLUSION

Today it is possible to discover ectopic pregnancies much earlier in their development than was possible in the past. Moreover, today techniques for transplanting developing unborn children into the womb have been perfected through the immoral experimentation carried out in connection with *in vitro* fertilization and embryo transfer. Consequently, I contend that it is morally imperative today to make every effort possible to discover and transplant into the uterus those unborn babies who have, unfortunately, implanted in the fallopian tube or other ectopic sites and not in the uterus where they belong.

If ectopic pregnancies are discovered at times when transplantation is not possible, some methods currently recommended for managing them must be repudiated as direct abortion and hence immoral. Among these are MTX "therapy," D&Cs, and, according to the present judgment of the magisterium, and in my own judgment, linear salpingo(s)tomies.

Some may wonder why we should bother about the morality of the different procedures advocated to manage ectopic pregnancies where there is no chance that the unborn child will become viable. It will die no matter what procedure is used. The end result will be a corpse, so what difference does it make whether its death comes about indirectly as a result, for instance, of a salpingectomy, or directly as a result of using MTX or a D&C?

The difference, one morally relevant, is that in one instance the unborn child's death, although foreseen, is not the object of one's act of choice—one does not choose to kill an innocent human person—whereas in the other instance its death is not only foreseen but is precisely the object of one's choice (however reluctantly one makes it). In the one instance its death is not the *means* to the good end of saving the mother's life; in the other its death *is* the *means chosen* to this end. And it is in and through the choices we freely make that we give to ourselves our identity as moral beings, our character. We ought not freely choose, however reluctantly, to kill an innocent human being, for by doing so we make ourselves *to be killers*, and we human beings, who are made in God's image and likeness, ought not to make ourselves killers.

If ectopic pregnancies are resolved by salpingectomy, segmental resection, ovarian resection or oophorectomy and abdominal hysterectomy, fetal tissues may be available for use in therapeutic experimentation—as there may be in spontaneous abortions or miscarriages. I believe that it would thus be morally permissible to use fetal tissue obtained in these ways in such experimentation.

146

References

American College of Obstetricians and Gynecologists. (1992). *Suspected Ectopic Pregnancy.* ACOG.

Aquinas, Saint Thomas. *Summa Theologiae.*

Bouscaren. (1944). *The Ethics of Extopic Operations.* Milwaukee: The Bruce Publishing Company.

Boyle, J. (1977). Double Effect and a Certain Kind of Crainiotomy. *Irish Theological Quarterly, 44*(4).

Cannon, L., & Jesionowska, H. (1991, June). Methotrexate Treatment of Tubal Pregnancy. *Fertility and Sterility, 55*(6).

Congregation for the Doctrine of the Faith (1990). *Instruction on the Ecclesial Vocation of the Theologian (Donum Veritatis).*

Fernandez, H., Rainhorn, J., & Papiernik et al, E. (1988). Spontaneous Resolution of Ectopic Pregnancy. *Obstetrics and Gynecology, 71.*

Finnis, J. (1972). The Rights and Wrongs of Abortion: A Reply to Judith Jarvis Thompson. *Philosophy and Public Affairs, 2.*

Flannery, K. (1993). What Is Included in a Means to an End? *Gregorianum 74*(3).

Grisez, G. (1970a). *Abortion: The Myths, the Realities, and the Arguments.* Cleveland/New York: Corpus Books.

Grisez, G. (1970b). Toward a Consistent Natural Law Ethic of Killing. *American Journal of Jurisprudence, 15,* 64–96, 73–75.

Grisez, G. (1983). *The Way of the Lord Jesus, Vol. 1, Christian Moral Principles.* Chicago: Franciscan Herald Press.

Grisez, G. (1987). The Definability of the Proposition: The Intentional Killing of an Innocent Human Being Is Always Grave Matter. In Citta Nuova Editrice (Ed.), *Persona, Verita e Morale: Atti del Congresso Internazionale di Teologia Morale* (pp. 291–313). Roma.

Leach, R., & Ory, S. (1987). Modern Management of Ectopic Pregnancy. *Clinical Obstetric Gynecology, 30.*

May, W. E. (1991). *An Introduction to Moral Theology.* Huntington, IN: Our Sunday Visitor Press.

National Conference of Catholic Bishops. (1971). *Ethical and Religious Directives for Catholic Health Care Facilities.* Washington, D.C.: United States Catholic Conference.

O'Donnell, S., Thomas J. (1991). *Medicine and Christian Morality.* Staten Island: Alba House.

Pius XII. (1944). Address La vostra presenza to the Italian Medical Biological Union of St. Luke, November 12, 1944. In *Enchiridion Familiae* (pp. 2.1306–1307, n. 25).

Pius XII. (1951). Nell'ordine to the National Congress of the "Family Front," November 26, 1951. In *Enchiridion Familiae* (pp. 2.1471–1472, n. 15).

Rock, J. A. (1992). Ectopic Pregnancy. In *TeLinde's Operative Gynecology.* Philadelphia: J.B. Lippincott Co.

Shettles, L. B. (1990, December). Letter. *American Journal of Obstetrics and Gynecology,* pp. 2026–2027.

Sultana, C. J., Easley, K., & Collins, R. L. (1992, February). Outcome of Laparoscopic Versus Traditional Surgery for Ectopic Pregnancies. *Fertility and Sterility, 57,* 2.

Wallace, C. (1917, 5 May). Transplantations of Ectopic Pregnancy from Fallopian Tube to Cavity of Uterus. *Surgery, Gynecology and Obstetrics,* pp. 578–579.

Zalba, M., S.J. (1976). Nihil Prohibet Unius Actus Duos Effectus. In *L'Agire Morale. Vol 5: Atti del Congresso Internazionale: Tommaso D'Aquino nel Suo Settimo Centenario.* Naples: Edizioni Dominicane Italiane.

Chapter 8

JUSTICE AND ALLOCATION
OF RESOURCES: A LOOK AT FETAL
TISSUE RESEARCH AND THERAPY

The Reverend Patrick Norris, O.P.

Editors' Summary: The Reverend Patrick Norris, O.P., considers the ethics of a Catholic network of human fetal tissue banks from the aspect of justice. Can a network of this sort which uses human fetal tissue for research and therapeutic purposes make its benefits available to the poor? Should the network exist if the poor are not able to benefit from it? The foundation for answers to these and like questions is provided in the first half of the chapter with an explanation of the concept of the "preferential option for the poor" and other principles of Catholic social justice. According to these principles, the human dignity of the poor and the demands of distributive justice necessitate that the Church's health care ministry reject any practices which discriminate against the poor. A fundamental right to health care is shown to be derived from the basic human good of health. Fulfilling this right is constrained by limited societal resources which may result in prioritizing the guarantee of a basic level of care over the development and use of cer-

tain health care technologies. The author cites five general criteria by which the proposed network should be tested for meeting the requirements of social justice, including the preferential option for the poor. Father Norris concludes that while the U.S. health care system as a whole does not fulfill the requirements of distributive justice, a human fetal tissue bank could be implemented so as to meet both the economic and medical demands of distributive justice in this question. An analysis of the current state of organ transplantation access is also provided with a view toward suggesting how a more fair and just access to fetal tissues would be required for their ethically permissible use.

Introduction

When one considers the ethical issues associated with the establishment of a Catholic sponsored fetal tissue bank for research and eventual therapeutic purposes, one immediately considers the issues of complicity with induced abortions, cooperation with evil, consent, scandal, and respect for the fetus. However, in accord with recent Church teachings, the advisability of such a project must also be analyzed from the perspective of the Church's preferential option for the poor. Specifically, is the pursuit of a potentially costly and highly technological mode of treatment appropriate when many people in contemporary society lack access to basic health care? Secondly, if the use of fetal tissue for research on and treatment of human diseases is an acceptable use of health care resources, can equitable access to and allocation of such treatment be accomplished consistent with the Church's mission to the poor and the marginalized?

THE VIEWING LENS: OPTION FOR THE POOR

THE CURRENT TEACHING

The establishment of a fetal tissue bank under the auspices of the Catholic Church has many social and ethical implications. Consequently, its establishment must be consistent with the tenets of Catholic social thought. The preferential option for the poor has emerged as a key paradigm by which to interpret social action. The U.S. Catholic Bishops' Pastoral Message and Letter on economic justice, "Economic Justice for All: Catholic Social Teaching and the U.S. Economy" (NCCB, 1986: 409–56), emphasizes that the Church has a special obligation to the poor and vulnerable (Pastoral Message, no. 16), that economic decisions

150

must be judged in light of what they do for the poor (Pastoral Letter, no. 24), that the Church maintains a preferential option for the poor (Pastoral Letter, no. 52), that the Church has duties to all, especially the poor (Pastoral Letter, no. 62), and that the poor have the single most urgent economic claim on the conscience of the nation (Pastoral Letter, no. 86). Although addressing the broader issue of economic justice, the Bishops' statement implies duties in regards to the poor in relation to the economics of health care. Economic practices are judged not only by what they produce but also by how they touch human life and whether they protect or undermine the dignity of the human person (Pastoral Message, no. 1). Therefore, the ethical analysis of fetal tissue research and therapy in its many facets must be filtered through the lens of its effect on the poor.

THE BACKGROUND THEORY

This emphasis on the concern or option for the poor originates in the teaching of the Scriptures, particularly the prophets and Jesus and his concern for the poor, for example, the parable of the last judgement (Mt. 25: 31–46) and the rich man and Lazarus (Lk. 16: 19–31).[1] Monica Hellwig points out that the outreach to the poor was often seen as a matter of justice rather than charity in the Church Fathers (Hellwig, 1984: 6–7). Papal teachings in the social encyclicals of the past one hundred years have always indicated a significant concern for the poor which gradually developed into the concept of a preferential option for the poor.[2] In addition, Hellwig points out that the Church in its health care ministry has always served the poor and the needy (Hellwig, 1984: 8). Thus, because of the intrinsic dignity and sanctity of human life as imaged in the poor, the Church must reject practices that discriminate against the poor in its health care ministry (Henriot, 1984: 21). Not surprisingly, the U.S. Bishops in their document on health and health care formally state that the option for the poor is particularly pertinent to the formal health apostolate of the Church (NCCB, 1981: 400). Economic considerations are not to be the determinant factor in the Church's health care ministry. Rather, service to the poor is to be pro-

---

[1] For a further development, see West (1987: 20–49).
[2] For the specific formulation of the preferential option for the poor, see Eagleson and Scharperr (1979: 264–67). See also Gremillion (1976: nos. 4–11). For a thorough study of the evolution of this concept, see Dorr (1983).

moted in order to build up the common good and prevent the further marginalization of the poor.

ASKING THE CONTEMPORARY QUESTIONS

With this hermeneutical approach to economic issues and in particular economic and allocation issues in Catholic health care in mind, one can analyze the appropriateness of the development of a fetal tissue bank for research and eventual therapeutic purposes. One must clearly define the effect of such a bank on the poor. Will such an endeavor advance human dignity or detract from it, especially in the lives of the poor and marginalized? Does the utilization of resources for fetal tissue research and therapy satisfy the requirements of distributive justice in the context of our health care crisis? To answer those questions, one must take into account the current state of affairs in health care.

DISTRIBUTION OF RESOURCES: FETAL TISSUE VS. OTHER NEEDS

THE CURRENT DISTRIBUTION OF RESOURCES

Although estimates vary, roughly 37 million United States citizens do not have medical insurance and another 26 million are underinsured and thereby lack access to certain basics of health care (Evans, 1990b: 975). Access to health care and health care expenditures have become a major political and social issue. Solutions to the crisis have included increasing taxes to offer greater coverage, rationing care, cost control, and cutting waste.[3] In the past six years, the state of Oregon has been at the forefront of tackling this problem through controversial adjustments in its Medicaid program. Engendering much ethical debate, in the spring of 1987, Oregon stopped covering bone marrow, heart, liver, and pancreas transplants for approximately 34 patients in order to expand its coverage of basic services for 1,500 additional citizens (Welch, Larson, 1988: 171–73). Recently, Oregon proposed a plan to expand Medicaid coverage for a greater percentage of the poor by rationing care through

---

[3]A recent edition of *Consumer Reports* indicated that almost a quarter of U.S. health care expenditures are unnecessary *Consumer Reports*, (1992: 435–48). See Dukakis, (1992: 1090–92) and Miles, et al., (1992: 1092–95).

the elimination of certain treatments previously funded by the program (Fox, Leichter, 1991: 7–27).[4] At first glance, these types of proposals for rationing health care and the public's growing awareness of the number of Americans with limited access to health care resources have raised questions about the appropriateness of pursuing costly technological research and therapy which may serve only to exacerbate the problems of an already overburdened system.

THE RIGHT TO HEALTH CARE

Underlying this questioning of the development and use of expensive treatments is the fundamental presumption that people have a right to health care which may be threatened by the development of such technology. Indeed, the public clamor to eradicate the great mass of uninsured Americans and subsequent federal and state reform proposals suggest a growing consensus that people have a right to basic health care. Interestingly, the President's Commission in 1983 indicated that individuals do not have a "right" to health care, but that society has an obligation to provide equitable care or an adequate level of health care (The President's Commission for the Study of Ethical Problems in Medicine and Biomedical and Behavioral Research, 1983: 20–34). On the other hand, recent Catholic magisterial teachings have acknowledged more forcefully the "right" of all people to health care. Pope John XXIII specifically mentioned the right to medical care.[5] The U.S. Bishops stated that "every person has a basic right to adequate health care. This right flows from the sanctity of human life and the dignity that belongs to all human persons. . . . It implies that access to that health care which is necessary and suitable for the proper development and maintenance of life must be provided for all people, regardless of economic, social or legal status" (NCCB, 1981: 402).

Joseph Boyle provides a philosophical undergirding for this magisterial teaching. Boyle maintains that the right to health care flows from the fact that health is a basic good which promotes human flourishing. The pursuit of this good is both individual and communal in nature. As

---

[4]See also Callahan, (1991: 78–87). There have been many critiques of the Oregon plans. The purpose in mentioning them is not to espouse them necessarily but to indicate that any reasonable system of equitable health care in consonance with other social goods will require some form of rationing and limitation of expenditures. See Dougherty (1991: 32–39).

[5]See John XXIII (1963).

153

members of the community, individuals have a responsibility to pursue health for the sake of the common good. Although there are many ways to pursue good health, today access to health care is integral to the endeavor. Consequently, because of the essential role of health care in actualizing the good of health, individuals have a right to "necessary" health care. As such, the right to health care requires that "members of a community committed to health be provided on an equal basis with the medical care they need" (Boyle, 1987a: 643–49). Although Boyle rightly asserts that the specifics of what the person is entitled to on an "equal basis" is less clear, society has an obligation to provide assistance for the sake of the common good. The President's Commission insists that equity of care implies that people are entitled to an adequate level of care. The Commission acknowledges this is an amorphous notion which has not lent itself to easy definition over the years (The President's Commission for the Study of Ethical Problems in Medicine and Biomedical and Behavioral Research, 1983: 20). Nevertheless, Boyle claims that when addressing the issue of adequate care, the provision of such care "takes priority in health care over more exotic treatments for those who can take for granted such minimally adequate health care" (Boyle, 1987b: 23).

Clearly then, people have a duty to promote their own well being and health. Given the role of medicine today, access to care is necessary to actualize one's health. This in turn gives birth to the right to health care. Someone might argue then that society has an obligation to provide the resources and funding for not only basic care but for all care which could potentially promote well being, including fetal tissue transplants. However, this would not necessarily be the case because the right to health care must be understood in a societal context. Larry Churchill comments that the right to health care is based on human need, but that need must be measured against the needs of the rest of the community. He says that "a just society cannot neglect the fact of our interdependence in a social world which precedes and nourishes the individualism we so highly prize" (Churchill, 1987: 61). Individuals should have equitable access based on need to effective care which society can reasonably afford (Churchill, 1987: 94). Consequently, basic care of all and other legitimate social goods may take precedence over the development of certain health care technologies.

Decisions regarding the development of new technologies which will benefit a limited segment of society must be weighed against the common good goal of providing access to basic care for all. Individual good cannot be separated from the common good; they are intertwined inextricably. This is the reason that the hard questions must be asked about the funding of programs.

154

Nevertheless, Churchill asserts that promoting the common good may be difficult because of a phenomenon called distancing. Human nature is such that it can block out the suffering of the unknown masses for the sake of a known individual or individuals (Churchill, 1987: 40). Thus, people may raise hundreds of thousands of dollars for a well publicized child in need of a transplant. Yet the plight of others who continue to lack basic care is ignored. This phenomenon of the human psyche makes it seem cruel and unjust not to help the individual sufferer (e.g., the Parkinson's patient who might benefit from fetal tissue transplant) over against helping the abstract, faceless members of the poor. However, one must not allow this psychological response to vitiate the ethical obligation to promote the common good. So one is left with the consideration, what does the right to health care demand of the community in regards to the distribution of health care resources, especially in light of our special responsibility to take care of the poor?

THE REQUIREMENTS OF DISTRIBUTIVE JUSTICE

To resolve the question of equitable distribution, the U.S. Bishops appealed to the concept of distributive justice. They indicated that distributive justice "requires that the allocation of income, wealth and power in society be evaluated in light of its effects on persons whose basic material needs are unmet" (NCCB, 1986: n. 70). The government has the responsibility to determine how to administer the various public goods and services to individuals and society. Distributive justice requires that burdens and benefits be distributed in a fair and equitable but not necessarily equal fashion. Such justice does not presume a Rawlsian approach to justice. John Rawls claimed that people are to be treated equally unless there are relevant differences among them or unless an unequal distribution would be to everyone's advantage (Rawls, 1971). Thus, the principle of the common good need not demand absolute equalitarianism. Distributive justice under the guidance of the common good merely insists that all have access to basic necessities and the provision of such necessities takes priority. The evolution of papal social thought is instructive on that point. Initially, Leo XIII wrote that individuals gave to the poor from their surplus wealth out of a sense of charity, not necessarily justice.[6] However, more recent documents suggest one must give out of one's necessities or substance, not just one's

---

[6]See Leo XIII (1892).

surplus. Rights to private property and the use of resources are constrained by the needs of the common good and particularly the needs of the poor.[7] Thus, some people may choose to use their wealth for extra health care rather than other material goods. However, a proper balance between the individual and common good suggests this can occur only as long as everyone has access to basic care necessary to promote human dignity (NCCB, 1981: 402).[8] Individuals then may not be able to exercise their right to certain types of expensive health care if to do so would place an undue burden on the rest of society, particularly the poor. The exercise of an inherent, individual right may be restricted by concerns of the common good. For example, one may have to move from one's own property for the sake of the construction of a new highway.

Unfortunately, restrictions on the right to pursue certain treatments may need to occur in the future because today's lack of basic health care for the poor indicates that the demands of distributive justice are not being met in our society (Boyle, 1987a: 648). As long as this condition perdures, one could conceivably argue that certain technologies should be foregone or delayed because their development may serve only to impede people's exercise of the right to health care. Despite the enormous potential goods of certain technologies, Catholic health care facilities must ascertain whether their time, energy, and resources could be better served by involvement in other more basic projects. To determine whether a particular project is ethically appropriate in relation to our duties of justice towards the poor, certain questions must be answered satisfactorily.

1) Does the proposed technology serve to make matters worse for the poor, the unemployed, and the marginalized? That is, could the resources utilized for an extravagant project be better used for basic services for the poor? Does the use of the resource exemplify a fair and equitable use of it?

2) Has the technological imperative—if we can do it, we must do it—unduly influenced the decision to pursue a project which would not help satisfy the requirements of distributive justice?

3) In assessing a new technology, can one be penny–wise but pound foolish? That is, one must guard against prohibiting the development of an expensive technology which may in the long run be less costly and improve people's lives more than the current therapy. For example, one

---

[7]See John Paul II (1987). Also see Paul VI (1967) and Vatican II (1965).

[8]The U.S. Bishops indicate that such basic care should place an emphasis on "the promotion of health, the prevention of disease, and the protection against environmental and other hazards to physical and mental health."

might assume that kidney transplants are too costly. Yet in the long run, the transplant is more cost efficient than dialysis. Often "transplant recipients lead better, more productive lives and may pay their taxes when they would otherwise consume health and social security budgets" (Sells, 1989: 1391–94).[9]

4) How does the use of resources for a new technology compare to other treatments? This is an important question to address with transplant technology because of the perception that it is extravagant in comparison with other treatments.

5) Are there viable changes in the current health care system which could help realize the requirements of justice, yet still allow for the development of new technologies? That is, should one eschew the development of technologies when so much wastage exists in the current system and other even more extravagant treatments are currently over-utilized?

The preceding questions must be considered in order to determine whether the establishment of a fetal tissue bank will help or hinder the poor to exercise the right to health care. Ultimately, will the development of such a project promote the common good?

THE TISSUE BANK AND DISTRIBUTIVE JUSTICE

In considering the above questions and the effect of fetal tissue research and therapy on the common good, I will distinguish between the research and therapeutic stages of the fetal tissue bank project, because they will involve different costs and utilizations of resources.

1) Will the project help or hinder the poor's access to health care? Like most research, it seems doubtful that experimental fetal tissue research will help the poor directly in acquiring the basics of health care. However, prior to the Clinton administration's lifting of the ban on using tissue from induced abortions, NIH officials estimated that feasibility studies using tissue from miscarriages (spontaneous abortions) could cost $24 million over five years, although the accuracy of such figures remain uncertain (Hilts, 1992).[10] Such expenditures are not excessive in the world of contemporary medical research. Moreover, the research performed would contribute to the general pool of scientific knowledge

---

[9]Live and related donor kidney transplants have been shown to be significantly less costly on a per year basis than center hemodialysis. See Roberts, Maxwell, and Gross (1980: 247).
[10]Estimates of costs at this point are estimates at best. This is a weakness of the assessment of the project to date.

thereby indirectly benefitting all in society including the poor. In general, one must be cautious about foregoing research which might lead to new technology. Kenneth Keller points out that "such an approach does not merely deprive us of the option of using the technology today, when it may indeed be inadvisable; it prevents us from having it in the future, when circumstances may change because of related technological breakthroughs or because the economic or social situation changes" (Keller, 1992: 19–24, 28). In addition, information garnered in one area of research may benefit other areas in a cross-fertilization process. With regards to the resultant therapies from tissue obtained from miscarriages, the NIH estimated that it may cost as much as $330 million per year (Hilts, 1992: A7). With the Clinton health care reform plan still unsettled, it remains uncertain as to what will be covered in a reformed system which will place a greater emphasis on preventative and basic care. Yet, compared to the current annual expenditure for health care in the U.S. of nearly $850 billion in 1992, such costs do not seem excessive. Of course, almost any program could make this claim. One must recognize that it is the accumulation of the costs of smaller programs which leads to the overburdened system which fails to adhere to the basic tenets of distributive justice. Boyle asserts that the current system of distribution of benefits as established by the government and the health care industry fails to provide adequately for the legitimate rights of the poor. Therefore, the Church has the obligation to be an advocate on behalf of the poor and to critique the *status quo* of the system (Boyle, 1987b: 19). Is this the case where for the sake of the common good, one finally says "no" to a new expensive program? To answer this question, one realizes that funds saved in foregoing fetal tissue therapy may not be translated into greater service for the poor. For example, an individual physician would not withhold an expensive treatment, naively believing that the funds would be employed necessarily and automatically for basic services. Indeed, in our current open system of health care, where no maximum expenditure cap has been set, such would not be the case.[11] Unfortunately, society has not reached a consensus whereby resources saved by not investing in certain projects would necessarily be utilized for basic health care for the poor. With the potential advent of global budgets in the Clinton plan, this may change. Consequently, money saved by restricting "high-tech" care could be utilized directly for basic care. However, even in a capitated system, it would be inappropriate to place all of the responsibility for health care reform on the fetal tissue

---

[11]In a closed system like Oregon's proposed Medicaid plan, society could guarantee more effectively that money saved on high-tech care would be utilized to care for the poor.

bank project, particularly given the amount of wastage that currently exists in the system which could be used for the poor. That is, without a concerted effort to examine other programs, it might not be expedient to proscribe the fetal tissue bank project as long as Catholic health care facilities and the government would continue to work towards a more just allocation of resources on other levels.

Ultimately, any participation in the therapeutic stage of the project must be a decision of prudence. In deciding upon which projects to expend time, energy, and resources, Catholic facilities must discern which ones will serve best the common good in light of the preferential option for the poor.

2) Has the technological imperative unduly influenced the call for fetal tissue transplant? Although preliminary research data remains limited, the research offers some reasonable hope for treating various diseases.[12] This study in itself suggests that careful consideration is being given to whether this is an appropriate and ethical use of science and technology. An obvious issue which emerges not so much in the research phase but in the subsequent therapy stage is whether the therapy will be self-limiting because of lack of supply of tissue given the number of potential uses. Would less self-limiting approaches to cures be more advisable? Consequently, other modalities of treatment which may not be as "technologically glamorous" should be researched simultaneously in order to justify the development of fetal tissue therapy.

3) In assessing a new technology, can one be penny-wise and pound-foolish? This question pertains more to the eventual therapeutic stages than the research stage because until the research is done, one does not know how cost effective the treatment will be. Given the number of patients who might be treated through fetal tissue or fetal cell transplants, the use of the technology may in fact be more cost efficient given the current outlay for maintenance care for such patients.[13] Of course, the needs of individuals served by such treatments cannot be seen as totally acceptable unless both rich and poor share in the benefits. Perhaps, then, the more problematic question is not whether to fund the

---

[12]For a thorough discussion of potential treatments and their chance of success, see Vawter, et al.(1990).

[13]Rough estimates indicate that 1.5 million Parkinson patients, 2.5–3 million Alzheimer patients, 6 million diabetic patients, and 0.4 million stroke patients could benefit from various fetal tissue treatments. See Hillebrecht (1989: 269–322). Moreover, future developments of cultured cells and other substances for transplant may minimize the need for the expensive process of fetal tissue procurement thereby decreasing costs substantially. And the treatments themselves may also be less costly and complicated than standard transplant procedures.

project but how does one guarantee that all will have access to the therapy once it is developed. The latter half of this essay will treat that particular issue.

4) How does the use of resources for this new technology compare with other research and therapies? Certainly, the research monies to be used do not appear excessive given expenditures on AIDS research (currently a proposed $2.7 billion) and given the comparable number of people who might be assisted by such research. With relation to the therapeutic stage, treatment for AIDS patients, TPN maintenance, and certain cancer therapies often exceed many transplant costs and would surpass undoubtedly costs for fetal tissue transplant (Evans, 1990a: 344–46). A prudential estimate suggests that such research and therapy is not exorbitantly expensive.

5) Is there wastage in the system which can be eliminated which would free up monies which could be used for other therapies? Clearly, the contemporary call to ration health care and restrict funding for research and therapy stems in part from the current misuse of funds in medicine (unnecessary tests, fraud, and excess administrative costs). Therefore, a practical approach to involvement in new programs necessitates a concomitant commitment to be more faithful stewards of health care resources by eliminating waste which hinders the poor's access to care.

In sum, in light of the preferential option for the poor, the requirements of distributive justice yield an indictment of the U.S. health care system. But they do not preclude necessarily the establishment of a fetal tissue bank without a more broad spectrum analysis of and political consensus about all treatments which contribute to the inadequacy of health care for the poor. The research stage of the project certainly seems warranted. Given the potential benefits of future therapies and the lack of foreseeable reform in the system, the therapeutic stage of the fetal tissue bank project could be justified. Nevertheless, the recent proposals to ration care in Oregon and other states as well as the ongoing national health care debate bring us closer to a more critical assessment of the use of technology which only marginally serves the common good.

ALLOCATION OF RESOURCES: THE ORGAN TRANSPLANT ANALOGY

CURRENT ALLOCATION SYSTEMS

Let us assume that a consensus could be reached that both fetal tissue research and subsequent therapeutic use would satisfy the broader

160

demands of distributive justice. Such a satisfaction would be **necessary but not sufficient** to satisfy the requirements of justice towards society and especially the poor. Specifically, a second criterion would require satisfaction. If the research proved promising, would the poor have access to the ensuing therapy or would it be limited to a select group of patients, namely the non-poor? The literature on fetal tissue research has yet to address this issue. It does mention that in its current experimental stage, some patients in order to participate in research must contribute $30,000–$40,000 to supplement private research funds (Donovan, 1990: 228).[14] Such up front costs seemingly would hinder the availability of such care to the poor. Consequently, to help in the analysis, one turns to the experience with organ transplantation as a helpful analogy.

Many questions have been raised about the fairness of the current methods of organ allocation. Criteria for allocation have been much debated. Should social worth, social class, intelligence, access to the media, or ability to pay enter into the distribution of organs? Should allocation be strictly a first come first serve process or a random lottery in order to insure fairness? Should only strict medical criteria be applied?

In order to maximize fairness, most people advocate an objective criteria be applied for the distribution. Thus, Thomas Starzl and his group in Pittsburgh have developed a point system that relies on a patient's time on the waiting list, the quality of the tissue match, medical urgency, logistical concerns, and presensitization to antibodies (Starzl, et al. 1987: 3073–75). However, others have suggested that since the organ supply is limited, every organ must be used most efficiently (Corry, 1988: 1011–13). The use of efficiency as a guiding principle introduces social factors into the analysis. For example, the success in organ transplantation depends on access to follow up care and the ability to purchase medications to prevent rejection. Obviously, the poor would be less likely to be able to fulfill those requirements. Moreover, because the poor often suffer from comorbidities like hypertension and diabetes, they are perceived as less optimal candidates for successful transplants. Still, others like H. Tristam Engelhardt believe that there will always be two tiers in medicine and the right to health care does not include the right to whatever might benefit the poor. He claims that it is unfortunate that the poor do not have access to transplant technology, but it is not unfair (Engelhardt, 1984: 68–71). Relying on an individualistic ethic, patients would be able to purchase the health care they desire in fulfillment of their rights to spend money as they see fit, just as parents can

---

[14]If the restrictions on government funding are lifted, then the need for such contributions might be alleviated in part.

choose or not choose to spend money on private education for children. Broader questions of justice would not be germane to that type of consumeristic and individual rights approach to health care.

In general, selection of recipients today is guided allegedly by medical criteria (Brock, 1988: 86–99).[15] This allows for a sufficiently fair distribution of organs once the person has made it to the selection process. Equitable allocation of donated organs should occur according to principles of justice and medical criteria. The reason for this is that as James Childress points out, the donated organs come from the whole community and thereby should be distributed amongst the whole community including the poor (Childress, 1989: 101–103). Thus, the issue of allocation of organs differs fundamentally from parental rights to use their wealth to finance private education. Therefore, the social context of organ donation would preclude an individualistic, consumeristic approach to allocation. Financial means or lack thereof would not be the determinative factor in distribution. Lack of access for the poor would be more than unfortunate, it would be unfair. Arthur Caplan further asserts that an equitable distribution of organs is necessary because procurement of the organs from the public rests on the general assumption that it will be used for both rich and poor. If only the rich received the organs, public support of the program might dwindle (Caplan, 1989: 3381).

THE PROBLEM OF DISCRIMINATION

On the surface, the medical criteria approach to organ allocation seems to satisfy the requirements of distributive justice in terms of the selection process once a person is on the waiting list. But getting on the waiting list — there is the rub! Caplan has been outspoken in his critique of the allocation system. Although distribution may be fair once patients get to the selection process, there has been a woeful lack of equity in the process of arriving at that point. Caplan says that "any assessment of the current system for distributing organs must look not simply at the pattern of organ distribution among those getting transplants but also at the values and principles that prevail at each of those stages of the allocation process" (Caplan, 1989: 3385). He identifies four stages in the process of receiving an organ: eligibility, admission, distribution, and selection. He insists that the most important decisions about organ transplant are made long before the patient's arrival at the transplant center

---

[15]Dan Brock points out that even the medical criteria are not completely value free.

(Caplan, 1989: 3383). First, eligibility is determined by exposure to a primary care physician who then is able to make the appropriate referrals. The poor and marginalized because of a lack of insurance and of money for medications are not referred or may not even have access to that primary physician. Second, admission to the process may discriminate on the basis of geography and the ability of the individual to pay upwards of $100,000 for the transplant up front through cash or insurance. This "green screen," as Caplan calls it, further prevents minorities, the poor, women, and the handicapped, from gaining access to the organ transplant system (Kjellstrand, 1990: 964).[16] In addition the rich often can have multiple listings on transplant lists because of their ability to travel. Caplan concludes that although there may be a sense of equity in certain parts of the process, overall the allocation system is unfair to the poor and disenfranchised. Clearly, the values and principles associated with the eligibility and admissibility criteria of allocation do not reflect a preferential option for the poor.

Consequently, organ transplant allocation fails to meet the broad criteria for distributive justice despite efforts to eliminate discrimination. The reason for this discrepancy is the relationship between social justice and distributive justice. Social justice governs distributive justice in that, if the social system and structures of society are ethically unjust, then no matter how fair individual methods of distribution seem to be within that system, the requirements of distributive justice will not be fulfilled. Thus, organs may be distributed fairly once one enters the system. But the poor are denied just entrance into the system because of poverty and the maldistribution of the goods of creation.

FETAL TISSUE/ORGAN TRANSPLANTS: COMPARED AND CONTRASTED

In applying the analogy of organ transplants to fetal tissue research and therapy, one must evaluate how well the model fits. In general, the same principles apply. Tissue that will be obtained from ectopic pregnancies and miscarriages will be donated to the public for the common good, and therefore, should benefit the common good and not just a limited section of society determined by financial means. To circumvent the problem of justice and the demands of the common good, some have

---

[16]Although many variables are involved including cultural and medical ones, still the rich receive before the poor, men before women, white before black.

suggested that remuneration could be provided to those willing to sell their organs or tissue (Hansmann, 1989: 57–85). Through the sale of tissue or organs, poor donors would be compensated. Tissue would thereby become "private property" whose disposal would not be regulated by norms of distributive justice and the ideals of the common good. However, the National Organ Transplantation Act has forbidden the sale of organs lest a distasteful market develop.[17] Moreover, George Annas comments that the sale of organs could have adverse effects. The sales would: put a price on the priceless gift; dilute the sense of altruism in society; treat the body as a mere thing; and exploit the poor through monetary coercion (Annas, 1984: 22–23). Therefore, the sale of tissue would not be a practical nor an ethical solution to the problem. One cannot avoid the criterion that the poor would need to have means to benefit from this therapy in accord with the principles of the common good in order for fetal tissue therapy to be acceptable.

One might argue that the organ transplant analogy does not apply to the issue of fetal tissue because it remains unclear whether a similar type of organ/tissue shortage will exist in any fetal tissue program as exists in the organ transplant field. However, barring the development of cell line technology which could obviate the need for large amounts of tissue, there will probably be a need to ration resources. Even if there were a plentiful amount of tissue, the same problems of eligibility and admissibility would remain because of financial constraints, unless the system were to change significantly. Therefore, the analogy between organ transplantation and fetal tissue transplantation is sufficiently adequate that one must be concerned vitally about the poor's ability to be eligible for and be admissible to transplant programs.

AN ASSESSMENT FOR ETHICAL DISTRIBUTION

Clearly, the current approach to distribution of organs seems inconsistent with the principles of distributive justice and the Church's clarion call to champion the rights of the poor. Thus, a Catholic facility engaging in fetal tissue research and eventual therapy would have to try to establish mechanisms to guarantee equitable and real access for the poor, minorities, unemployed, the disabled, and other marginalized

---

[17]Public Law 98–507, October 19, 1984. See "National Organ Transplant Act," section 372, in Mathieu (1988).

groups. A Catholic health care facility would need to be an advocate on behalf of the poor to enhance the eligibility and admissibility standards for them. Certainly, any Church affiliated program could not overcome all of the structural inequities which hinder the poor's exercise of their right to health care. Definitely, some of the poor still will be excluded no matter how sensitive the Catholic facility is to its call to be in solidarity with the poor. Nevertheless, even though the remedy to the problem of access to care is beyond the principle influence of the Church, Catholic health care facilities cannot remove themselves totally from the complexities and inadequacies of the overall system. The Church's health care facilities in their establishment of a fetal tissue bank can act as an advocate for the poor. They can give witness to a concerted effort to increase access to care for the marginalized of our society. Accompanying an exploration of fetal tissue transplantation must be an active promotion of reform of the system in order to guarantee better access to care for the poor.

AN OVERALL EVALUATION

The Catholic Church approves of scientific and medical progress. The Church's presence in the field of fetal tissue research provides a valuable witness to the sanctity of life through its insistence on avoiding complicity with the evil of induced abortion. Moreover, it seeks to promote healing and the relief of suffering of individual members of society. Simultaneously, Catholic facilities also should evaluate such advances and progress in light of the preference for the poor and a dedication to the common good of all in society. This is particularly important because the U.S. system of medicine is dominated by principles of individuality and the technological imperative wherein the needs of the poor may be left unaddressed or, at best, addressed inadequately.

Any development of technology should reflect the Church's mission of charity. However, as a prerequisite of charity, the Church's health care facilities and programs must promote the virtue of justice. Specifically, the requirements of distributive justice should be realized. Those requirements should give us pause to consider the long range ethical appropriateness of investing in this new technology. However, as understood currently, fetal tissue research and the development of subsequent therapies reflect an acceptable use of health care resources. This is provided that in the short range, Catholic facilities continue to promote appropriate reform of the health care system. Also, any fetal tissue program sponsored by the Church will have to modify substantially the approach to transplantation access and allocation currently in existence in U.S. health care. This will help to assure that the lives of the poor and their ability to gain access to care will not be further undermined and burdened.

References

Annas, G. (1984, February). Life, Liberty, and the Pursuit of Organs. *Hastings Center Report.*

Boyle, J. (1987a). The Right to Health Care and its Limits. In D. McCarthy (Ed.), *Scarce Medical Resources and Justice.* Braintree: The Pope John Center.

Boyle, J. (1987b). The Concept of Health and the Right to Health Care. In S. Lammers & A. Verhey (Eds.), *On Moral Medicine.* Grand Rapids: William B. Eerdmans Co.

Brock, D. (1988). Ethical Issues in Recipient Selection for Organ Transplantation. In D. Mathieu (Ed.), *Organ Substitution Technology: Ethical, Legal, and Public Policy Issues.* Boulder: Westview Press.

Callahan, D. (1991, Summer). Ethics and Priority Setting in Oregon. *Health Affairs.*

Caplan, A. (1989). Problems in the Policies and Criteria Used to Allocate Organs for Transplantation in the United States. *Transplantation Proceedings, 21.*

Childress, J. (1989). Ethical Criteria for Procuring and Distributing Organs for Transplantation. *Journal of Health Politics, Policy, and Law, 14.*

Churchill, L. (1987). *Rationing Health Care in America: Perceptions and Principles of Justice.* Notre Dame: University of Notre Dame Press.

Corry, R. (1988). Public Policy and Organ Distribution. *Transplantation Proceedings, 20.*

Donovan, P. (1990). Funding Restrictions on Fetal Research: The Implications for Science and Health. *Family Planning Perspectives, 22.*

Dorr, D. (1983). *Option for the Poor: A Hundred Years of Vatican Social Teaching.* Maryknoll, NY: Orbis Books.

Dougherty, C. (1991, October). Ethical Problems in Healthcare Rationing. *Health Progress.*

Dukakis, M. (1992). The States and Health Care Reform. *New England Journal of Medicine, 327.*

Engelhardt, H. T. (1984). Allocating Scarce Medical Resources and the Availability of Organ Transplantation. *New England Journal of Medicine, 311.*

Evans, R. (1990a). Organ Transplantation: Costs, Insurance Coverage, and Reimbursement. In P. Terasaki (Ed.), *Clinical Transplants.* Los Angeles: UCLA Tissue Typing Lab.

Evans, R. (1990b). The Private Sector Vis-a-vis Government in Future Funding of Organ Transplantation. *Transplantation Proceedings 22.*

Fox, D., & Leichter, H. (1991, Summer). Rationing Care in Oregon: The New Accountability. *Health Affairs.*

Hansmann, H. (1989). The Economics and Ethics of Markets for Human Organs. *Journal of Health Politics, Policy, and Law, 14.*

Hellwig, M. (1984). Scriptural and Theological Bases for the 'Option for the Poor'. In M. J. Kelly (Ed.), *Justice and Health Care.* St. Louis: Catholic Health Association.

Henriot, P. (1984). Service of the Poor: A Basis for Spirituality and Mission. In M. J. Kelly (Ed.), *Justice and Health Care.* St. Louis: Catholic Health Association.

Hillebrecht, J. (1989). Regulating the Clinical Uses of Fetal Tissue. *Journal of Legal Medicine, 10.*

Hilts, P. (1992, July). Fetal-Tissue Bank not Viable Option, Agency Memo Says. *New York Times,* p. A7.

John XXIII. (1963). *Pacem in terris, no. 11.*

John Paul II. (1987). *Sollicitudo rei socialis, nos. 31, 42.*

Keller, K. (1992, Spring/Summer). Confluence of Ethical and Economic Issues in the Development and Adoption of High Technology Approaches in Clinical Care. *Trends in Health Care, Law and Ethics.*

Kjellstrand, C. (1990). The Distribution of Renal Transplants: Are Physicians Just? *Transplantation Proceedings, 22.*

Latin American Episcopate. (1979). A Missionary Church Serving Evangelization in Latin America. In J. Eagleson & P. Scharperr (Eds.), *Puebla and Beyond.* Maryknoll, NY: Orbis Books.

Leo XIII. (1891). *Rerum novarum, no. 36.*

Miles, S., et al. (1992). Health Care Reform in Minnesota. *New England Journal of Medicine, 327.*

National Conference of Catholic Bishops. (1981). Pastoral Letter on Health and Health Care. *Origins, 11.*

National Conference of Catholic Bishops. (1986). Economic Justice for All: Catholic Social Teaching and the U.S. Economy. *Origins, 16.*

National Organ Transplant Act. (1988). In D. Mathieu (Ed.), *Organ Substitution Technology: Ethical, Legal, and Public Policy Issues.* Boulder: Westview Press.

Paul VI. (1967) *Populorum progressio, nos. 22–23.*

Poverty of the Church. (1976). In J. Gremillion (Ed.), *The Gospel of Peace and Justice.* Maryknoll, NY: Orbis Books.

Rawls, J. (1971). *A Theory of Justice.* Cambridge: Belknap Press.

Roberts, S., Maxwell, D., & Gross, T. (1980). Cost-Effective Care of End-Stage Renal Disease: A Billion Dollar Question. *Annals of Internal Medicine, 92.*

Sells, R. (1989). Ethics and Priorities of Organ Procurement and Allocation. *Transplantation Proceedings, 21.*

Starzl, T., et al. (1987). A Multifactorial System for Equitable Selection of Cadaver Kidney Recipients. *JAMA, 257.*

The President's Commission for the Study of Ethical Problems in Medicine and Biomedical and Behavioral Research. (1983). *Securing Access to Health Care.* Washington, D.C.: Govt. Printing Office.

The Use of Human Fetal Tissue: Scientific, Ethical and Policy Concerns (D. Vawter, et al., Ed.). (1990). Minneapolis: University of Minnesota Press.

Vatican II. (1965). *Gaudium et spes, no. 69.*

Wasted Health-Care Dollars. (1992, July). *Consumer Reports.*

Welch, H., & Larson, E. (1988). Dealing with Limited Resources: The Oregon Decision to Curtail Funding for Organ Transplantation. *New England Journal of Medicine, 319.*

West, C. (1987). The Common Good and the Participation of the Poor. In O. Williams & J. Houck (Eds.), *The Common Good and U.S. Capitalism.* Lanham, Maryland: The University Press of America.

Chapter 9

THE GOOD THINGS SOUGHT IN THE FETAL TISSUE PROJECT: SHOULD CATHOLIC INSTITUTIONS COOPERATE IN THIS PLAN?

The Reverend Ronald Lawler, O.F.M. Cap.

Editors' Summary: Father Ronald Lawler begins his chapter by setting Catholic moral theology within the context of the great commandment to love God and neighbor. For it is on the basis of Christian love that a Catholic network of fetal tissue banks is being proposed. There is, it is explained, a two-fold requirement of love to pursue those goods which will truly enable human flourishing and to do so in such a way that those goods are not eclipsed by gravely harmful consequences of our actions. Moreover, love cannot allow for actions which are intrinsically wrong. It is in light of the demands of love that the good things sought by the network are then examined. Certainly the hope of treating a number of debilitating diseases such as Alzheimer's and Parkinson's disease, constitutes a real good. The witness to the sacred dignity of human life which Catholic institutions can make by their involvement in such a project is an important good. This institutional witness will have the effect of fostering a greater general respect for human life in society. Another achievable good is the opportunity for Catholic institutions to show that there are reliable, creative ways of reaching good ends which do not employ evil means. Proof may once again be given that sound medicine and moral restraints are quite compatible. The proposed network will also enable parents to find comfort and peace from the tragedy of miscarriage by giving consent to the use of tissues from their deceased loved one. The chapter concludes with the cautionary note that while there are a number of definite goods attainable by the network, the possibility of good ends is not the final determination of a project's moral status. Care must be taken at every phase to ensure that the work of the network does not, even unintentionally, lead to cooperation with the immoral use of human fetal tissue. This being taken into account, the network appears to be a morally sound one.

This paper seeks primarily to explore the nature and value of the good things that are or can be pursued in the fetal tissue project being studied by the Pope John Center. Then it wishes to investigate whether these good things can be pursued in this project faithfully and well, neither obtaining the goods to be pursued by immoral means, nor causing any excessive unwanted harms in its pursuit of its good ends. Finally it points out that the morality of the project will depend on the determination, sought in the course of many papers written by those studying the issue for the Center, of whether the project does pursue good things in such responsible and good ways.

CATHOLIC MORALITY AND THE PURSUIT OF HUMAN GOODS

Clearly Catholic moral life is centrally concerned with doing the works of love, with pursuing what is really good for our brothers and sisters on this earth. The Gospel sharply insists that the "great commandment" for believers is that they love God, and so love also their brothers and sisters (Cf. Matthew 22. 37–40). Our first principle is love, and a primary concern of Christian life is doing the works of love, doing what helps our brothers and sisters in their need (Cf. Matthew 25. 34 ff.). When the Second Vatican Council spoke of the desired reform in moral theology, it called for fresh emphasis that should be placed on the positive pursuit of what is really good. "[Moral theology] should show the nobility of the Christian vocation of the faithful, and their obligation to bring forth fruit in charity for the life of the world" (Second Vatican Council, 1965b: n. 16).

170

Hence we shall seek first to point out the various kinds of goods that can be achieved by Catholic institutions when they work together to further a project like this. This shall be the first major section of our paper.

It is true, of course, that the pursuit of good ends must be a responsible pursuit if it is to be morally upright. A pursuit of good ends would not be responsible if one did or encouraged immoral actions in the pursuit of one's good ends. Certain kinds of actions are "infamies indeed,"[1] are intrinsically wrong, and would not be right in the service of any end whatever. Moreover, even actions good in themselves can be immoral if they are foreseen as likely to bring about such grave evil consequences that it would be unreasonable to pursue the good ends sought at so high a cost. (To say this does not imply that we can directly add up diverse kinds of goods and evils, and neatly determine whether the balance favors good and evil. But there are broader principles one can invoke: should evils so great threaten as one pursues good things in a given context, then the golden rule would urge that one not act in such a way.)[2]

For love requires both that we act out of generous love, seeking to help others flourish in good, and also that we pursue what is good in ways that do no intrinsically evil deeds, nor bring about irresponsibly measures of harm that in the circumstances we have a duty not to bring about. Love requires the negative precepts of the decalogue as certainly as it requires positive works of love. "Love does no harm to the neighbor" (Matthew 13.10). Hence a Christian should not find an enterprise morally upright, following the requirements of responsible love, if it involved participating in acts of killing the innocent, or acting directly against basic human goods, or if in the context it threatens such great harms that it would be unreasonable to pursue particular goods by such a path.

Hence, when we pursue the question of the moral appropriateness of urging Catholic professionals and institutions to assist in doing research in fetal tissue, two moral considerations arise. First, what are the good things that love pursues "for the life of the world" in undertaking such research? Secondly, are we striking against love in any other way in doing this: does this activity threaten to involve its participants in any kind of behavior incompatible with love?

---

[1]See: Second Vatican Council (1965a: n. 27).
[2]Cf. Grisez (1983: 189).

171

1. Good Things Aimed at in Pursuing Fetal Research

A. Substantive life and health goods

Research entered into on the uses of fetal tissue clearly aims at many important goods. The field is very young, and what can actually be achieved is uncertain, but the goods hoped for are great ones indeed.

Already we know that fetal tissue has remarkable properties. Fetal tissue has the vigor of its youth: it has a greater adaptability, considerable regenerative power, and is less likely to be rejected. It seems to be more able to adapt and grow in transplants in ways that are needed in the living organism into which it is placed.

Some have great and reasonable hopes that it can be of great service in handling many of the more fearful diseases, like Altzeimer's and Parkinson's diseases. Great hope is held out in the case of other neurological disorders, of diabetes, and of a large array of other disorders. Experience seems to have shown that in a number of forms of fetus–to–fetus transplants, where both the host organism and the donated tissue or organs have such adaptability, there is promise of the greatest possible success. And there is reason to hope that fetal tissue transplants in certain areas will be more likely to succeed in benefiting a patient than transplants from more mature persons.

The field is a young one, but one in which expectations seem to be high.

Now physicians can certainly engage in this research as an act of great love. Research is not necessarily an act of fraternal love, but it clearly can be. Specialists need by no means be confined to less noble motives, efforts to promote their careers or achieve status, fame, or wealth. Even should such less noble motives be present in modest measure, the labors can be essentially works of love for one's suffering brother.

B. Other important goods such cooperative efforts of Catholic institutions can further

Catholic institutions, joined together in projects promoting research in the ways in which fetal tissue can benefit human life, can be signal witnesses to the sacredness and dignity of young life, even in young fetuses. They can provide an added public witness to the concern of Catholic institutions to provide positive goods for society. They can pursue an important comfort to parents of children from miscarriages,

172

in seeking to discover ways in which the pain of loss these parents experience may be lightened by awareness that these children can be sources of great assistance to the health and life of others. And in such a project they may also well reveal again how the good ends sometimes sought through evil means can also be sought in ways that are morally irreprehensible.

1. Increasing respect for life. In *Donum Vitae,* the Holy See urges: "The Gift of life, which God the Creator and Father has entrusted to man, calls him to appreciate the inestimable value of what he has been given and to take responsibility for it" (CDF, 1987: n. 1).

In many ways Catholic institutions uniting together to promote more acceptable forms of fetal tissue research can help to assure fuller respect for every human life. They can undertake an enterprise which may provide great benefits to mankind in a way that shows also entire respect for every human person, and for every human value that should be taken into account in such a task.

For example, they may institute procedures to make certain that no living human fetus is deprived of tissue or organs while the fetus is yet living. They can see to it that in pursuing the goods fetal tissue transplants can achieve they do not participate in killing the innocent. When directly aborted fetuses are used for tissue, they are treated without respect. Human persons are deliberately killed, and their bodies used without any form of reasonable and legitimate consent. But Catholic institutions can surround the use of such tissue (from miscarriages) with immense respect. They will do nothing deliberately to hasten the death of the fetus, however certain and close death may be. They will seek to gain precise awareness of when death of the organism occurs, so that the yet living organs and tissues may be able to be used well, and with consent of those reasonably judged the right persons to make available the precious living gifts from very young human persons whom they have always reverenced and loved, and never treated with violence or neglect.

2. Persistent Catholic concern for achieving positive goals. They can show in fresh ways the positive concern of the Catholic health world for achieving important specific good things, even when original ways of achieving such good involved morally dubious conduct. The concern of Catholic science is not merely to avoid evil, but to find creative ways of achieving good ends by good means in the world. If the world today is moving toward something frightening in fortifying the abortion industry and encouraging the use of those slain by a society that largely does not honor their personality and worth, and if it is willing to use the slain without any credible consent to improve the lives of the other citizens, who are encouraged by their political and personal stances on the aborting of the innocent, still (while not at all supporting such a fearful attitude) we will struggle to find how the substantive goods pursued by those who would cooperate with the abortion industry may rather be obtained in legitimate ways, ways that respect fully the human person.

3. They can help parents of children from miscarriages to find a certain comfort in bringing good things to others when they tragically lose their own children. One of the perils of the use of tissue from aborted children is that it gives a certain false dignity and reassurance to those who deliberately abort their children, and to a society that encourages people to abort their children.

But there is a certain real good lurking here. Elective abortions do not have to occur, and seeming to honor the direct killing of innocent human beings by suggesting that assistance to furthering the health of others by some involvement with so deadly an industry leads mankind by an unfortunate path. But seeking to take advantage of tissue made available by miscarriages is morally of a very different nature.

For miscarriages were tragic happenings, not the result of immoral choices. Parents who loved their children, and in no way acted to end their lives, can be rightly comforted if tissue or organs from their children can be used to support the health and lives of others.

4. Shared Catholic efforts to advance health through promoting fetal research support the proper claim that adherence to moral demands does not inhibit advancement in scientific knowledge and human medical practices. The contention that sound moral principles serve medicine and the good ends it seeks has been established in many ways; still it constantly needs to be reinforced. When medicine uses immoral means to acquire knowledge, it is inclined to argue that the restraints of a sound ethic make medical advances too slow. Experimentation has often run past ethical limits in the history of modern science, and never to the advantage of medicine or humane concerns. The tragic record of Nazi doctors is far from the only mass of immoral activities in experimentation, in which persons are abused, and any kind of informed consent neglected.

To perform experimental work within necessary moral requirements could limit in some circumstances the speed and efficiency with which work can be done. But untimely speed that neglects ethical guidelines tends to bring far greater harms to the experimenter. When the community becomes aware of the refusal to remain within ethical limits in the pursuit of knowledge, really major harms and delays are stirred up for researchers.

It is true that ethicists can be found who would approve the use of tissue and organs from aborted fetuses, as there will be those who approve abortion and other kinds of direct killing of living human beings. Ethical justification from some sources has always been accessible to justify any research, however inhuman, that pretends to offer some significant pragmatic advantages. But medicine suffers deeply if it does not attend earnestly to all serious arguments that proposed policies are gravely wrong. Mistakes might tragically be made, but they ought not be made because one is unwilling to take seriously all important considerations, or because one is so fascinated by hoped for immediate goods that one becomes unable to weigh realistically the moral consideration raised by many.

2. PURSUING GOOD ENDS ONLY IN MORALLY GOOD WAYS

A moral issue is not resolved by showing that some great good can be achieved by a procedure being considered. Sometimes great goods can be reached by doing evil things. Some acts are so directly opposed to the good human persons should honor in all their acts that they are not reasonable or human or legitimate in any circumstances.

Sometimes too it is immoral to do good actions, aimed at good ends, if one foresees a greater likelihood of evil consequences far more significant that the goods reasonably to be expected. Thus if it should appear that cooperating with a fetal tissue research project would very likely lead to serious (even if unintended) bad effects, care must be taken in determining whether the likelihood or seriousness of these effects is so great that the enterprise itself would be immoral.

Many of the papers in this study by the Pope John Center explore possibilities of these kinds. For example, it is well known that it is often difficult to determine whether a spontaneously aborted fetus is now alive or not. Can the difficulties here be mastered, or can cases in which fetuses *might* be alive be so isolated from others (and care taken that possibly living fetuses are not killed in pursuit of tissue)? Or is involvement in this project very likely to lead in fact to the killing of living and innocent human persons?

What is likely to happen if research with fetal tissue from miscarried fetuses proves successful? Is there much likelihood that in that case the demand for fetal tissue would be so great that there would be almost unanswerable demands for fetal tissue, far more than could be satisfied by miscarriages? One must take into account, however, the consideration that such a demand might not be created specifically by research done in a project like ours, and that the demand would not really be created by the kind of research people engaged in this project would be doing.

3. DETERMINING WHETHER THIS PROJECT IS A MORALLY GOOD ONE

Thus it is evident that the determination of the moral suitability of a project like this one is quite complex. One needs to take seriously into account all that one can reasonably expect to be done and achieved in such a project.

An important element is the matter focused on in this paper. What, and how great, are the good things that such a project can be expected to achieve. It would seem that very substantive health goods may be achieved, while there remains a certain real doubt at this time, because the use of fetal tissue is at so early a stage. But the goods hoped for are very great ones, and there are other goods, noted above, that are very important also. Great goods are indeed being sought by this project.

The fear that entering this project might lead participants into participating in intrinsically immoral acts seems very speculative at this time. Still, when undertaking, and continuing, such a project, these considerations must be kept in mind.

The danger that this research would lead to bad consequences like those suggested here also does not now appear to be very serious. Still, it is a question that should be investigated with some care if Catholic institutions are to take part in such a project.

Prudential judgments seem to be all one can obtain, and to be sufficient for guiding one's judgment. But those who would make such prudential judgments ought to take into careful consideration all the relevant questions that this whole study by the Center has been raising. The fact that great goods may be reached by such a project does not finally determine that it is a good one. Still, this is a deeply important consideration, and does lead one to lean toward a judgment that the project appears to be morally suitable.

References

Congregation for the Doctrine of the Faith. (1987). *Instruction on Respect for Human Life in Its Origin and On the Dignity of Procreation.*

Grisez, Germain. (1983). *The Way of the Lord Jesus: Vol. 1. Christian Moral Principles.* Chicago: Franciscan Herald Press.

Second Vatican Council. (1965a). *Pastoral Constitution on The Church in the Modern World.*

Second Vatican Council. (1965b). *Decree on Priestly Formation.*

In February, 1992, the Pope John XXIII Medical-Moral Research and Education Center sponsored a Workshop for the Bishops of North and Central America on the theme of "the interaction of Catholic bioethics and secular society." During this week-long symposium, the bishops heard twenty-one talks on various bioethical issues ranging from physician assisted suicide to chemical abortion, the human genome initiative and healthcare reform.

In the United States of America in 1992, much discussion was taking place regarding the continuation of the government moratorium on fetal tissue research and transplantation. Therefore, of special interest to many of the bishops assembled for this symposium was the presentation of Maria Michejda, M.D. about the scientific realities and realistic clinical possibilities of such research.[1]

As I reflected on her presentation, it occurred to me that the Church should make a contribution to the conversation that was taking place in our society about whether or not, or under what precise conditions the government moratorium on fetal tissue research should be lifted or modified. I discussed this concern with Dr. Michejda and with Father Russell Smith, the President of the Pope John Center. Together we concluded that this would be a most worthy topic for which the Pope John Center should conduct a task force examination. A generous benefactor was also eager to assist in this project.

---

[1]See Michejda (1992).

And so this ambitious project was launched. Under the direction of Father Smith and Peter Cataldo, Ph.D., the Center's Director of Research, approximately thirty scholars, representing various branches of the biological sciences, law, philosophy and theology, were assembled from throughout the United States and Europe. The Pope John Center hosted two plenary sessions in Braintree and specialist sessions for the scientists in Washington, D.C., and the ethicists in Pittsburgh respectively throughout 1992 and 1993.

The fruit of their study is contained in this volume. The substance of this work was submitted to the National Institutes of Health, which were conducting hearings on this question throughout 1994. It is my hope that this book, the fruit of that work, will benefit all parties interested in these issues.

The Catholic Church recognizes and affirms that scientific investigation is to be conducted according to its proper method. This method, however, must always be open to clear moral criteria which correctly directs the very process of research itself. "These criteria are the respect, defense and promotion of man, his 'primary and fundamental right' to life, his dignity as a person who is endowed with a spiritual soul and with moral responsibility and who is called to beatific communion with God" (CDF, 1987: Introduction). The Christian faith has consistently and insistently taught that all human beings inherently have these rights and characteristics from conception to death.[2] In light of the confluence of the biomedical possibilities and the ethical safeguards, it is the government's responsibility to assure proper protection for every subject of any experimentation, especially should those subjects be embryos and fetuses who are among the most vulnerable members of the human family.

Among the fundamental rights to be protected, safeguarded and fostered by any government are "a) every human being's right to life and physical integrity from the moment of conception until death; b) the rights of the family and of marriage as an institution and, in this area, the child's right to be conceived, brought into the world and brought up by his parents" (CDF, 1987: III). Furthermore, concerning research and experimentation on the corpses of human embryos and fetuses: "the moral requirements must be safeguarded, that there be no complicity in deliberate abortion and that the risk of scandal be avoided" (CDF, 1987: I.4.). With this in mind, the ethical conclusions with regard to fetal tissue research clearly follow from these rights. This clarity is made manifest by the interdisciplinary work contained in this volume. I am personally de-

---

[2]See CDF (1987: I.1. and *passim*).

lighted by the quality of the task force's research, and by the promise of the contribution this volume can make to the ongoing societal deliberation about government sponsorship of fetal tissue research and transplantation. Its conclusion that scientific research and medical progress will in no way be hindered, but in fact fostered in every way, by clear ethical conclusions is the patrimony of the best philosophical wisdom and the constant teaching of the Church.

In the words of the *Instruction* from the Congregation for the Doctrine of the Faith: "In the light of the truth about the gift of human life and in the light of the moral principles which flow from that truth, everyone is invited to act in the area of responsibility proper to each and, like the good Samaritan, to recognize as a neighbour even the littlest among the children of men (Cf. *Lk* 10:29–37). Here Christ's words find a new and particular echo: 'What you do to one of the least of my brethren, you do unto me' (*Mt* 25:40)" (CDF, 1987: Conclusion).

It is my prayerful hope that this volume and the diligent work of its contributors will very soon inspire and make concretely possible a network of fetal tissue banks which derive their tissues in morally upright ways. I commit this work to the intercession of the Blessed Virgin of Guadalupe, patroness of the Americas, that as she expressed her Divine Son's love for the poor of the new world, so she will foster in us His love for the voiceless and poor on the frontiers of new technology.

Bernard Cardinal Law
Archbishop of Boston

References

Michejda, Maria, M.D. (1992). Transplant Issues. In Russell E. Smith (Ed.), *The Interaction of Catholic Bioethics and Secular Society: Proceedings of the Eleventh Bishops Workshop* (pp. 115–130). Braintree, MA: The Pope John Center.

Congregation for the Doctrine of the Faith. (1987). *Instruction on Respect for Human Life in its Origin and on the Dignity of Procreation: Replies to Certain Questions of the Day (Donum vitae)*.

ETHICAL CRITERIA

The folowing ethical criteria for a proposed Catholic Network of Human Fetal Tissue Banks are to be followed:

1. Fetal tissues from induced abortions are not used.
2. The tissues or cells are obtained from miscarriages or ectopic pregnancies (aquired in an ethically acceptable manner) which meet specified medical requirements and the embryo or fetus is certifiably deceased.
3. Appropriate consent has been obtained from the mother or proxy.
4. The participating hospitals have the proper equipment and trained personnel to carry out the requisite procedures.
5. Effective public relations programs are mounted to instruct hospital staff, the medical and nursing communities as well as the general public regarding the nature of the fetal tissue network, its moral acceptability, and its avoidance of complicity with induced abortions.
6. It can be judged by the organizers that the proposed network would not contribute to false expectations and lead to increased demand for induced abortions.
7. Efforts are made so that the poor and others without adequate financial resources would have reasonable access to fetal tissue transplants for the management of their treatable medical disorders.

MAJOR COMPONENTS OF A PROPOSED CATHOLIC NETWORK OF HUMAN FETAL TISSUE BANKS

I. Network Structure

The network will consist of various Catholic hospitals around the United States which will serve as collection sites for tissue. Tissue specimens will be shipped from these sites on a continuing basis to a central processing, storage, and distribution site at which research will also be conducted and from which tissues will be distributed to other sites for research and transplantation (see Appendix C). The institutions receiving tissues for research and transplantation need not be Catholic.

II. Policy and Education

The success of any Catholic network will depend upon the development of clear, comprehensive policies to be implemented both on the level of the individual participating institutions and on the network level. In addition to proper scientific and medical education required for the work of the network, a sound education in the ethics of the enterprise will be critically important. This education should certainly include an explanation of the moral difference between utilizing tissues from miscarriages and from induced abortions. Ethics educational programs should include patients, staff, and boards. Cross-training of personnel is also advisable.

III. Collection Site Components

Each collection site will have specially trained physicians and technicians to obtain proper consent from parents, perform tissue dissection, and to process, store, and ship tissues. A thorough, comprehensive, and universal protocol will be established for each step of the process to ensure ethical propriety and the highest quality control. The specifically trained staff at each site will be on call for rapid response. Each site will have a fully equipped dissection area. A central phone number will be set-up to call in and coordinate cases and collect data.

IV. Cost Categories and Central Administration

Collection site costs will include salaries for technician-coordinators, educational material, medical supplies, maternal laboratory tests, and transportation. Costs at the central distribution facility will include salaries for a network director and clerical services, travel, rent, office equipment and furniture. Costs will also be incurred for the scientific work to be performed at the central facility. Administration of the network will consist in a network director who will implement policy and coordinate both the banking work of the participating physicians, technicians, and researchers and the distribution of tissues to users.

Appendix C

Proposed Catholic* Network of Human Fetal Tissue Banks

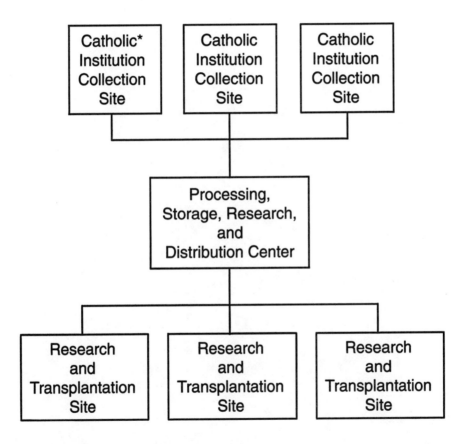

---

*Non-Catholic institutions will be included who accept Catholic teaching regarding the sanctity of human life and also the Network's ethical criteria.

Abortion, xvi, xix, 15–17, 22, 23, 30, 31, 33, 62–67, 70, 71, 73–77, 99, 100, 106, 111, 124, 126, 129, 134, 139, 143, 145, 146
   decision, 72–74
   direct, 122, 129, 133, 137, 138, 142–145
   elective, 61, 62, 66, 72, 73, 94
   ethical problems of, 2
   incomplete, 96
   indirect, 137, 138, 142, 145
   induced, xviii, 61, 62, 64, 65, 67, 70, 71, 75, 78, 150
   industry, 64–77
   inevitable, 96
   legal problems of, 2
Accomplices, 16, 31
Act
   involuntary, 17
   voluntary, 17
Agent, 37, 44, 47, 51
Allocation of resources, 159–160
Alzheimer's disease, 21
Amnion membrane, 42
Anencephalic infant, 108, 114
Aquinas, Saint Thomas, 18, 100, 134–136, 138, 139
Aristotlean, 44
Aristotle, 17
Asexual reproduction, 48, 51
Authority, 20, 23, 27, 28, 31
Autonomy, 15, 17–19

Blackstone, William, 23
Blastomere, 34, 37, 39, 40, 43, 48, 49, 53, 54
Blood transfusions, 20, 28
Body, 20, 23, 24, 27
Bone marrow, 2, 4, 5, 7, 9, 10
Bouscaren, T. Lincoln, 121, 128–130, 133, 137
Boyle, Joseph, 101, 102, 139, 140, 142, 143
Brain, 37, 45–47, 49, 51, 104–106, 108–111, 113, 115

Catholic
   Church, 33, 35, 50
   health care facility, 165
   hospitals, xx
   institutions, 169, 171–173, 176
Cells, fetal, 1, 7
   hematopoietic stem cell, 6, 8, 9
   pancreatic, 7
Charity, 151, 155, 156
Child(ren), 16, 20–23, 28–31, 172, 174
Choice, 17, 31
Chorion membrane, 42
Christ, 99
Chromosome, 41, 53, 54
Cleavage, xviii, 34, 38–40, 43, 47–49, 53
Clinic, 30, 66, 74, 77, 78
Common good, 152, 154–160, 163–165

Compaction, 40, 100
Compassion, xi, xiii, 93, 98, 99,
    101, 117
Complicity, xix, 62, 64, 65, 69–71,
    150, 165
Conception, xviii, 34, 35, 37, 38, 41,
    42, 50, 52, 54
Consciousness, 107–109
Consent, 15–23, 25–31
Cooperation, xix, 81–86, 90, 91
    contingent, xix, 82, 86
    formal, xix, 81, 84–87, 90, 91
    immediate, 86, 87
    material, xix, 81–83, 85, 86, 91
    mediate, xix
    necessary, xix, 86
    proximate, xix, 82, 86, 91
    remote, 86
    with evil, 150
Counseling, 74
Court, 22, 24, 28
Critical system of the brain (CSB),
    111–114
Curettage, 63, 96
Cytogenetic screening, 10
Cytoplasm, 38–40, 43, 47–49

Death, 16, 19, 21, 22, 24, 29, 31, 45–
    47, 94, 99–107, 109, 110, 112–116
    brain, 46, 53, 106–108, 110, 113
    definition of, 97, 101, 103,
        105–108
    determination of, 101, 103, 105,
        113, 117
    event, 103
    process, 103
Declaration on Procured Abortion,
    xvi, xvii
Declaration of Independence, 16
Delayed hominization, 35–37
Diabetes, 21
Differentiation, 39, 40, 47, 48, 50, 51
Disease, 3, 7, 8
    graft-versus-host, 8
    neurological, 7
Distributive justice, 149, 152, 155–
    158, 160–165

Dolan, Joseph V., 140
Dominant, 49
Donation, 20, 25–29
    organ, 16, 23
Donee, 26
Donum Vitae, xvii, 173
Dopamine, 3
Double effect, 82, 83, 134
    principle of, 134
Duty(ies), xvi, xvii, 26

Ectopic pregnancies, xix, 21, 121–
    124, 127, 128, 132, 137, 144, 146
    abdominal, 125
    ovarian, 125, 145
    tubal, 123, 130, 132
Effects
    bad, 175
Embryo, 35–43, 46, 50, 52–54
Embryogenesis, 38
Ends, 170, 171, 173–175
Ethical and Judicial Affairs, Council
    of, 4
Euthanasia, 99, 100
Evil, 170, 171, 173, 175
    actions, 171
Experimentation, 87, 88, 90
Extra uterine gestation, 95, 97

Faculties, 51
Fees, 75
    processing, 74
Fertilization, xviii, 34, 35, 47, 48,
    52, 53
Fetal death, xx, 94, 95, 97
Fetal gasps, 96
Fetal heart beat, 95, 96, 98, 104, 105
Fetal tissue, xv, xvii, xix, xx, 16, 20,
    21, 29, 30, 61, 62, 64, 65, 67,
    70–78
    collection, 62, 63
    research, 71, 73, 74, 151, 152, 157,
        160, 163–165
    therapy, 158, 164
Fetus, 16, 20, 23, 30, 93–98, 101,
    106, 110, 114–117
    nonviable, 94, 114–116

Fetus (*cont.*)
  viable, 114
Flannery, Kevin, 142–145
Food, 77
Funding ban, xi, 4

Gastrulation, 41, 42
Gaudium et spes, xvi
Genes, 38–41, 47–49
Genome, 39, 49, 51, 52
God, 35, 37, 50, 52
Good, 169–171, 176
  actions, 175
  ends, 170, 171, 173–175
  human, 170, 171
Goods, xx, 169–175
Grafts, neural, 3
Grisez, Germain, 101, 102, 122, 133,
    134, 137–140, 142–144
Guidelines, ethical, 2
Guidelines, legal, 2

Hamilton, Alexander, 16
Health, 172–174, 176
Heartbeat, 95, 96, 98, 104, 105
Holocaust, 67–70
Hominization, 34–37, 46, 52
Hormones, 51
Hospital, xviii, xix, 26, 31
  Catholic, xx
Human life, xv–xviii, 93, 98, 107,
    109, 110, 113
  conservation of, 99, 117
  ex utero, 96, 114
  in utero, 95, 114
  inviolability of, 94, 117
Human organism, 94, 102, 104–106,
    110–113, 117
Human person, 34–36, 50–53
Hydatidiform moles, 37, 47

Imaging
  ultrasound, 7
Immunology, 7
Implantation, 34, 35, 37, 38, 41, 42,
    53, 54
In vitro fertilization, 35, 52

Inborn errors, 7
Individuation, 37
  developmental, 37
  genetic, 37
Infection, 5, 7
Inner cell mass, 40–43, 48, 49, 54
Ischemic changes, 2, 9
Islet cells of Langerhans, 7, 9

John Paul II, Pope, xv, 99, 117
Jurisprudence, 17
Justice, xx, 150, 151, 157, 162, 163, 165

Kant, Immanuel, 18
Killing, 171, 173–175

Law, 16
Lawler, Ronald, 141, 143
Liberty, 15, 19
Locke, John, 15, 19
Love, 169–174
Lumen gentium, 127

Madison, James, 15
Magisterium, 122, 126, 127, 133, 135,
    137, 139, 144, 146
  relating to ectopic pregnancies,
    121–124, 127, 137, 144
Medicine, preventive, 7
Membranes, 39, 41, 42, 50, 53, 54
Miscarriage, xv, xviii, xix, xx, 1, 2,
    4–6, 8–10, 20, 21, 29, 37, 47,
    158, 163, 170, 172–175
Moral life, 170
Moral rights, 53, 54
Morula, 40, 41
Mother, 16, 22, 23, 28
Motor function, 3
MPTP, 3
Murder, 64, 66, 67, 71

National Institutes of Health, 30
National Organ Transplantation
    Act, 164
Nature, 15, 17, 18, 21, 24, 31
Nazi doctors, 67, 70
Network, 169

Neurotansmitter, 7
Nucleus, 39, 47, 49, 52

O'Donnell, Thomas, 125, 130,
    131, 145
Oocyte, 38
Organ of central control (OCC), 45–
    47, 49, 51, 52
Organ transplantation, 150, 161, 164
Organism, xviii, 34, 36, 38, 40–53
Organs, 23, 25–28
Ovum, 38, 39, 46, 47, 52
Oxytocin, 96

Parent, 20, 22, 27, 31
Parkinson's disease, 21
Patient, 16, 26, 28
Persistent vegetative state (PVS),
    111–113
Person, xvii, 16, 17, 19, 20, 23, 24,
    26–29, 34, 35, 99, 101, 104, 107–
    111, 113,
Pius XII, Pope, 99, 100, 126, 127,
    135, 138
  teachings on abortion, 126, 127
Placenta, 41, 50, 54
Polls, 73, 74
Preferential option for the poor, 149–
    151, 159, 160, 163
Pregnancy, 22, 28, 31
President's Commission, 153, 154
Primitive streak, 41, 42, 54
Principle, 47, 51, 52
Processors, 62, 65, 66, 71, 75
  rental of, 62, 75
Pronuclei, 53, 54
Prostaglandins, 96
Proxies, 27
Prudential judgments, 176
Public attitudes, 73

Rationing, 152
Regulation, 39, 41–43, 48, 52
Research, 82, 83, 85, 87, 88, 90, 91
Researcher, 62–66, 71
Respiration, 95, 96, 104, 105

Right to health care, 149, 153–157,
    161, 165
Rights, xviii, 15–19, 22–24, 27, 29,
    31, 34
Rock, John A., 123
Roe v. Wade, 23

Salvifici doloris, 99
Scandal, 91, 150
Scientific community, 6
Self-development, 45, 46
Semen, 37
Somatic cells, 39
Soul, 34, 36, 37, 50–52
Spermatozoa, 38
Spermatozoon, 38, 46, 47, 52
Spinal cord injury, 3, 7
Spontaneous abortions, 157
Statutes, 21
Subject, 34–36, 52–54
Substantial form, 34, 50, 51
Substrate, 107–109, 111–114
Surgery, 17, 18, 20, 23, 25, 28, 29

Technological imperative, 156,
    159, 165
Therapeutic modalities, 4, 7, 10
Tissue banks, xx, 2, 4, 5, 10, 16, 21,
    22, 27, 29, 30, 31, 169
Tissues, 1, 2, 4, 6, 9, 10, 23, 26
  lymphoid, 7
  neuralogical, 3, 6, 7
Toleration, 85
Totipotentiality, 37, 40, 42, 48
Transplants, 26
Trimester
  first, 2, 8, 9
  second, 2, 5, 9
Trophoblast, 40–42, 48–50, 54
Truths, 16–18, 27
Twinning, 37, 40–43, 48, 50–52

Ultrasound, 95
Uniform Anatomical Gift Act, 16, 25
United States Supreme Court, 22
Uterus, 41

Vatican Council II, 127, 170
Viral vectors, 4

Wallace, C. J., 131, 132
Womb, 21, 29, 31

Xenotransplantations, 4

Zona pellucida, 34, 53, 54
Zygote, xviii, 35, 37–40, 46, 47, 49,
    52–54